MathWorks 11
Workbook

MathWorks 11
Workbook

Pacific Educational Press
Vancouver, Canada

MathWorks 11 Workbook

Published by Pacific Educational Press
University of British Columbia
www.pacificedpress.ca

Writer: Katharine Borgen, PhD, Vancouver School Board and University of British Columbia
Design, Illustration, and Layout: Sharlene Eugenio, Eva Neesemann, Five Seventeen
Editing: Katrina Petrik, Nancy Wilson, Jordie Yow

Copyright © 2011 Pacific Educational Press
ISBN 978-0-9867141-3-9

All rights reserved. No part of this publication may be reproduced, stored in a retrieval system, or transmitted in any form or by any means, electronic, mechanical, photocopying, recording, or otherwise without the prior written permission of the publisher or a licence from Access Copyright. Pacific Educational Press is a member of Access Copyright. For a copyright licence, visit www.accesscopyright.ca or call toll-free 1-800-893-5777.

Every effort has been made to identify copyrighted material, obtain permission from copyright holders, and credit sources. We will gladly correct any errors or omissions in
future printings.

We acknowledge the financial support of the Government of Canada through the Canada Book Fund (CBF) for our publishing activities.

Printed and bound in Canada.
21   20   19   18   9   10   11   12

Contents

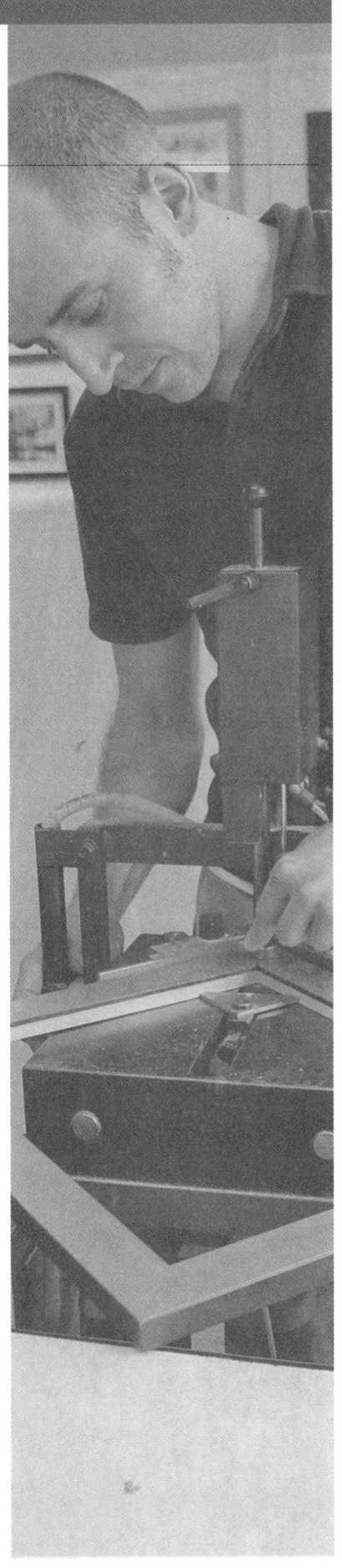

How to Use this Book — 7

1 Slope and Rate of Change — 9

1.1 Rise Over Run — 9
1.2 Grade, Angle of Elevation, and Distance — 20
1.3 Rate of Change — 36
Chapter Test — 55

2 Graphical Representations — 58

2.1 Broken Line Graphs — 58
2.2 Bar Graphs — 80
2.3 Histograms — 100
2.4 Circle Graphs — 109
Chapter Test — 119

3 Surface Area, Volume, and Capacity — 124

3.1 Surface Area of Prisms — 124
3.2 Surface Area of Pyramids, Cylinders, Spheres, & Cones — 149
3.3 Volume and Capacity of Prisms and Cylinders — 170
3.4 Volume and Capacity of Spheres, Cones, and Pyramids — 182
Chapter Test — 194

Contents continued

4 Trigonometry of Right Triangles — 197

- **4.1** Solving for Angles, Lengths, and Distances — 197
- **4.2** Solving Complex Problems in the Real World — 214
- Chapter Test — 226

5 Scale Representations — 231

- **5.1** Scale Drawings and Models — 231
- **5.2** Two-Dimensional Representations — 245
- **5.3** Three-Dimensional Representations — 259
- Chapter Test — 273

6 Financial Services — 279

- **6.1** Choosing an Account — 279
- **6.2** Simple and Compound Interest — 290
- **6.3** Credit Cards and Store Promotions — 305
- **6.4** Personal Loans, Lines of Credit, and Overdrafts — 315
- Chapter Test — 325

7 Personal Budgets — 329

- **7.1** Preparing to Make a Budget — 329
- **7.2** The Budgeting Process — 342
- **7.3** Analyzing a Budget — 354
- Chapter Test — 367

Glossary — 373

Credits — 375

How to Use This Book

This workbook is a companion to *MathWorks 11* student resource, the authorized resource for the Western and Northern Canadian Protocol (WNCP) course, Apprenticeship and Workplace Mathematics. The *MathWorks 11 Workbook* is a valuable learning tool when used in conjunction with the student resource, or on its own. It emphasizes mathematical skill-building through worked examples and practice problems.

Here, you will learn and use the practical mathematics required in the workplace. Whether you plan to enroll in college, learn a trade, or enter the workforce after graduating from secondary school, the mathematical skills in this workbook will support you at work and in your daily life.

The *MathWorks 11 Workbook* contains seven chapters. Chapters are divided into sections, each focusing on a key mathematical concept. Each chapter includes the following features.

Review

Each chapter opens with a review of mathematical processes and terms you will need to understand to complete the chapter's lessons. Practice questions are included.

Example

Each example includes a problem and its solution. The problem is solved step by step. Written descriptions of each mathematical operation used to solve the problem are included.

New Skills

The chapter's core mathematical concepts are introduced here. This section often includes real-world examples of where and how the concepts are used.

Build Your Skills

This is a set of mathematical problems for you to solve. It appears after each new concept is introduced and will let you practise the concepts you have just learned about. Build Your Skills questions often focus on workplace applications of mathematical concepts.

Practise Your New Skills

The section's key concepts are presented as review problems at the end of each chapter section.

Chapter Test

At the end of each chapter, a chapter test is provided for review and assessment of learning.

Definitions

New mathematical terms are defined in the sidebar columns. They are also included in the glossary at the back of the book.

Glossary

Definitions for mathematical terms are provided here. To increase understanding, some glossary definitions include illustrations.

Chapter 1

Slope and Rate of Change

This skier is practising tricks at Whistler Mountain in British Columbia. How would you calculate the slope of the jump?

1.1 Rise Over Run

REVIEW: WORKING WITH RATIO AND PROPORTION

In this section, you will calculate ratios and solve for unknown values in proportions.

A **ratio** is a comparison between two numbers measured in the same units. For example, if an engine runs on a mixture of gas and oil and needs 15 L of gas for every 1 L of oil, the ratio of gas to oil is 15 to 1. This can be written as 15:1 or $\frac{15}{1}$.

A **proportion** is a statement of equality between two ratios. For example, if an engine twice the size of the one above needs the same mixture of gas and oil, it will need 30 L of gas for 2 L of oil. The ratio of gas to oil is still the same. The following proportion shows this equality.

$$\frac{15}{1} = \frac{30}{2}$$

ratio: a comparison between two numbers with the same units

proportion: a statement of equality between two ratios

Example 1

A recipe for vegetarian chili contains:

- 56 oz of chopped tomatoes
- 30 oz of kidney beans
- 15 oz of whole kernel corn

a) What is the ratio of corn to kidney beans?

b) What is the ratio of tomatoes to kidney beans?

SOLUTION

a) The recipe contains 15 oz of corn and 30 oz of kidney beans. The ratio can be written as follows.

corn:kidney beans = 15:30

corn:kidney beans = (15 ÷ 15):(30 ÷ 15)   Divide both sides by a common factor.

corn:kidney beans = 1:2

The ratio of corn to kidney beans is 1:2.

ALTERNATIVE SOLUTION

A ratio can also be written as a fraction or in words:

- The ratio of corn to kidney beans is $\frac{1}{2}$.
- The ratio of corn to kidney beans is 1 to 2.

b) The recipe contains 56 oz of tomatoes and 30 oz of kidney beans.

tomatoes:kidney beans = 56:30

tomatoes:kidney beans = (56 ÷ 2):(30 ÷ 2)

tomatoes:kidney beans = 28:15

> A ratio can have a numerator larger than the denominator. Because a ratio compares two numbers, do not rewrite it as a mixed fraction.

Chapter 1 Slope and Rate of Change

BUILD YOUR SKILLS

1. In a juice mixture, 750 mL of water are mixed with 250 mL of juice concentrate. What is the ratio of concentrate to water?

   1 : 3

2. To mix a certain shade of green paint, a painter mixes 2.3 L of blue paint with 1.7 L of yellow paint. What is the ratio of blue paint to yellow paint? Express your answer as a fraction.

   $\dfrac{23}{17}$

3. A cereal mixture contains 6 cups of oats, 2 cups of almonds, 1 cup of raisins, and $\dfrac{3}{4}$ cup of coconut.

   a) What is the ratio of oats to raisins?

   6 : 1

   b) What is the ratio of almonds to coconut?

   8 : 3

   c) What is the ratio of oats to the total ingredients in the recipe?

   8 : 13

Example 2

A big-screen TV has an aspect ratio of 16:9, which means that for every 16 inches of width, the TV is 9 inches high. What is the height of a TV that is 40 inches wide?

SOLUTION

Set up a proportion to solve for x, the height of the TV.

$$\frac{40}{x} = \frac{16}{9}$$

$$9 \times x \times \frac{40}{x} = \frac{16}{9} \times x \times 9 \quad \text{Multiply by a common factor.}$$

$$9 \times 40 = 16x \quad \text{Simplify.}$$

$$\frac{9 \times 40}{16} = x$$

$$22.5 = x$$

The TV will be 22.5 inches wide.

BUILD YOUR SKILLS

4. A dirt bike requires 15 L of gas to be mixed with 4 L of oil. If you use 20 L of gas, how much oil will you need?

   5.3 L

5. If 10 cm on a map represents 25 km of actual ground, how many centimetres would 45 km of actual ground be on the map?

   18 cm

6. A recipe for corn chowder includes 3 cups of corn, 2 cups of water, and $1\frac{1}{2}$ cups of cream. If you increase the yield of the recipe and use $4\frac{1}{2}$ cups of cream, how much corn will you need?

   9 cups

NEW SKILLS: WORKING WITH SLOPE

You may have heard the words pitch, slant, or steepness. What do these terms mean? They are words to describe **slope**. Slope is a ratio that compares the change in a vertical distance to the change in a horizontal distance. It is a ratio between these two numbers.

Slope can be expressed as follows.

$$\text{slope} = \frac{\Delta \text{ vertical distance}}{\Delta \text{ horizontal distance}}$$

The variable *m* is used to represent slope. The change in vertical distance is also called the rise, and the change in horizontal distance is also called the run. Slope can therefore be expressed as follows.

$$m = \frac{\text{rise}}{\text{run}}$$

For more details, see page 12 of *MathWorks 11*.

slope: a ratio of rise to run which indicates how steeply something is slanted

The symbol Δ is the Greek letter delta, and it means "change" or "difference."

Example 3

Calculate the slope of a line that has a rise of 12 cm for a run of 8 cm.

SOLUTION

Use the formula for slope.

$$m = \frac{\text{rise}}{\text{run}}$$

$$m = \frac{12}{8} \quad \text{Substitute in the known values.}$$

$$m = \frac{12 \div 4}{8 \div 4} \quad \text{Divide by a common factor.}$$

$$m = \frac{3}{2}$$

The slope is $\frac{3}{2}$.

Slope does not have units because it is a ratio, not a measurement.

ALTERNATIVE SOLUTION

The slope can also be expressed as a decimal.

$$\frac{3}{2} = 1.5$$

The slope is 1.5.

BUILD YOUR SKILLS

7. Calculate the slope in the following situations.

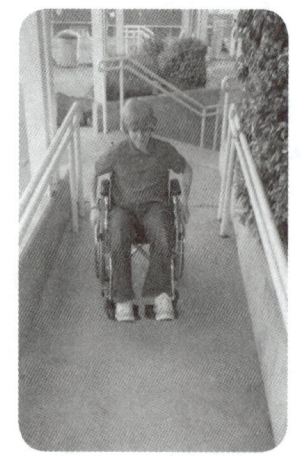

Building codes specify how steep a wheelchair ramp can be.

a) A wheelchair ramp has a rise of 3 feet and a run of 18 feet.

$\frac{1}{6}$

b) A snowboard jump rises 1.25 m over 5 m of horizontal distance.

$\frac{1}{4}$

c) A roof rises 8 feet over a horizontal distance of 18 feet.

$\frac{4}{9}$

d) A hill rises 10 metres over a horizontal distance of 8 metres.

$\frac{5}{4}$

e) A slide covers 3.5 m of ground and is 2.4 m tall.

$\frac{24}{35}$

Example 4

The slope of a line is $\frac{7}{20}$. What is the rise if the run is 100 metres?

SOLUTION

Use the formula for slope.

$$m = \frac{\text{rise}}{\text{run}}$$

$$\frac{7}{20} = \frac{\text{rise}}{100} \quad \text{Substitute in the known values.}$$

$$100 \times \frac{7}{20} = \frac{\text{rise}}{\text{run}} \times 100 \quad \text{Multiply to isolate the rise.}$$

$$100 \times \frac{7}{20} = \text{rise} \quad \text{Simplify.}$$

$$35 = \text{rise}$$

The rise is 35 m.

BUILD YOUR SKILLS

8. The slope of a hill is $\frac{3}{190}$. The hill has a rise of 400 m. What is the horizontal distance covered by the hill?

   25 333 m

9. The slope of a staircase is 0.95. If it rises 210 cm, what is the run?

   221 cm

10. The slope of a street is 0.54. If it covers 28 m of horizontal distance, what is the rise of the street?

15.1 m

Example 5

Harbinder is building a ramp in two sections, both with the same slope. If one section rises 2 m for a run of 6.5 m, how much will it have to rise for the remaining run of 9.8 m?

SOLUTION

Calculate the slope of the first section.

$$m = \frac{\text{rise}}{\text{run}}$$

$$m = \frac{2}{6.5}$$

The slope of the second section is also $\frac{2}{6.5}$. Set up a proportion to solve for x, the rise of the second section.

$$\frac{2}{6.5} = \frac{x}{9.8}$$

$$9.8 \times \frac{2}{6.5} = \frac{x}{9.8} \times 9.8 \quad \text{Multiply to isolate } x.$$

$$\frac{9.8 \times 2}{6.5} = x$$

$$\frac{19.6}{6.5} = x$$

$$3.02 \approx x$$

The rise of the remaining section is approximately 3.02 m.

BUILD YOUR SKILLS

11. Leslie works for a shipping company. He regularly carries boxes up and down several stairs and has decided that it would be easier if he built a ramp. The stairs have a rise of 3.5 m for a run of 6.0 m. What is the slope of the stairs?

    $\frac{7}{12}$

12. Harry is building a staircase with a slope of 0.89. If the total rise of the staircase is 203 cm, what is the total run of the stairway?

    228 cm

13. The slope of a slide for a playground is to be $\frac{17}{10}$. If the maximum space available for the slide is a horizontal distance of 1.5 m, how high will the slide be?

    2.55 m

Builders need to consider the slope when building a new staircase.

PRACTISE YOUR NEW SKILLS

1. Calculate the slope as a fraction in the simplest form and as a decimal.

Rise	Run	Slope As a fraction $\left(m=\frac{\text{rise}}{\text{run}}\right)$	As a decimal
18 m	63 m	$\frac{2}{7}$	0.29
21 m	49 m	$\frac{3}{7}$	0.43
1.2 cm	0.6 cm	2	2
12.4 mm	4.6 mm	$\frac{62}{23}$	2.70
300 ft	900 ft	$\frac{1}{3}$	0.33

2. Use the information given to complete the table.

Rise	Run	Slope
15 ft	60 ft	$\frac{1}{4}$
12 cm	32 cm	0.375
28.8 m	16 m	$\frac{9}{5}$
192 in	42 in	$\frac{32}{7}$
63 m	21 m	3.0
19.5 ft	78 ft	0.25

3. Zane is designing a small waterslide for children to play on. If the slide has a run of 120 inches and a height of 56 inches, what is the slope of the slide?

$\frac{7}{15}$ or approx. 0.47

4. A safe slope for a ladder is 1 ft of run for every 4 ft of rise. Vincent needs to use a ladder to reach a window sill that is 22 ft above the ground. How far from the house should the base of the ladder be?

5.5 ft

5. Harj is digging a drainage ditch. It must drop 3 cm for every 1.5 m of horizontal distance. How much will it drop in a horizontal distance of 25 m?

50 cm

6. The slope of a hill is an average of 0.64. How many metres will it rise for a horizontal distance of 32 metres?

    20.5 m

7. Hazuki needs to calculate the slope of the water table—the elevation at which water is found under the ground. One well has water at 752 m elevation and the another has it at 895 m elevation. If the wells are 1.2 km apart, what is the slope of the water table?

    $\frac{143}{1200}$ or approx. 0.12

8. Calculate the slope of the roof and of the diagonal trusses.

    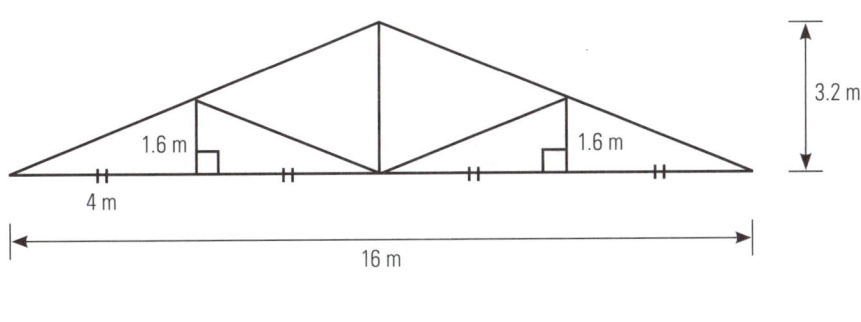

    $\frac{2}{5}$ or 0.4

9. Alfred wants to make a doll house that is a copy of his own house. The roof of his house is 10.8 m wide and is 2.4 m higher at the centre than the edges. If the doll house is 1.6 m wide, what will be the rise of the roof?

    0.36 m

1.2 Grade, Angle of Elevation, and Distance

REVIEW: THE PYTHAGOREAN THEOREM AND THE TANGENT RATIO

In this section, you will work with the Pythagorean theorem and the tangent ratio.

The Pythagorean theorem states the relationship between the sides of a right triangle. In right triangle ΔABC shown below, the Pythagorean theorem states the following.

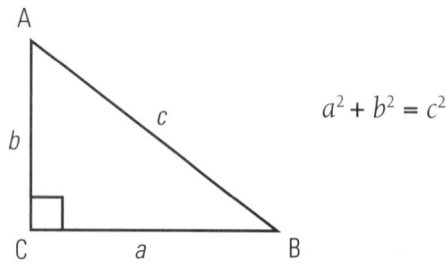

$$a^2 + b^2 = c^2$$

The tangent ratio is a trigonometric ratio that applies to right triangles. It is a ratio of the side opposite an acute angle to the side adjacent to the angle. For angle A, the ratio can be stated as follows.

$$\text{tangent } \angle A = \frac{\text{length of side opposite } \angle A}{\text{length of side adjacent to } \angle A}$$

This can be abbreviated as:

$$\tan A = \frac{\text{opp}}{\text{adj}}$$

For triangle ABC shown above, tan A can be stated as:

$$\tan A = \frac{a}{b}$$

Example 1

Use the diagram to calculate the following:

a) the length of the hypotenuse; and

b) the measure of ∠A.

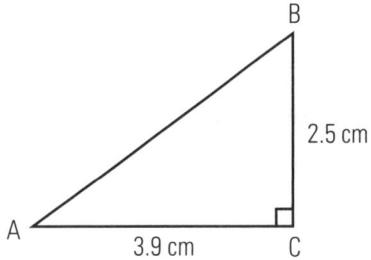

SOLUTION

a) Use the Pythagorean theorem to solve for the length of the hypotenuse.

$a^2 + b^2 = c^2$

$2.5^2 + 3.9^2 = c^2$ Substitute in the known values.

$6.25 + 15.21 = c^2$

$21.46 = c^2$

$\sqrt{21.46} = c$ Take the square root of both sides.

$4.6 \approx c$

The length of side c, the hypotenuse, is about 4.6 cm.

b) Use the tangent ratio to solve for ∠A.

$\tan A = \dfrac{\text{opp}}{\text{adj}}$

$\tan A = \dfrac{2.5}{3.9}$ Substitute in the known values.

$A = \tan^{-1}\left(\dfrac{2.5}{3.9}\right)$ Use the inverse function to find the angle.

$A \approx 32.7°$

∠A is about 32.7°.

> Use the "inverse" tangent operation on your calculator to solve for an unknown angle.

22 MathWorks 11 Workbook

BUILD YOUR SKILLS

1. In each diagram, calculate the indicated side using the Pythagorean theorem and find the indicated angle using the tangent ratio.

a)

G = 23.8°
h = 4.7 cm

Triangle with legs 1.9 cm and 4.3 cm, hypotenuse h, angle G at the right end.

b)

S = 46.4°
R ≈ 11.3 m

Right triangle with vertex S at top, legs 7.8 m and 8.2 m, hypotenuse r.

c)

E = 55.3°
f = 11.4 in

Right triangle with vertex E at top, sides 6.5 in and 9.4 in, side f opposite the right angle.

NEW SKILLS: WORKING WITH SLOPE AND THE TANGENT RATIO

In section 1.1, you saw that slope is equal to the ratio of rise to run.

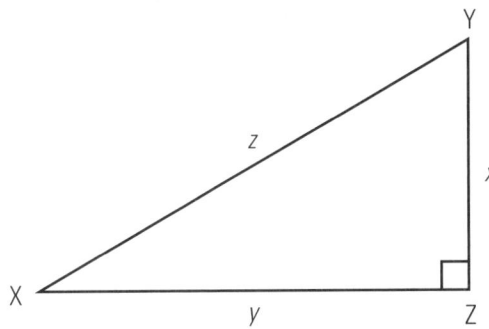

In the right triangle ΔXYZ, the slope of the segment z is the ratio of the rise, x, to the run, y.

$m = \dfrac{\text{rise}}{\text{run}}$

$m = \dfrac{x}{y}$

The tangent of $\angle X$ is the ratio of the opposite side, x, to the adjacent side, y.

$\tan X = \dfrac{\text{opp}}{\text{adj}}$

$\tan X = \dfrac{x}{y}$

Thus, the slope of segment z, the hypotenuse of the triangle, is the same as the tangent of $\angle X$.

$\angle X$ can be referred to as the angle of elevation of segment z. $\angle Y$ is called its angle of depression.

For more details, see page 26 of *MathWorks 11*.

Example 2

In trigonometry, the Greek letter theta (θ) is used to label an unknown angle.

Find the slope of the hypotenuse as a fraction, and use it to find the angle of elevation.

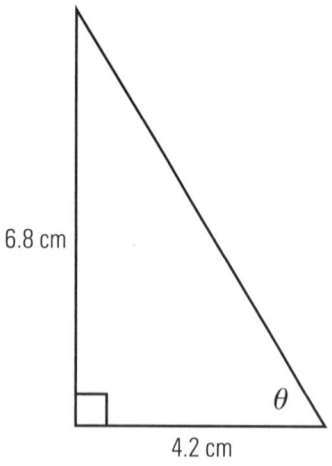

SOLUTION

The slope of the hypotenuse will be the rise, 6.8 cm, divided by the run, 4.2 cm.

$m = \dfrac{\text{rise}}{\text{run}}$

$m = \dfrac{6.8}{4.2}$ Substitute in the known values.

$m = \dfrac{68}{42}$ Multiply the numerator and the denominator by 10 to eliminate decimals.

$m = \dfrac{34}{21}$ Divide the numerator and the denominator by 2.

Use the tangent ratio to solve for the angle of elevation.

$\tan \theta = \dfrac{\text{opp}}{\text{adj}}$

$\tan \theta = m$

$\tan \theta = \dfrac{34}{21}$

$\theta = \tan^{-1}\left(\dfrac{34}{21}\right)$

$\theta \approx 58.3°$

The angle of elevation is about 58.3°.

Chapter 1 Slope and Rate of Change 25

BUILD YOUR SKILLS

2. Calculate the angle of elevation and the slope of the hypotenuse.

a) 11 ft, 25 ft, θ

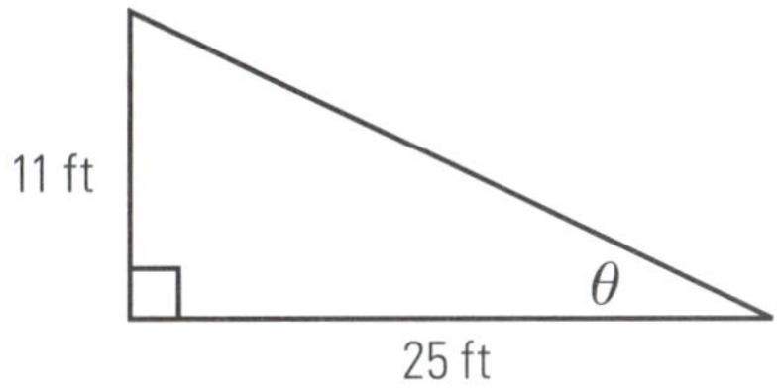

$\theta = 23.7°$, $m = \frac{11}{25}$ or 0.44

b) 29 cm, 14 cm, θ

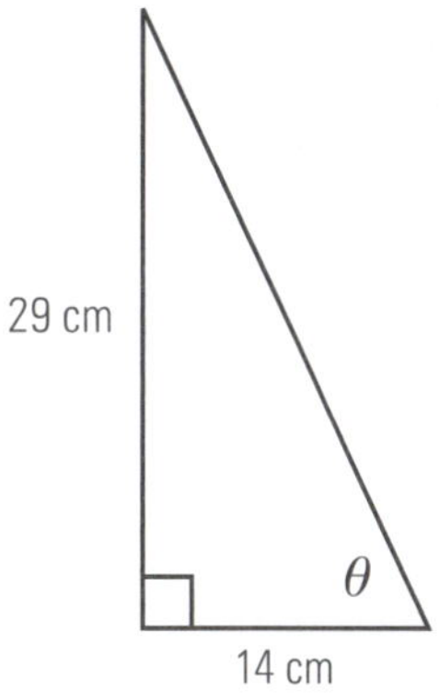

$\theta = 64.2°$, $m = \frac{29}{14}$ or 2.07

3. A ski jump rises 3 feet over a run of 7 feet.

   a) What is the length of the surface of the jump?

   7.6 ft

   b) What is the angle of elevation of the jump?

   23.2°

4. A driveway rises 2.2 m from the street level to the carport, which is a horizontal distance of 5.8 m from the street.

   a) How long is the driveway?

   6.2 m

   b) What is its angle of elevation?

   20.8°

5. A wheelchair ramp is being built to rise to a landing that is 2.4 m above the ground. Building regulations say that the ramp can have a maximum rise of 2.5 cm per 30 cm of run.

   a) What is the total run for the wheelchair ramp?

   28.8 m

   b) How long will the ramp be?

   28.9 m

NEW SKILLS: WORKING WITH GRADE

When talking about the slope of a road, it is usually called the road **grade**. Grade is commonly expressed as a percentage. The steeper the road, the higher its percent grade. The following formula can be used to calculate grade.

$$\text{percent grade} = \frac{\text{rise}}{\text{run}} \times 100$$

For more details, see page 25 of *MathWorks 11*.

grade: the slope of a physical feature such as a road or hill, often expressed as a percentage

Example 3

Martin is driving his truck on the Trans-Canada Highway. There is a sign indicating a 7% grade.

a) What is the slope of the road, as a fraction?

b) Find the angle of elevation of the road.

SOLUTION

a) A grade of 7% means a rise of 7 units for a run of 100 units.

$$\text{percent grade} = \frac{\text{rise}}{\text{run}} \times 100$$

$$7 = \frac{\text{rise}}{\text{run}} \times 100$$

$$\frac{7}{100} = \frac{\text{rise}}{\text{run}}$$

$$\frac{7}{100} = m$$

The slope of the road is $\frac{7}{100}$.

Road grades must be kept to a minimum because a steeper grade limits the size of load that can be hauled. A 1% grade halves the load that can be hauled by a locomotive!

b) Use the tangent ratio to solve for the angle of elevation.

$$\tan \theta = \frac{\text{rise}}{\text{run}}$$

$$\tan \theta = \frac{7}{100}$$

$$\theta = \tan^{-1}\left(\frac{7}{100}\right)$$

$$\theta \approx 4.0°$$

The angle of elevation is approximately 4.0°.

BUILD YOUR SKILLS

6. Heckman Pass is a very steep section of highway connecting Anahim Lake and Bella Coola, BC. At its steepest section, it rises 900 m over a run of 5 km. What is the percent grade of this section?

    18%

7. So that water will drain properly, a patio attached to a house should slope downward about $2\frac{1}{2}$ inches for every 10 feet of run. Calculate:

    a) the slope; and

    $-\frac{1}{48}$ or -0.021

    b) the percent grade.

    2.1%

8. One of the steepest railways in the world is the Lisbon tram in Portugal. In one section, it has a grade of 13.5%.

   a) Express this as a slope.

   0.135

   b) Calculate the angle of elevation.

   7.7

The tramway in Lisbon, Portugal, has been in operation since 1873.

   c) What is the rise for a run of 15 m?

   2.03 m

NEW SKILLS: WORKING WITH PITCH

The slope of a roof is often referred to as its pitch. A roof with a pitch of 5:8 is a roof with a rise of 5 and a run of 8, or a slope of $\frac{5}{8}$.

Example 4

How wide is the shed in the diagram below if the pitch of the left side is 3:4 and the pitch of the right side is 8:9?

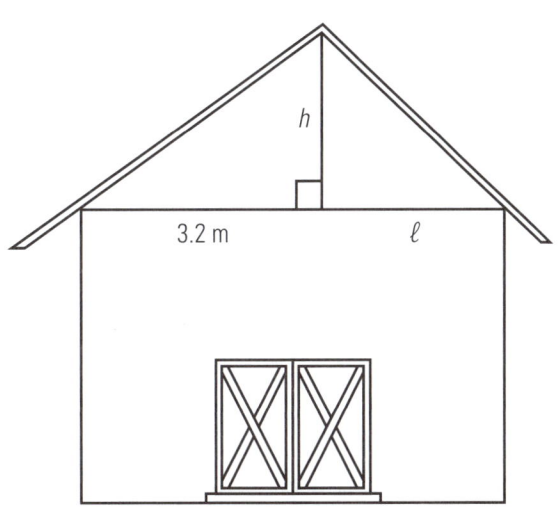

You could say that the slope on the left side of the roof is positive and the slope on the right side is negative because they go in different directions. For construction purposes, though, it is only the measurements that are important.

SOLUTION

A pitch of 3:4 is a slope of $\frac{3}{4}$. Find h, the rise of the roof.

$$m = \frac{\text{rise}}{\text{run}}$$

$$\frac{3}{4} = \frac{h}{3.2}$$

$4 \times 3.2 \times \frac{3}{4} = \frac{h}{3.2} \times 3.2 \times 4$ Multiply both sides by the same number.

$9.6 = 4h$ Simplify.

$\frac{9.6}{4} = \frac{4h}{4}$ Divide both sides by 4.

$2.4 = h$

Use this height to find ℓ.

$$m = \frac{\text{rise}}{\text{run}}$$

$$\frac{8}{9} = \frac{2.4}{\ell}$$

$9 \times \ell \times \frac{8}{9} = \frac{2.4}{\ell} \times \ell \times 9$ Multiply both sides by the same number.

$8\ell = 21.6$ Simplify.

$\frac{8\ell}{8} = \frac{21.6}{8}$ Divide both sides by the same number.

$\ell = 2.7$

Add to find the total width of the shed.

$3.2 + 2.7 = 5.9$

The width of the shed is 5.9 m.

BUILD YOUR SKILLS

9. The pitch of a roof on a lean-to that Dianna is building is 2:5. If the lean-to touches the ground 4.8 m from the base of the building, how high up the building does it reach?

   1.92 m

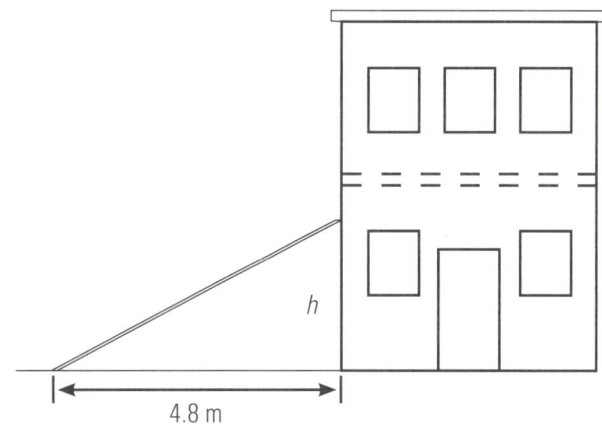

10. What is the pitch of the roof of an A-frame building if its height is 3.6 m and its width is 5.4 m?

    4:3

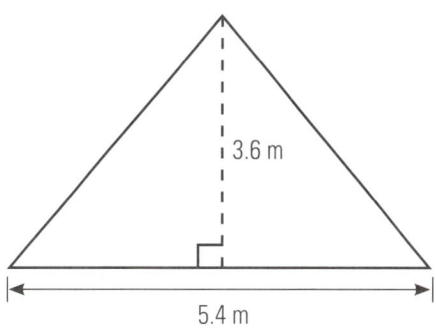

11. The roof of a tool shed has a pitch of 2:5. If the shed is 7 feet wide, what is the rise of the roof?

    1.4 ft

PRACTISE YOUR NEW SKILLS

1. Calculate the missing angles and the slope of the hypotenuse.

A = 50.4°, B = 39.6°
M = 29/35 or approx. 0.83

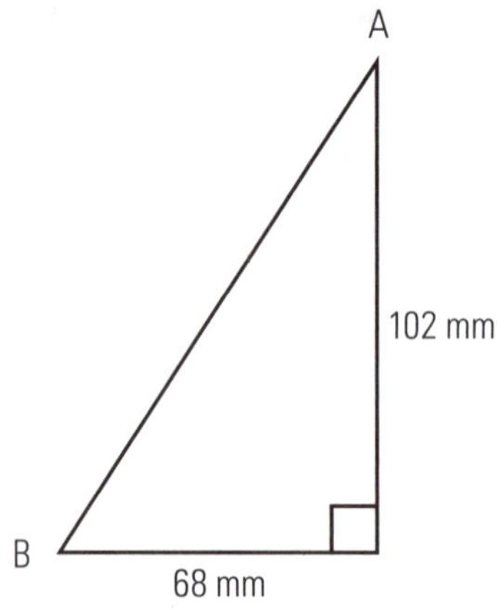

a)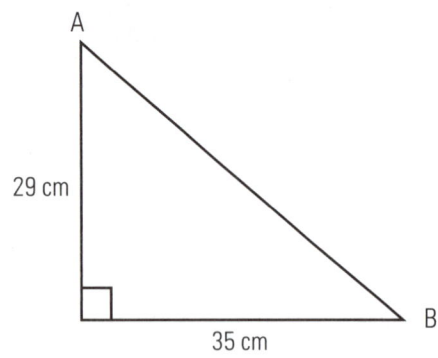

b) A = 33.7°, B = 56.3°
M = 3/2 or 1.5

c) A = 53.8°, B = 36.2°
M = 19/26 or 0.73

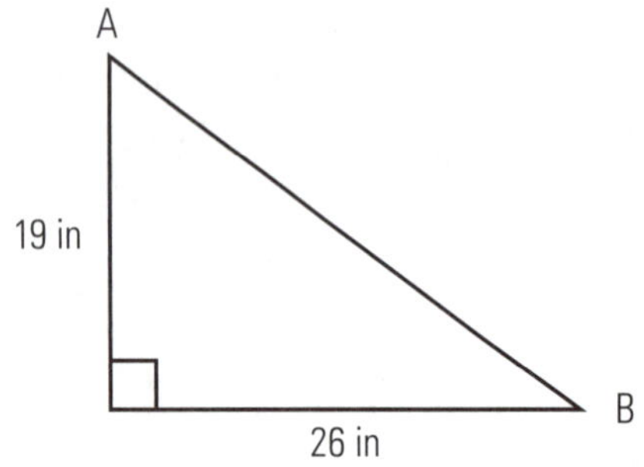

d) A = 54.0°, B = 36.0°
M = 8/11 or approx. 0.73

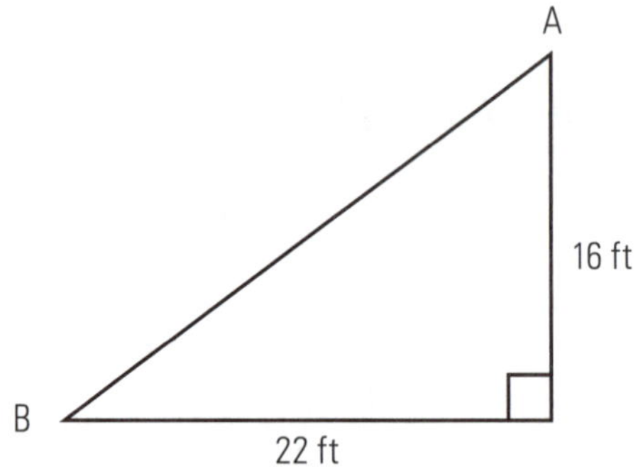

2. Jon is building a wheelchair ramp at his grandmother's house. The ramp will rise 1.2 m over a run of 7.2 m. Jon will purchase roll roofing to lay on the ramp to create a non-slip surface.

   a) What length of roll roofing will Jon have to purchase to cover the wheelchair ramp?

    7.3 m

   b) What is the angle of elevation of the ramp?

   9.5°

3. Akiko works as a ski instructor. He has read that human-triggered avalanches occur most often on slopes with angles of elevation between 35° and 45°.

   a) What are the slopes of these two angles of elevation?

   For 35°, m ≈ 0.7, for 45° m = 1

   b) What are the percent grades?

   70% and 100%

Whether an avalanche will occur depends on many factors, including the slope of the hill, the moisture content in the snow, and the temperature.

4. Aurena is installing a pipe for drainage. The system requires a drop of 1.5 cm for every 2.5 m of horizontal distance.

   a) What is the slope of the pipe?

   $m = \dfrac{3}{500}$ or 0.006

   b) How much drop will she need if the horizontal distance is 12 m?

   7.2 cm

   c) What is the angle of elevation of the pipe?

   $0.34°$

5. Joel drove his truck 3 km along a road. During this drive, his altitude increased from 982 m to 1257 m.

   a) What horizontal distance did he travel?

   2987 m

   b) What was the percent grade of the road?

   9.2%

6. A roof rises 2 ft for every 5 ft of run.

   a) What is the pitch of the roof?

   2:5

   b) What is the slope of the roof, as a decimal?

   0.4

   In areas that get a lot of snow, roofs are usually steeper to allow snow to fall off.

   c) What is the percent grade?

   40%

7. The roof of one house has a pitch of 4.2:12. The roof of a second house has a pitch of 7.8:20. Which roof is steeper?

   roof of the second house

8. One straight section of road rises from an elevation of 1070 m to 1132 m. The run is approximately 1.3 km. What is the percent grade of the road?

   4.8%

1.3 Rate of Change

NEW SKILLS: USING COORDINATES TO CALCULATE SLOPE

Slope is calculated as the change in vertical distance divided by the change in horizontal distance. If you are calculating the slope of a line plotted on a graph, how would you calculate these values?

You can do this using any two points on the line. Choose two points, (x_1, y_1) and (x_2, y_2), then use the following formula.

$$m = \frac{y_2 - y_1}{x_2 - x_1}$$

If a line on a graph rises from left to right, as in the following graph, the slope is positive.

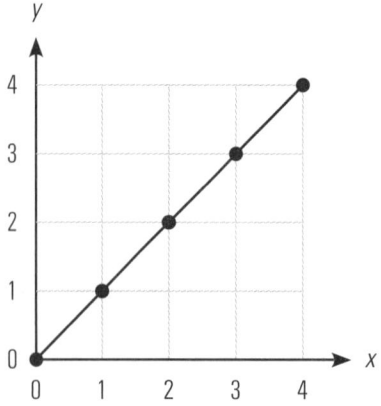

If a graph falls or goes down from left to right, the slope is negative because the "rise" is downward, or in the negative direction. The graph below has a negative slope.

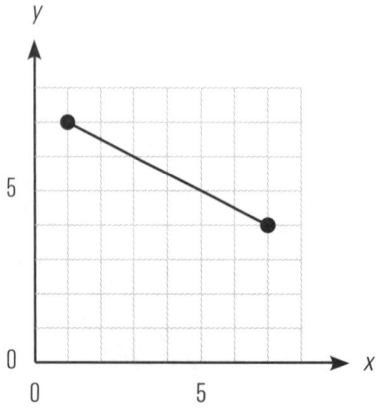

For more details, see page 35 of *MathWorks 11*.

Example 1

Consider each of the following graphs. Are the slopes positive or negative? Calculate each slope, as a fraction.

a)

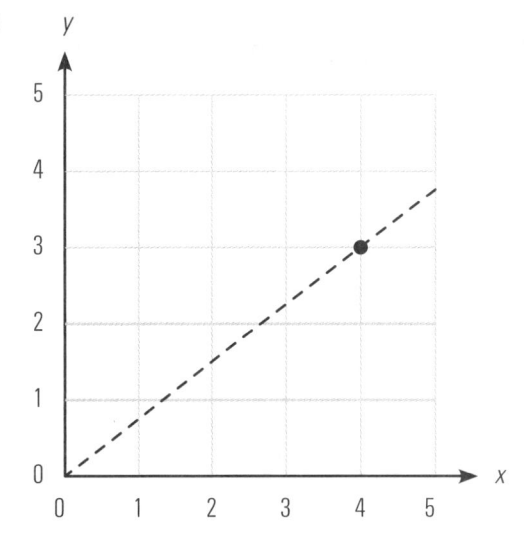

b)

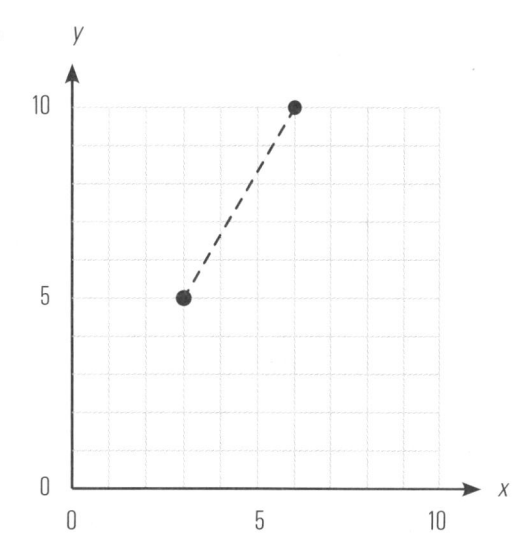

c)

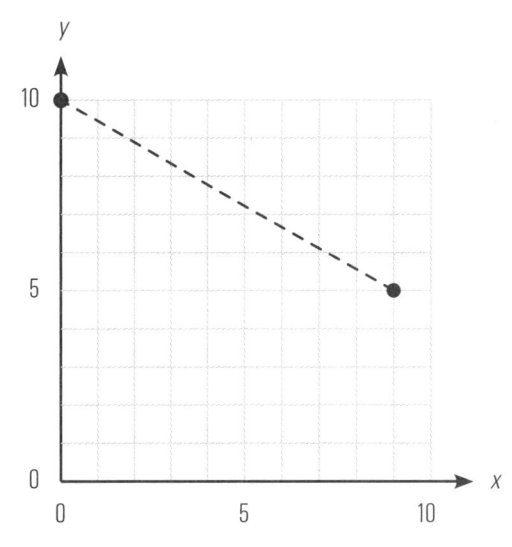

SOLUTION

a) This graph has a positive slope because it rises from left to right. To calculate the slope, choose two points on the line, such as (0, 0) and (4, 3).

$$m = \frac{y_2 - y_1}{x_2 - x_1}$$

$$m = \frac{3 - 0}{4 - 0}$$

$$m = \frac{3}{4}$$

b) This graph has a positive slope. Choose two points on the line, such as (3, 5) and (6, 10).

$$m = \frac{y_2 - y_1}{x_2 - x_1}$$

$$m = \frac{10 - 5}{6 - 3}$$

$$m = \frac{5}{3}$$

c) This graph has a negative slope, because it decreases from left to right. Choose two points on the line, such as (0, 10) and (9, 5).

$$m = \frac{y_2 - y_1}{x_2 - x_1}$$

$$m = \frac{5 - 10}{9 - 0}$$

$$m = \frac{-5}{9} \text{ or } -\frac{5}{9}$$

BUILD YOUR SKILLS

1. Calculate the slope of the two lines on the graph. Which is steeper?

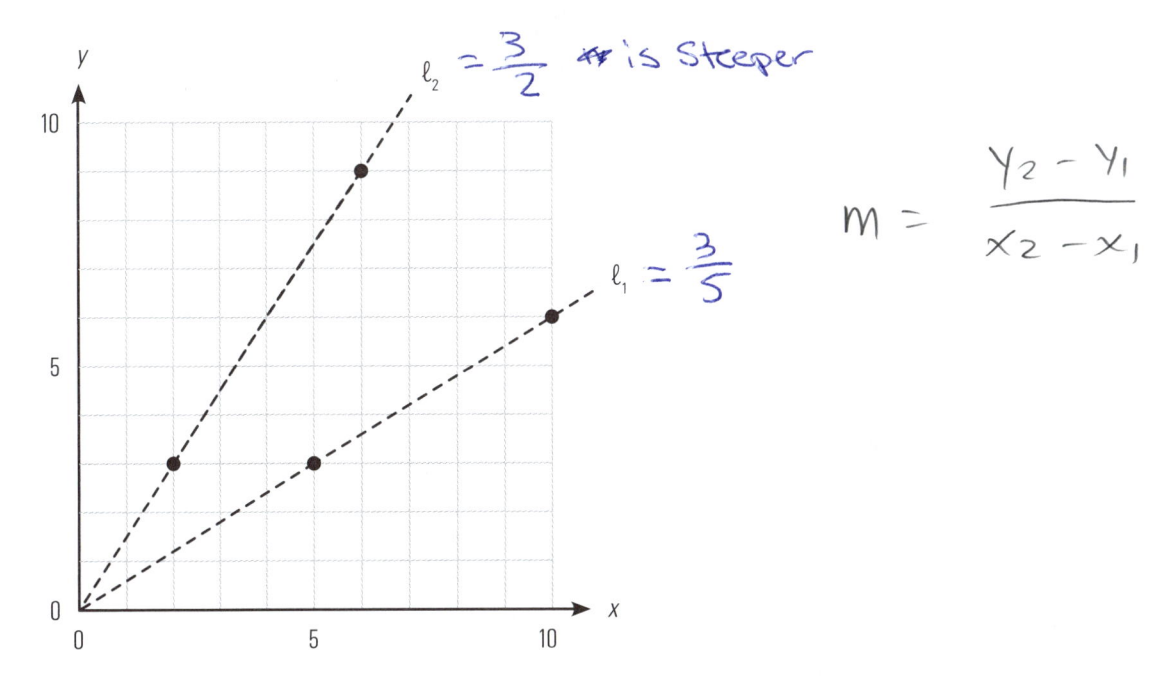

$\ell_2 = \frac{3}{2}$ ℓ₂ is steeper

$\ell_1 = \frac{3}{5}$

$$m = \frac{y_2 - y_1}{x_2 - x_1}$$

2. Calculate the slopes of the two lines on the graph.

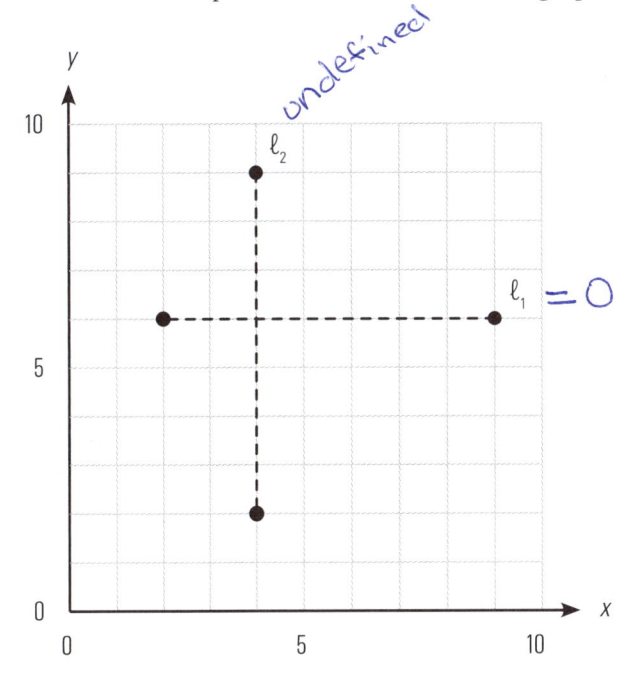

ℓ_2 = undefined

$\ell_1 = 0$

3. On the graph below, draw:

   a) a solid line that passes through point A and has a slope of $\frac{6}{5}$; and

   b) a dotted line that passes through point A and has a slope of $-\frac{3}{2}$.

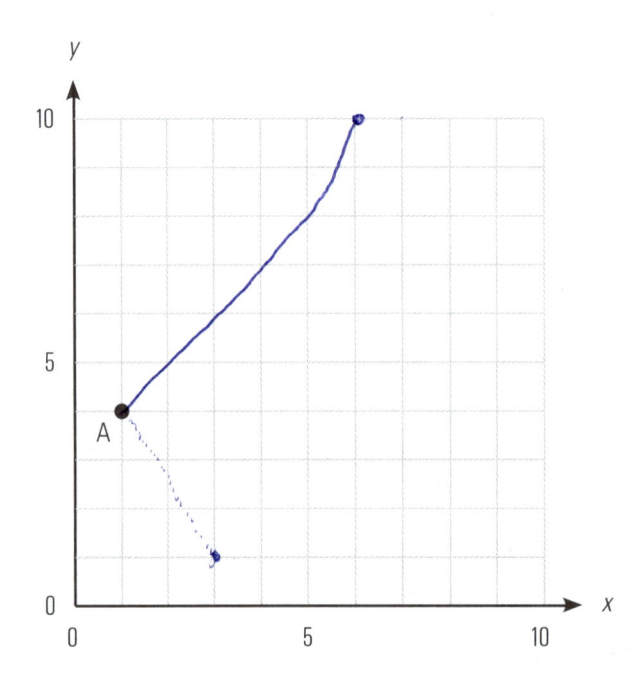

NEW SKILLS: WORKING WITH SLOPE AS A RATE OF CHANGE

If you travel in a car at a constant speed of 50 km/h for a length of time, you will have travelled 50 km in one hour, 100 km in two hours, 150 km in three hours, and so on. If you travel at 75 km/h, you go 75 km in one hour, 150 km in two hours, and so on.

You can plot these rates on a graph with time on the horizontal axis and distance on the vertical axis. You will get straight lines.

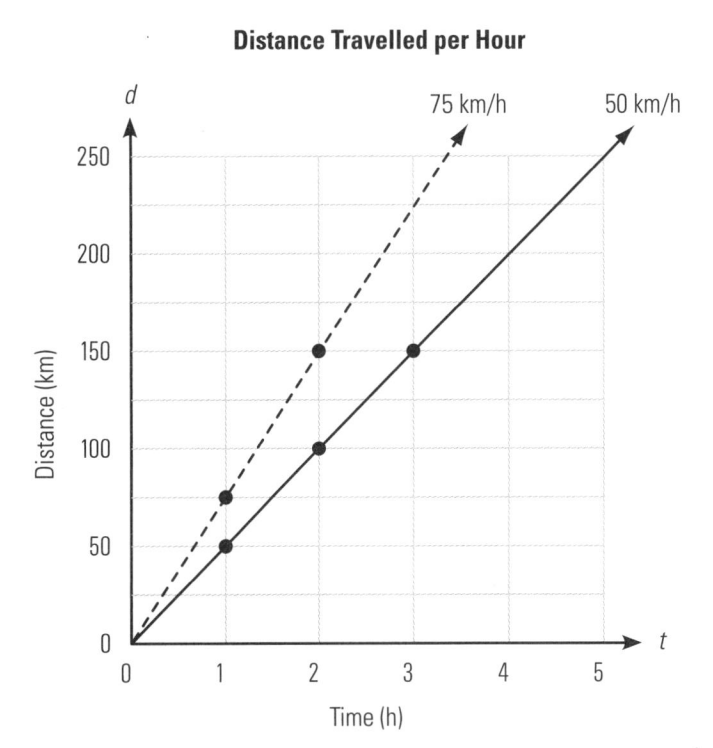

Distance Travelled per Hour

You can join the dots because this is a continuous function.

If you choose any two points on the solid line and calculate the slope, the fraction will always reduce to $\frac{50}{1}$. Similarly, if you choose two points on the dotted line, the rise divided by the run will always be $\frac{75}{1}$. The slope of the line is the rate at which you are travelling. It is the **rate of change** of distance to time. Time is the **independent variable** and distance is the **dependent variable**.

The relationship between distance and time for these two sets of data can be written as the following equations.

$d_1 = 50t$
$d_2 = 75t$

For more details, see page 35 of *MathWorks 11*.

rate of change: the rate at which one variable changes compared to another variable

independent variable: a variable whose value can be freely chosen and which is not dependent on any other value

dependent variable: a variable whose value relies on the value of another variable

Example 2

Willard works as an electrician's assistant and earns $12.25 per hour.

a) What is the dependent variable? Write an equation that shows the relationship between hours worked and income.

b) Graph the equation.

c) What is the slope of the graph and what does it represent?

d) How much will Willard earn in 5 hours?

e) If he earned $183.75 on a job, how many hours did he work?

SOLUTION

a) The dependent variable is Willard's total earnings.

Let e represent Willard's income and h the hours he works. The equation is then as follows.

$e = \$12.25h$

b) **Willard's Earnings per Hour**

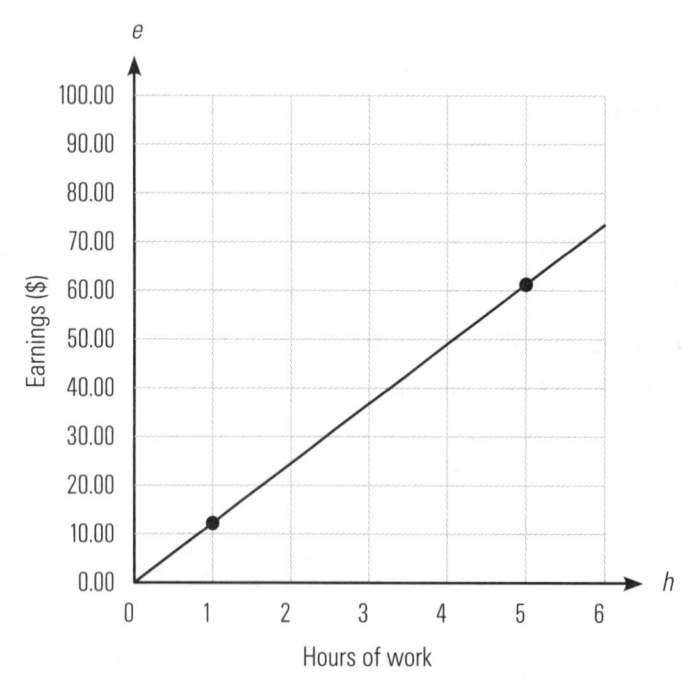

c) Choose two points on the graph, such as (0, 0) and (1, 12.25).

$$m = \frac{y_2 - y_1}{x_2 - x_1}$$

$$m = \frac{12.25 - 0}{1 - 0}$$

$$m = 12.25$$

The slope of the graph is 12.25. It represents Willard's earnings per hour.

d) Use the equation for Willard's total earnings to calculate how much he would earn in 5 hours.

$e = \$12.25h$

$e = \$12.25 \times 5$

$e = \$61.25$

Willard would earn $61.25 in 5 hours.

e) Use the equation for Willard's total earnings.

$$e = \$12.25h$$

$$183.75 = 12.25h$$

$$183.75 \div 12.25 = h$$

$$15 = h$$

Willard worked 15 hours.

BUILD YOUR SKILLS

4. Reggie is starting to practise for a marathon.

   a) If he walked 3 km in 30 minutes, what is his average rate in km/h?

   6 km/h

   b) Which is the independent variable?

   Time

   c) If he does not change his pace, how long will it take him to walk a 36-km marathon?

   6 h

5. Jenita's car needs repairing, and she borrows $600.00 from her brother to pay the bill. She repays her brother $40.00 a week.

   a) Write an equation that shows the relationship between how much she owes her brother and how much she pays each week.

   P be the amount owed and W be the # of weeks

   $$P = 600 - 40W$$

b) Graph the information. What is the slope of the line and what does it represent?

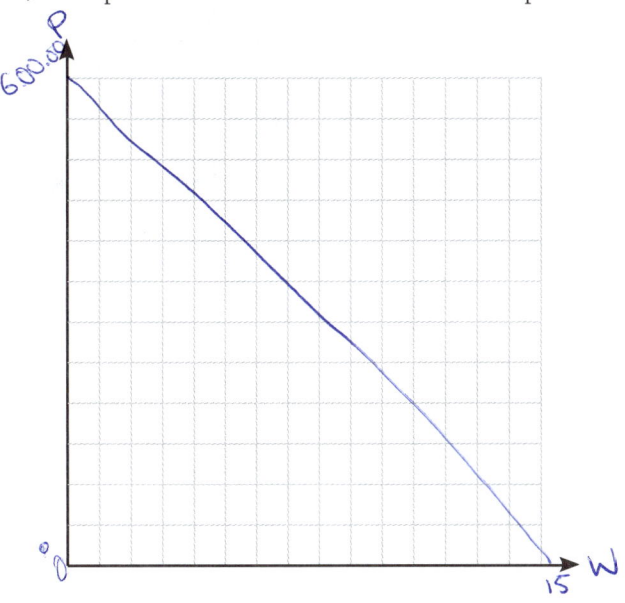

The line is -40. The slope represents the amount of money Jenita pays per week.

(Graph: P-axis starting at 600.00, W-axis with point at 15, line decreasing from (0, 600) to (15, 0))

6. George works in a furniture store where he earns a commission of 12% on all his sales.

   a) Calculate how much commission George will earn if he makes sales of $500.00, $1000.00, or $2000.00.

   $60.00, $120.00, $240.00

   b) Write an equation that shows the relationship between his sales and his commission. Which is the independent variable?

   earnings = 0.12 × sales
   independent variable is the sales

c) Sketch a graph that shows George's income from sales of \$500.00, \$1000.00, and \$2000.00. What is the slope?

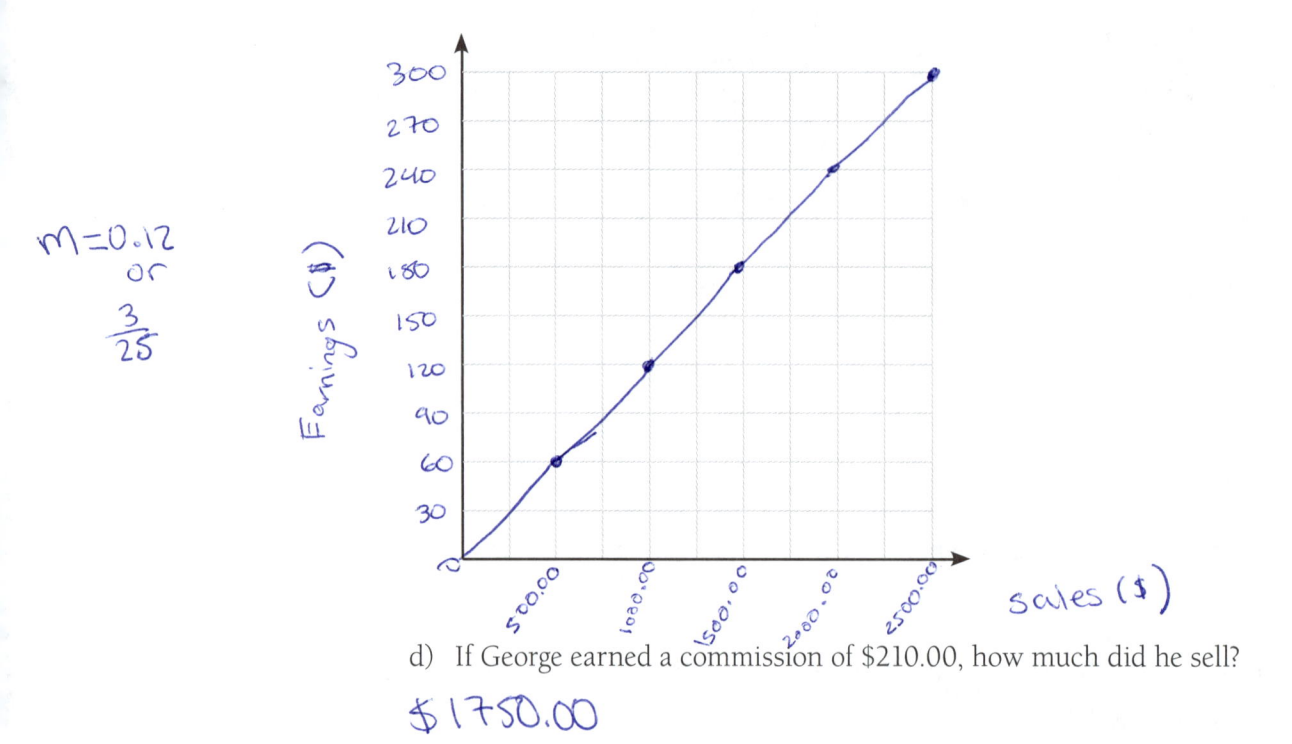

$m = 0.12$ or $\frac{3}{25}$

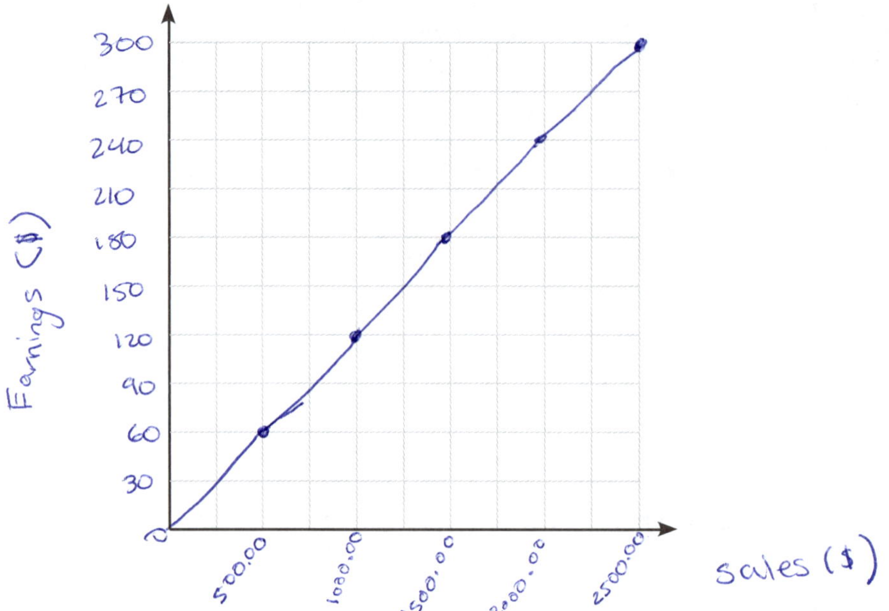

d) If George earned a commission of \$210.00, how much did he sell?

\$1750.00

Chapter 1 Slope and Rate of Change 47

Example 3

Reg timed himself jogging on a race course. He passed the 300-m point 1.5 minutes after starting, and the 600-m point after 2.8 minutes.

a) Show this on a graph.

b) What was his average rate in m/min for this portion of the race?

SOLUTION

(x, y)

a) The graph will pass through (0, 0), because he ran 0 distance in 0 time. It will also pass through points (1.5, 300) and (2.8, 600).

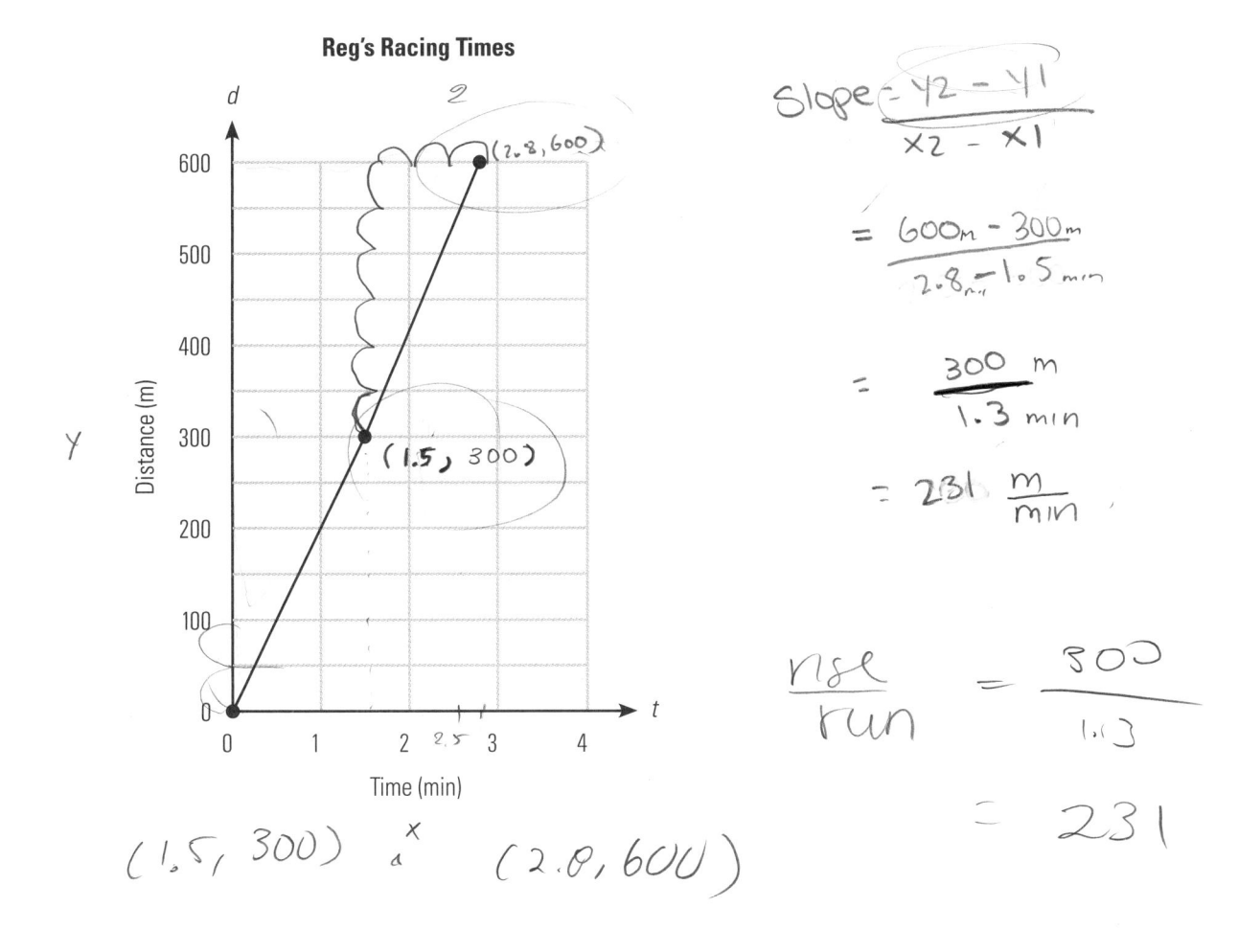

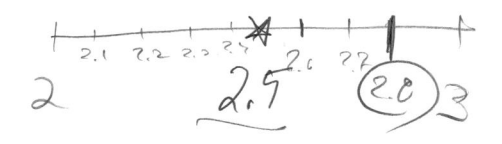

Reg's Racing Times

[Graph: Distance (m) vs Time (min), showing points (1.5, 300) and (2.8, 600)]

$$\text{Slope} = \frac{y_2 - y_1}{x_2 - x_1}$$

$$= \frac{600\,m - 300\,m}{2.8\,m - 1.5\,min}$$

$$= \frac{300\,m}{1.3\,min}$$

$$= 231 \frac{m}{min}$$

(1.5, 300)   (2.8, 600)

$$\frac{rise}{run} = \frac{300}{1.3}$$

$$= 231$$

b) The rate of change is equal to the slope of the graph.

$$m = \frac{y_2 - y_1}{x_2 - x_1}$$

$$m = \frac{600 - 300}{2.8 - 1.5}$$

$$m = \frac{300}{1.3}$$

$$m = \frac{300}{13}$$

$$m \approx 23.1$$

Reg ran at a rate of about 23.1 m/min.

ALTERNATIVE SOLUTION

Slope can be calculated using the change in rise (represented by the distance Reg ran) over the change in run (represented by the time).

Calculate the change in distance.

600 − 0 = 600

Calculate the change in time.

2.8 − 0 = 2.8

$$m = \frac{\text{rise}}{\text{run}}$$

$$m = \frac{600}{2.8}$$

$$m \approx 23.1$$

Reg ran at a rate of about 23.1 m/min.

BUILD YOUR SKILLS

7. Mariya is filling a rectangular swimming pool with water. She knows that the pool will hold about 13 500 gallons of water. After 45 minutes she estimates that there are approximately 2250 gallons of water in the pool.

   a) At what rate was the pool being filled?

   50 gal/min or 3000 gal/h

   b) How long will it take to fill the pool at this rate?

   270 min or 4.5 h

8. Tom is a long-haul truck driver. On the first leg of his current trip, he travelled 380 km in 5 hours.

   a) If he drove at a constant speed, what was his rate of travel?

   76 km/h

   b) After the 5th hour, he sped up. After 9 hours he had travelled a total of 764 km. What was his average rate of travel after he sped up?

   96 km/h

9. Maryam is reading a book at a rate of 0.6 pages/minute.

   a) How long will it take her to read the entire 321-page book?

   535 minutes or 8 hours 55 mins

   b) After 2 hours, how many pages will she have read?

   72 pages

PRACTISE YOUR NEW SKILLS

1. The line on a graph has the following points. Calculate the slope of the line.

   a) (0, 0) and (4, 204)

   51

   b) (12, 3) and (16, 4.5)

   $\frac{3}{8}$ or 0.375

   c) (150, 3) and (25, 6)

   $-\frac{3}{125}$ or −0.024

2. a) Draw a solid line on the graph that passes through point (0, 0) and has a slope of $\frac{5}{4}$.

   b) Draw a dotted line on the graph that passes through point (2, 1) and has a slope of $\frac{2}{3}$.

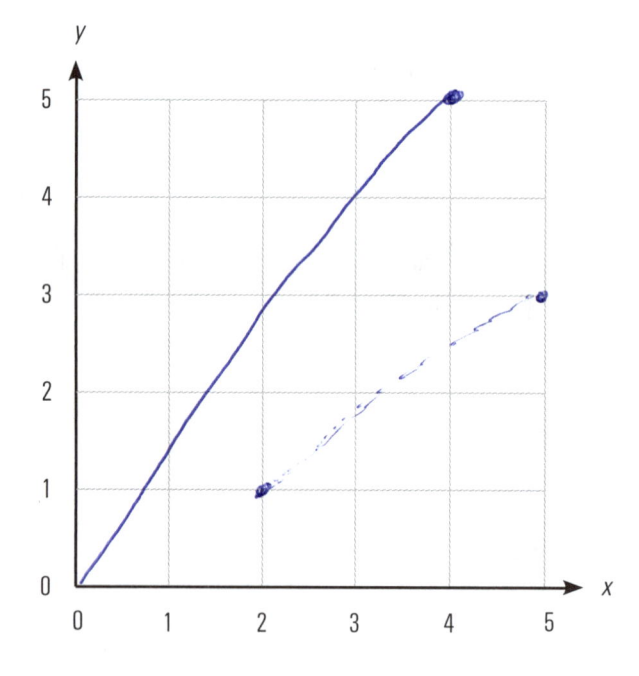

3. Henrik earns $73.20 in 6 hours at his weekend job. Javier earns $55.50 in 5 hours.

   a) Calculate their earnings for five different lengths of time.

Hours	Henrik	Javier
1	$12.20	$11.10
2	$24.40	$22.20
3	$36.60	$33.30
4	$48.80	$44.40
5	$61.00	$55.50

   b) On the same graph, draw a solid line indicating Henrik's earnings and a dotted line showing Javier's earnings.

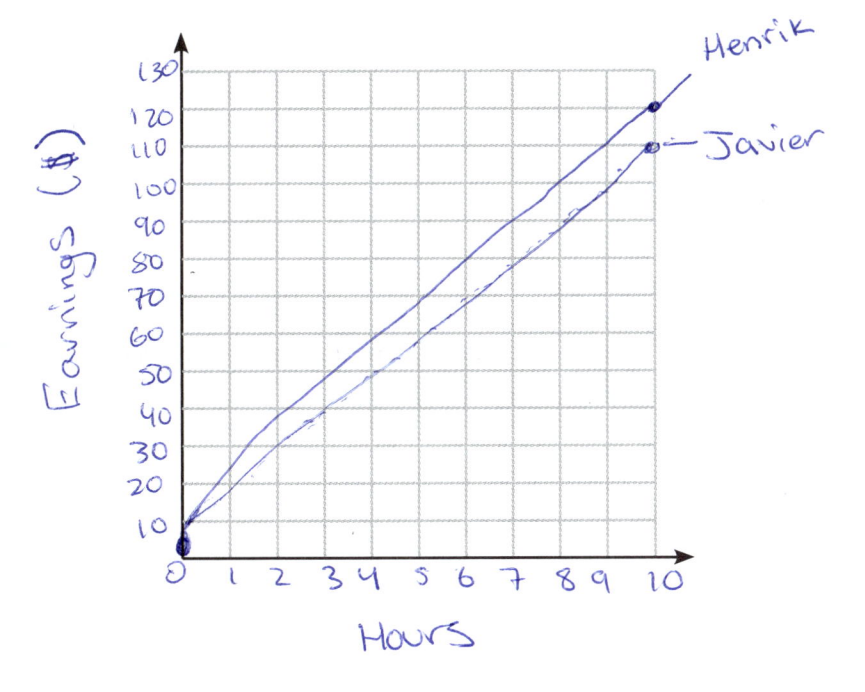

c) Who makes more money after an 8-hour shift?

Henrik did

d) Calculate Henrik's and Javier's rate of earning.

= $12.20/h   *= $11.10/h*

4. Janice is a real estate agent. When she makes a sale, she earns a commission of 4% of the value of the house. She earned $7560.00 on the sale of a house. What was the selling price?

$189 000.00

5. Rita is participating in a cycling trip. After 2 hours and 15 minutes of cycling, she takes a rest. She has travelled 40 km. She then continues cycling and stops at a location 75 km from her starting point. She has cycled a total of 4 hours.

a) What was her average rate of travel between the 40-km stop and the 75-km stop?

20 km/h

b) If she continues cycling at the same rate, how far will she have travelled after 6 hours of cycling in total?

115 km

Travelling by bicycle can be a great way to see the scenery and get some exercise.

6. Sheila and Brandy are on a backpacking trip.

   a) If Sheila walked 28.8 km in 6 hours and Brandy walked 32.2 km in 7 hours, who is the faster walker?

   Sheila is the fast walker

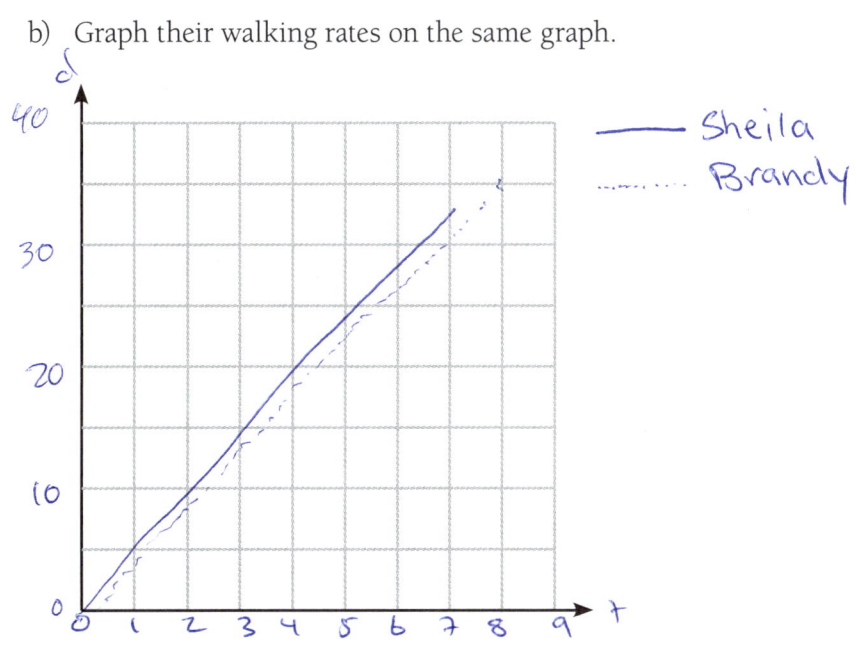

   b) Graph their walking rates on the same graph.

   —— Sheila
   ······ Brandy

   c) How long does it take each of them to walk 10 km?

   Sheila = 2.1 h
   Brandy = 2.2 h.

7. Water flows from a tank at a rate of 1500 litres per minute. The tank has a volume of 480 000 L.

   a) Fill in the following table showing how much water is left in 30-minute intervals.

Time elapsed (minutes)	Volume of water remaining (L)
0	480 000
30	435 000
60	390 000
90	345 000
120	300 000
150	255 000

   b) Draw a graph of the data.

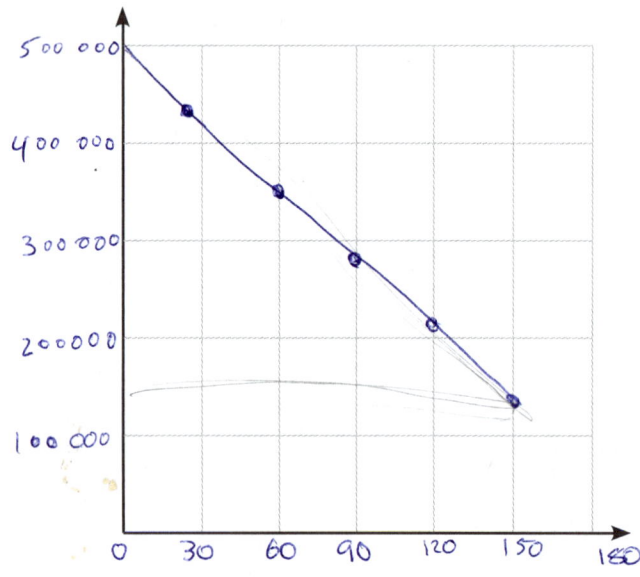

   c) Calculate the slope. What does it represent?

   M = -1500

   The slope is the rate at which the water volume decreases, -1500 L/min

   d) When will the tank be empty?

   320 min

CHAPTER TEST

1. Calculate the slope of a ramp rising to a deck that is 1.8 m high and starts a horizontal distance of 4.5 m from the deck.

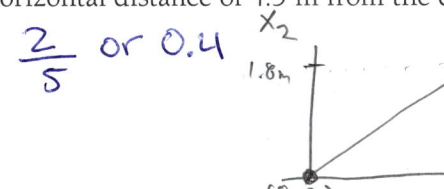

   $\frac{2}{5}$ or 0.4

   $$\text{slope} = \frac{1.8\text{m} - 0\text{m}}{4.5\text{m} - 0\text{m}} = 0.4$$

2. On a set of stairs, the slope of the railing is $\frac{2}{3}$. How much higher will the railing be a horizontal distance of 250 cm from the base?

   167 cm

   slope = $\frac{2}{3}$, $x_2 = 250$ cm

   $$\frac{2}{3} = \frac{y_2 - 0}{250 - 0} = \frac{y}{250}$$

   $\frac{2}{3} = \frac{y_2}{250}$ → 166.7 = **167 cm**

3. A waterslide has an angle of elevation of 20°. What is the rise for a run of 2.6 m?

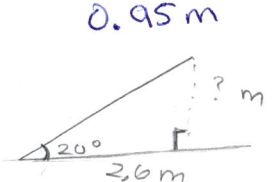

   0.95 m

   $2.6\text{m} \cdot \tan 20° = \frac{\text{rise}}{2.6\text{m}} \cdot 2.6\text{m}$

   rise = 0.946 = **0.95 m**

4. Garry is making a temporary ramp from the ground to the top of his patio so that he can roll a cart up it to move furniture in. The surface of the patio is 3 feet 9 inches above the ground and Garry wants the ramp to have a slope of no more than 0.375.

   ×12: 1 ft = 12 in, ? ft = 9 in (÷12)

   0.75 ft + 3 ft = 3.75 ft

   a) What is the shortest horizontal distance he can have from the base of the patio to the base of the ramp?

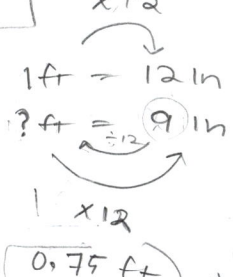

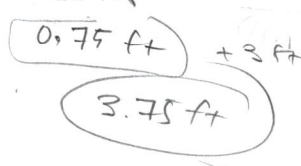

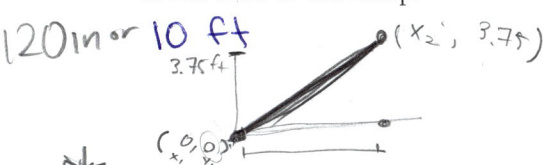

   120 in or 10 ft

   Slope = $\frac{y_2 - y_1}{x_2 - x_1}$

   $0.375 = \frac{3.75 - 0}{x_2 - 0}$

   $\frac{8}{3} = \frac{x_2}{3.75}$

   x = 10

   b) What is the shortest length the surface of the ramp can be?

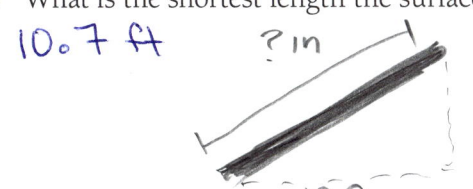

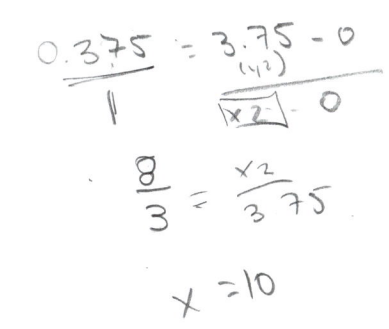

   10.7 ft

   (45 in, 120 in)

   c) What will be the angle of elevation of the ramp?

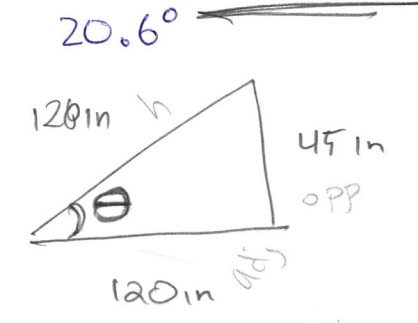

   20.6°

   $\tan\theta = \frac{45\text{ in}}{120\text{ in}}$

   $\tan\theta = 0.375$

   $\theta = \tan^{-1}(0.375) = $ **20.6°**

5. Shandra has a greenhouse in her backyard. The pitch of the roof is 4:12.

   a) What is the slope of the roof?

   $\frac{1}{3}$ or about 0.33

   b) What is the angle of elevation?

   18.4°

6. One section of the Crowsnest Highway has a 6% grade. What will be the vertical change for a horizontal change of 15 km?

   0.9 km or 900 m

7. a) How long will a section of railroad track be if it rises 6.8 metres for a run of 125.9 metres?

   126.1 m

   b) What is the percent grade of the road?

   5.4%

   slope = $\frac{rise}{run}$
   = 0.054 × 100%

   5.4%

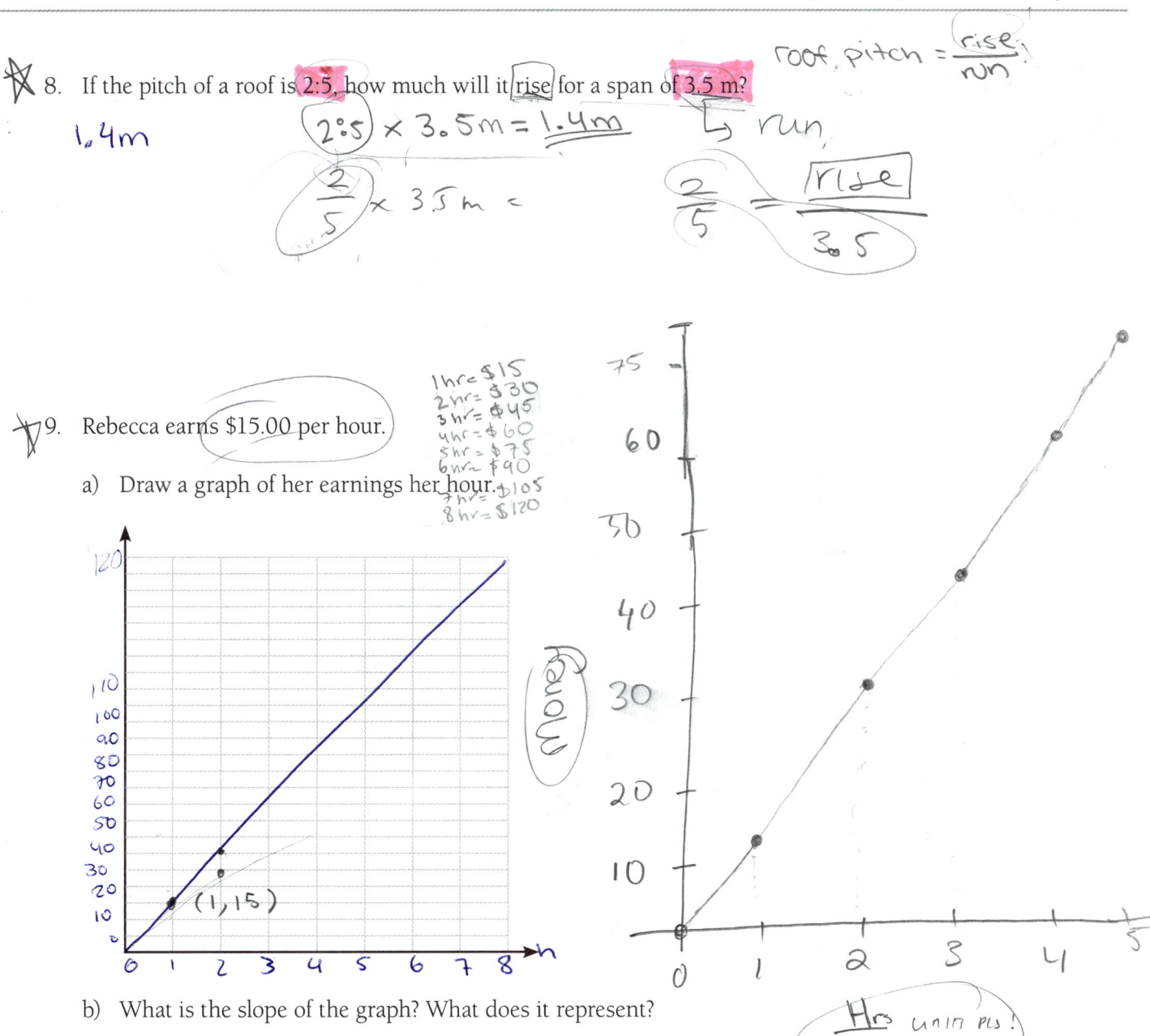

Chapter 1   Slope and Rate of Change   **57**

8. If the pitch of a roof is 2:5, how much will it rise for a span of 3.5 m?

    1.4 m

    (2:5) × 3.5 m = 1.4 m

    $\frac{2}{5} \times 3.5\,m =$

    roof pitch = $\frac{rise}{run}$

    ↳ run

    $\frac{2}{5} = \frac{rise}{3.5}$

9. Rebecca earns $15.00 per hour.

    1 hr = $15
    2 hr = $30
    3 hr = $45
    4 hr = $60
    5 hr = $75
    6 hr = $90
    7 hr = $105
    8 hr = $120

    a) Draw a graph of her earnings her hour.

    (1, 15)

    Hrs unit p.s.!

    b) What is the slope of the graph? What does it represent?

    m = 15 representing how much dollars earned per hour.

    c) How much will Rebecca have earned after 8 hours?

    $120.00

Chapter 2

Graphical Representations

Graphs are useful tools in many types of work. They can be used to track profits, expenses, product sales, and many other kinds of data.

2.1 Broken Line Graphs

NEW SKILLS: WORKING WITH BROKEN LINE GRAPHS

broken line graph: a graph that uses points joined by line segments to display data

In the last chapter you used graphs to show slope and rate of change. In this section you will learn about **broken line graphs**. A broken line graph shows information by plotting values and joining them with line segments.

The title of a graph and the labelling of the horizontal and vertical axes tell you about the data shown. If you are drawing the graph, you have to decide what variables to display on each axis, as well as a scale for them. The independent variable goes on the horizontal axis, and the dependent variable goes on the vertical axis.

Broken line graphs are useful for showing a trend over time. They can also be used to compare sets of data, using multiple lines on the same graph.

For more details, see page 56 of *MathWorks 11*.

Example 1

The graph below shows the average snowfall in Regina, Saskatchewan, by month.

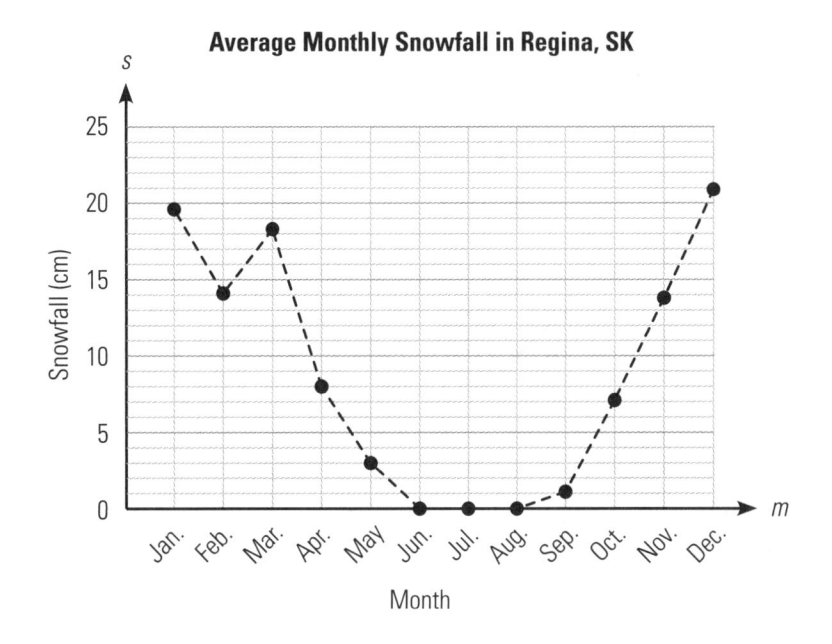

Average Monthly Snowfall in Regina, SK

a) What month has the highest average snowfall? How much snow fell that month?

b) During what three months is there no snowfall in Regina?

c) During what month is the average snowfall approximately twice as much as the average October snowfall?

SOLUTION

a) December has the highest average snowfall at approximately 21 cm.

b) There is no snowfall recorded in June, July, or August.

c) Use the graph to find October's average snowfall. It is just over 7 cm, so you need to find what month has approximately double that snowfall, or about 14 cm. February's average snowfall is just over 14 cm.

BUILD YOUR SKILLS

1. The following graph shows Tom's spending on lunches for the past week.

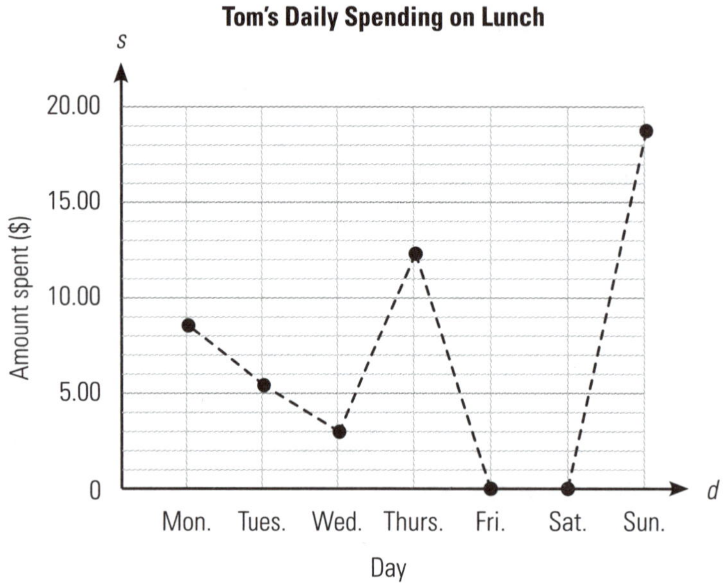
Tom's Daily Spending on Lunch
s
20.00
15.00
10.00
5.00
0
Amount spent ($)
d
Mon.
Tues.
Wed.
Thurs.
Fri.
Sat.
Sun.
Day

a) How much did he spend on lunch on Wednesday? Friday?

W = $3.00 F = $0

b) On what day did he spend the most on lunch, and how much was it? Give one possible reason why he might have spent so much that day.

He spent about $19.00 for lunch on Sunday. May had gone out with friends.

2. Use the graph provided to answer the following questions.

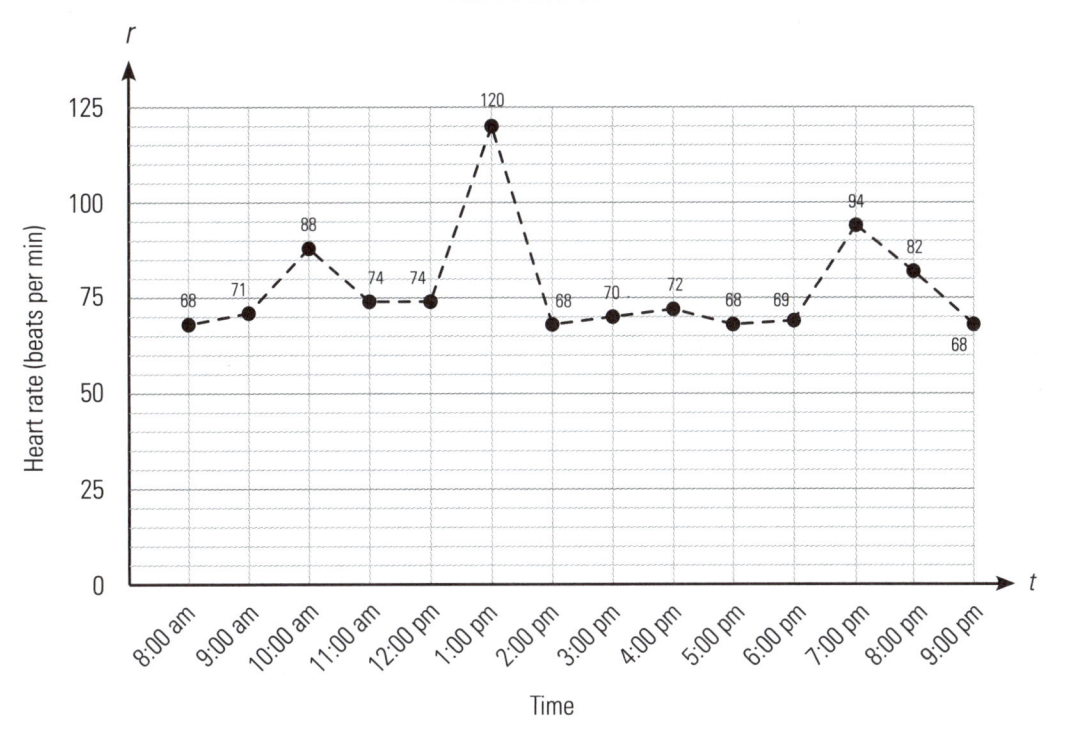

Katie's Heart Rate

a) What does the graph show?

Katie's heart rate in beats per minute each hour from 8:00am to 9:00pm.

b) When was Katie's heart rate the lowest and what was it?

8:00 am, 2:00 pm, 5pm and 9pm, 68 beats per minute.

c) When was her heart rate the highest? Why might this have been so?

Her highest was at 1pm. She may have just been involved in some physical activity.

3. The graph below shows the value of a particular stock that Vince bought, over a 10-week period. If Week 1 is when Vince bought the stock, use the graph to answer the following questions.

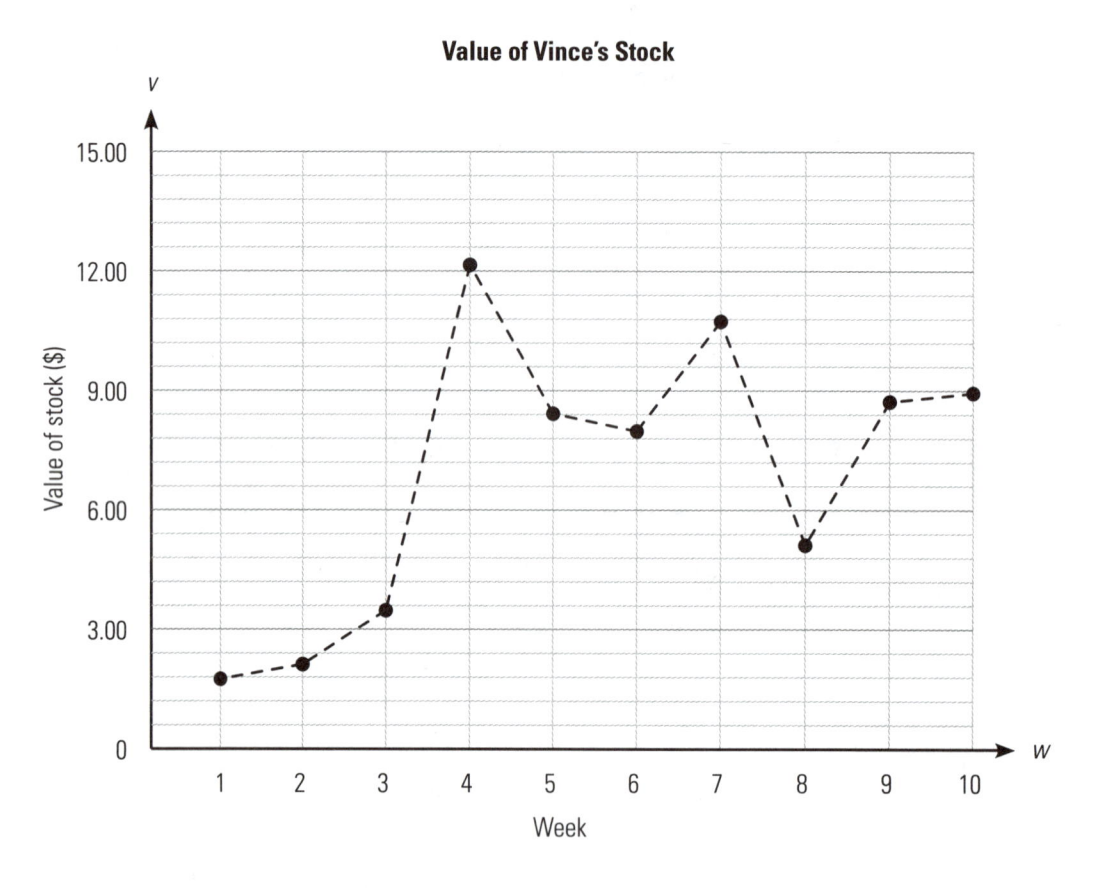

Value of Vince's Stock

a) At what price did Vince buy the stock?

Approx. $1.75

b) When was the stock worth the most? If Vince had sold it then, what would have been his profit?

Stock was worth most ($12.15) in week 4. He would have earned $10.40 per share of the stock.

Example 2

Jacob owns a small appliance repair company. He tracked the company's net profits over a 10-year period. He is examining the data to see if there is a trend and to decide if he can increase the salaries of his employees.

COMPANY'S NET PROFIT, 2000–2009

Year	2000	2001	2002	2003	2004	2005	2006	2007	2008	2009
Profit (thousands of dollars)	5	15	18	35	40	38	42	20	58	65

a) Graph the data on a broken line graph.

b) Is there a general trend in the data? If so, what is it? Are there any exceptions to the trend?

SOLUTION

a) The year is the independent variable and should be displayed on the horizontal axis. The net profit is the dependent variable and will be along the vertical axis. A suitable choice for scale would be 1 along the horizontal axis and 5 along the vertical axis.

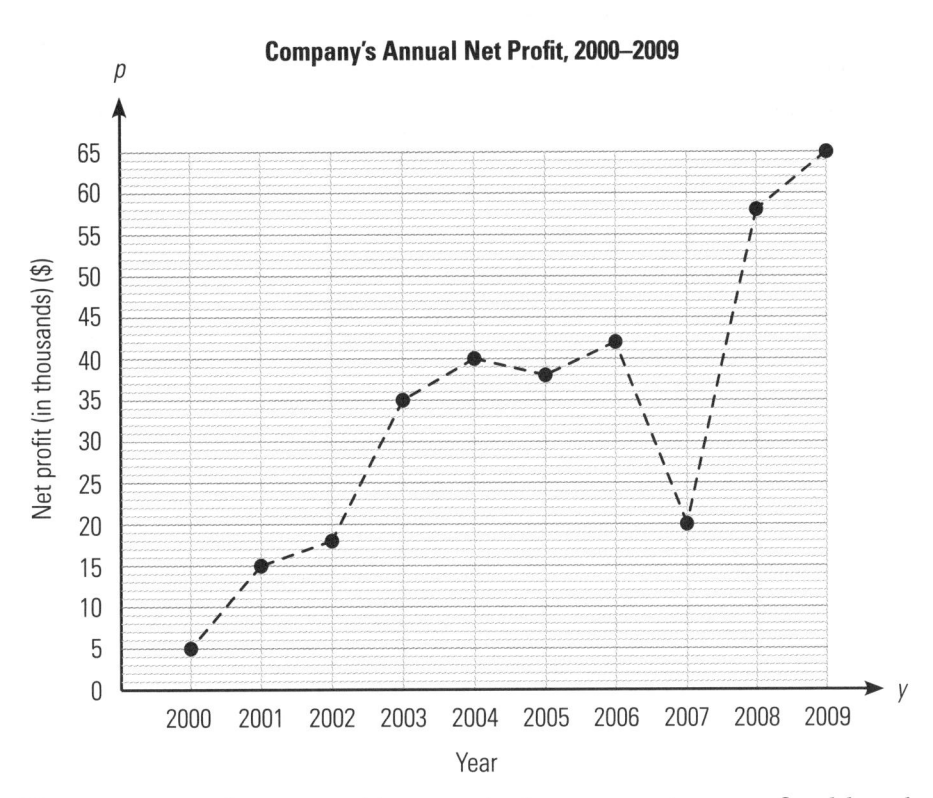

b) There appears to be a general increase in the company's net profit, although there was a big decline in 2007.

BUILD YOUR SKILLS

4. *Canadian Review* magazine is published once a week. The company keeps track of the number of magazines sold from different outlets to determine the market trend. The following data show the number of *Canadian Review* sales at a local store over the past eight weeks.

CANADIAN REVIEW MAGAZINE SALES								
Week	1	2	3	4	5	6	7	8
Number of copies sold	20	22	18	15	30	26	32	28

Draw a broken line graph to display the data. Are sales of the magazine increasing or decreasing?

5. Stephanie works in a pediatrician's office. One of her jobs is to track the growth rate of the babies the doctor treats. The table below shows baby Jessica's weight for the first twelve weeks of her life. Draw a broken line graph of the data and discuss the trend.

WEIGHT CHART, JESSICA, WEEKS 0–12													
Age (weeks)	0	1	2	3	4	5	6	7	8	9	10	11	12
Weight (kg)	2.4	2.2	2.6	2.9	2.9	3.1	3.5	3.6	4.0	4.0	4.2	4.4	5.1

6. A long-distance truck driver recorded the distances he drove each day for two weeks.

DISTANCE DRIVEN PER DAY

Day	1	2	3	4	5	6	7	8	9	10	11	12	13	14
Distance (km)	450	235	406	0	0	560	325	386	264	453	0	0	356	289

a) Graph the data using a broken line graph.

Saskatchewan provides 10% of the world's exported wheat. The wheat is delivered to market by truck and train.

b) Are there any data points that seem unusual? What might have caused them?

c) Do you think this graph is a good representation of the data?

NEW SKILLS: DISCUSSING TRENDS AND ESTIMATING VALUES

interpolate: to estimate a value between two known values

extrapolate: to estimate a value beyond a known range of values

A broken line graph may help you discover a regular pattern in the data. It may show a generally increasing or decreasing trend, which can allow you to **interpolate** or **extrapolate** a value.

Interpolating means to estimate a value between two values shown on the graph. Extrapolating means to predict a value from beyond the given data shown on the graph.

For more details, see page 60 of *MathWorks 11*.

Example 3

The following graph shows the growth rate of a bean plant that David planted in his vegetable garden.

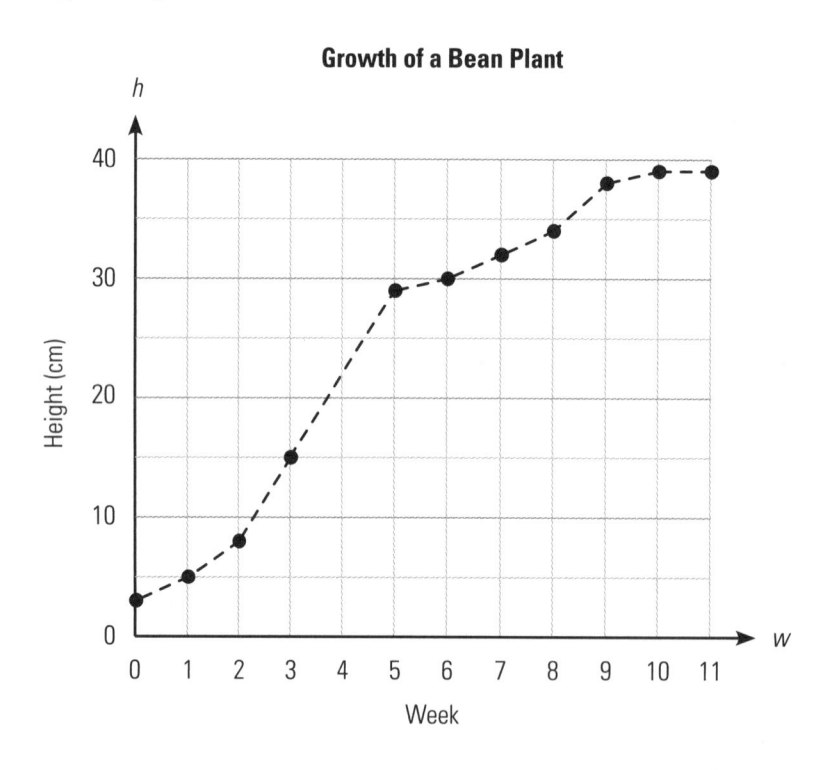

Growth of a Bean Plant

(Graph: Height (cm) vs. Week, with data points approximately at (0,3), (1,5), (2,8), (3,15), (4,?), (5,29), (6,30), (7,32), (8,34), (9,38), (10,39), (11,39))

a) David forgot to record the height of the bean plant in Week 4. Use the graph to interpolate the height of the plant that week.

b) What might the height of the plant be in Week 12?

c) Write a statement describing trends in the bean plant's growth rate from Week 0 to Week 11.

SOLUTION

a) Between Week 2 and Week 5, the bean plant seems to have grown at a fairly steady rate. Its height in Week 4 was probably between the heights in Weeks 3 and 5. Add the heights at Weeks 3 and 5, and divide by 2.

$(29 + 15) \div 2 = 22$

The height of the plant in Week 4 was probably around 22 cm.

b) The plant's growth seems to have slowed or stopped in Weeks 9 to 11. It might stay at 39 cm in Week 12, or grow slightly, maybe to about 40 cm.

c) The plant grew at a fairly steady rate for the first two weeks, and had a rapid growth from Week 2 to Week 5. The growth was then fairly steady until Week 9, when it seemed to stop growing.

BUILD YOUR SKILLS

7. Thérèse is on a road trip and is keeping track of her car's fuel consumption. The graph below shows the amount of gas in Thérèse's car at different times of the day. Use the graph to discuss what she may have been doing during the different time frames.

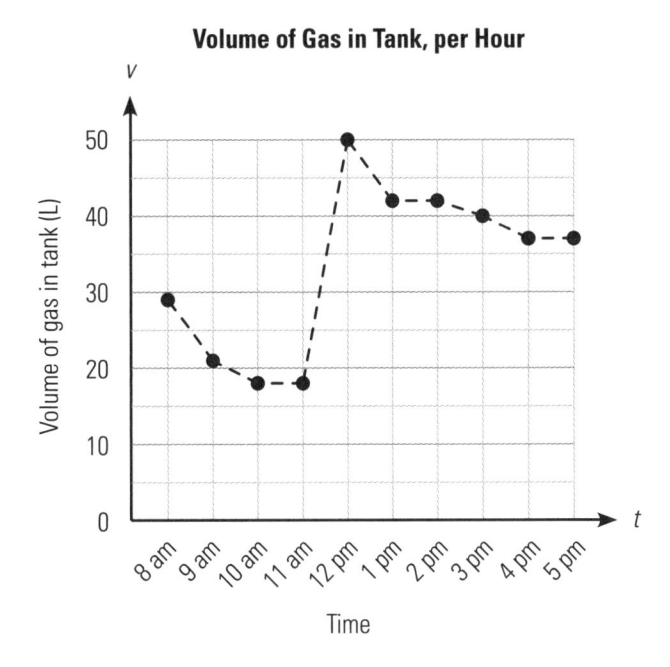

8. Lumber is often priced in board feet. A board foot is a piece of lumber 1 foot long by 1 foot wide by 1 inch thick. The graph below represents the cost per board foot of kiln-dried spruce over a period of one year.

Cost of Kiln-Dried Spruce

a) What is the general trend in cost of kiln-dried spruce?

b) The graph does not show the cost in August. Use the graph to interpolate the cost of kiln-dried spruce that month.

c) Based on the general trend in the data, what would you estimate the cost of kiln-dried spruce to be the following month, March?

Example 4

Brett is a real estate agent and is comparing the average listed price for houses in Vancouver to those in Regina from 2006 to 2010.

HOUSE PRICES, REGINA AND VANCOUVER, 2006–2010

Year	2006	2007	2008	2009	2010
Regina	$132 000.00	$166 000.00	$230 000.00	$230 000.00	$232 000.00
Vancouver	$571 000.00	$594 000.00	$592 000.00	$665 000.00	$685 000.00

a) Display the information on a broken line graph.

b) What conclusions can you draw from the table about house prices in the two cities?

c) What can you tell from the graph more readily than from the table?

SOLUTION

a) Drawing a multiple broken line graph is just like drawing a single one, except that you put two or more lines on the same set of axes. You must also use a legend to indicate which line represents which data.

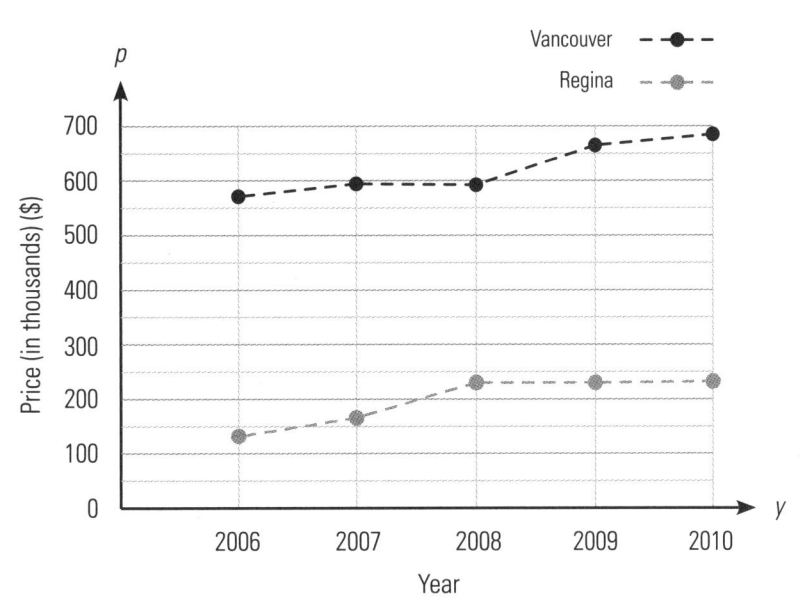

House Prices in Vancouver and Regina, 2006–2010

b) From the table, you can tell that house prices in Vancouver are much higher than in Regina.

c) From the graph, you can tell that the prices in Regina increased more rapidly than in Vancouver from 2006 to 2008. After 2008, the prices increased more rapidly in Vancouver.

BUILD YOUR SKILLS

9. Raquel is an agent for a cell phone company. The data below indicates the number of cell phones sold to males and females in the last year.

CELL PHONE BUYERS BY GENDER												
Month	Jan.	Feb.	Mar.	Apr.	May	Jun.	Jul.	Aug.	Sep.	Oct.	Nov.	Dec.
Male	53	150	75	238	105	167	102	309	298	76	153	398
Female	21	222	89	174	309	111	76	398	442	123	67	299

a) Use the data to draw a double line graph.

b) Write a statement describing the general trend in cell phone purchases over the year.

c) Does the graph indicate any relationship between the number of cell phones purchased by males compared to females? Why or why not?

d) Do you think this graph is a useful representation of the data? If so, why? If not, what might be a better way to show trends in cell phone purchases?

10. At the end of every month, Suzanne keeps a record of the price of two stocks she bought.

Month	Jun.	Jul.	Aug.	Sep.	Oct.	Nov.	Dec.	Jan.	Feb.	Mar.	Apr.	May
Stock A	$2.75	$2.95	$1.43	$0.89	$0.76	$0.98	$1.14	$1.28	$0.65	$0.45	$0.76	$0.53
Stock B	$1.25	$1.11	$1.32	$1.45	$1.20	$1.25	$1.87	$1.59	$1.76	$1.43	$1.38	$1.21

a) Draw a double broken line graph.

b) Use the graph to discuss the trends in the prices of the two stocks and how the prices of the two stocks compare.

c) If Suzanne were to sell one and buy more of the other, which would you suggest she sell? Why?

NEW SKILLS: WORKING WITH MISLEADING GRAPHS

The scale and the size of a graph can influence the way you interpret the data. By changing the scale on an axis or changing the starting point of an axis, you can change how a viewer interprets the graph; while the graph will still be right, you can influence a person's perception of the data.

Example 5

The graph below indicates the approximate cost of sheet metal per tonne over a period of time.

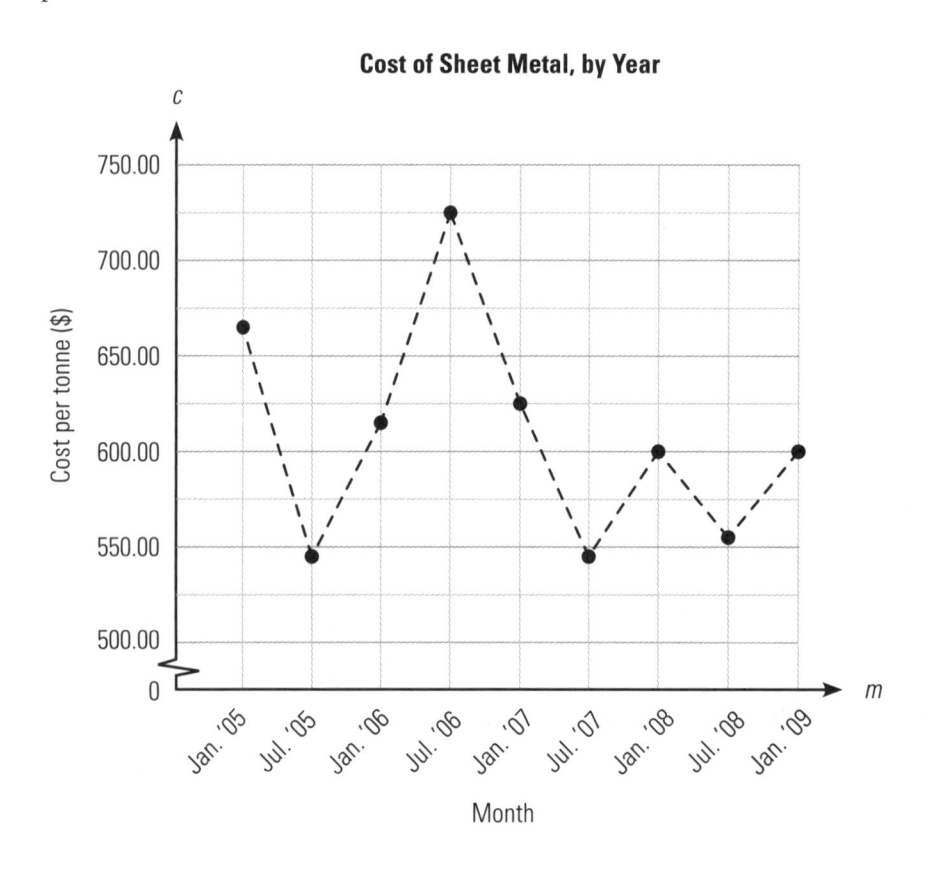

Cost of Sheet Metal, by Year

a) What does it appear has happened to the price of sheet metal over time?

b) What are the scale and starting point of the vertical axis?

c) Redraw the graph starting the vertical axis at zero and using the same scale. What does this new graph show about the fluctuation in prices?

SOLUTION

a) The graph seems to show that there was a lot of fluctuation in the price of sheet metal over time.

b) The vertical axis begins at 500 and is divided into groups of 50.

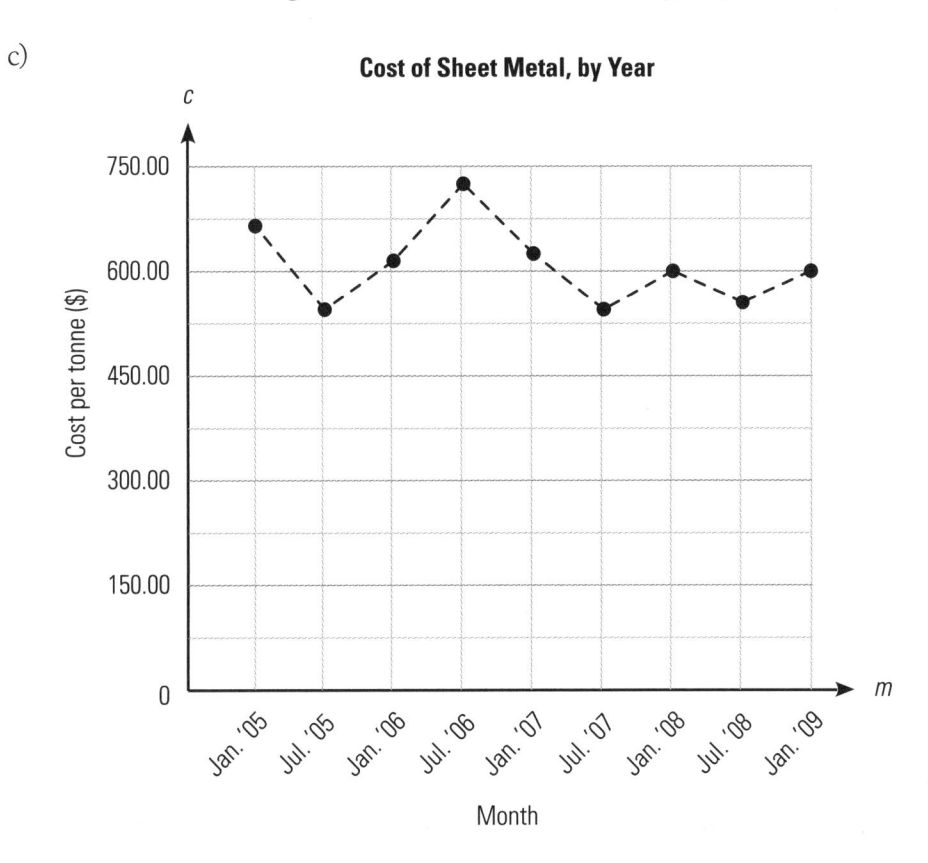

c)

Cost of Sheet Metal, by Year

[Graph: Cost per tonne ($) vs. Month, with vertical axis from 0 to 750.00 in increments of 150.00, and horizontal axis from Jan. '05 to Jan. '09 in 6-month intervals. Data points approximately: Jan. '05: 670, Jul. '05: 550, Jan. '06: 610, Jul. '06: 735, Jan. '07: 620, Jul. '07: 550, Jan. '08: 600, Jul. '08: 570, Jan. '09: 600.]

When the vertical axis starts at zero, the fluctuations in price don't look as large.

BUILD YOUR SKILLS

11. Consider the graph below.

Marcia's Weekly Grocery Expenditures

Groceries are a significant weekly expense. If you plan your meals and look for new recipe ideas, you can keep your food costs down.

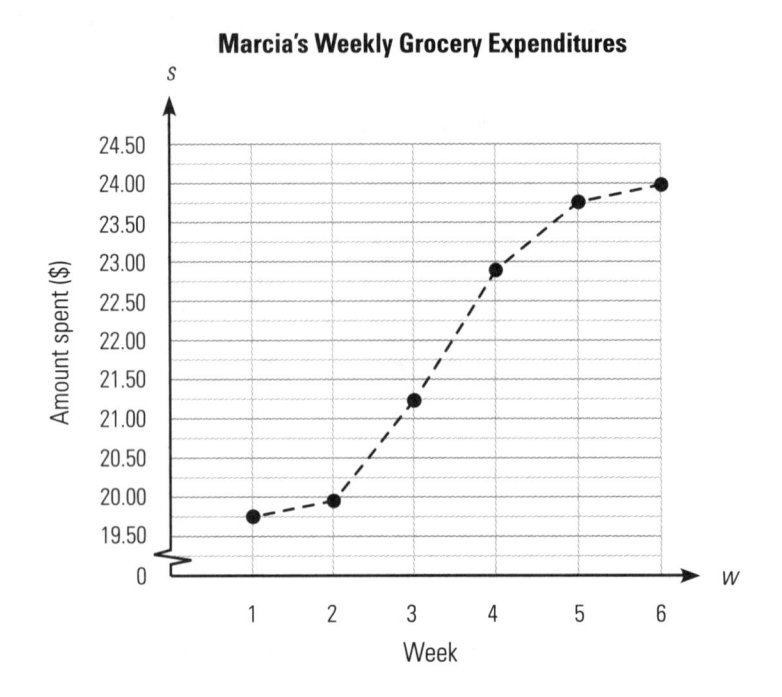

a) What does it represent?

b) What is the general trend in Marcia's weekly grocery expenditures?

c) What is misleading about the graph?

d) Draw a graph that better represents her expenditures.

12. Consider the two graphs below that show the percentage of the population of Alberta living in rural areas.

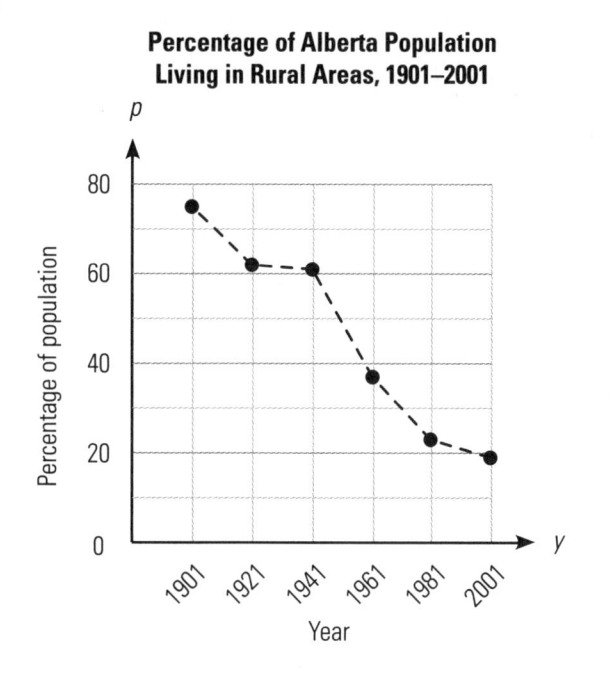

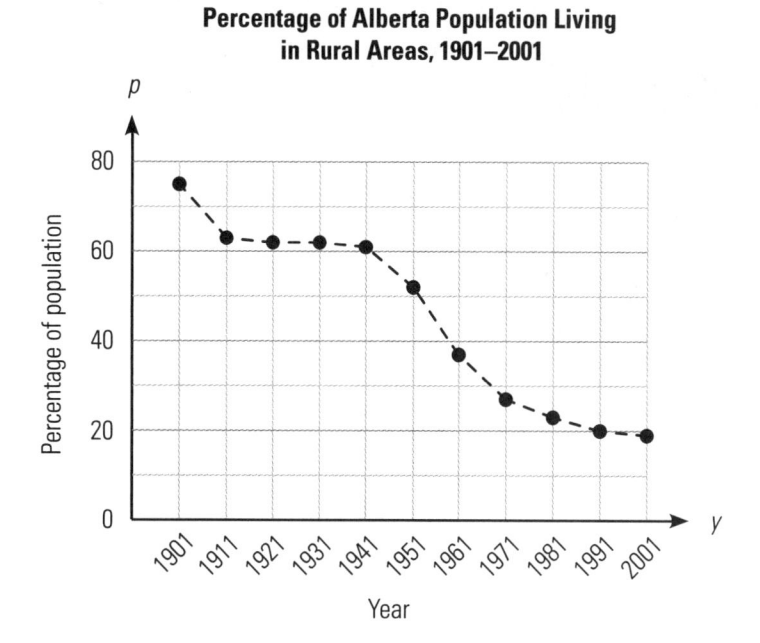

Percentage of Alberta Population Living in Rural Areas, 1901–2001

Percentage of Alberta Population Living in Rural Areas, 1901–2001

a) Which graph makes it appear that the decrease in rural population was more rapid? Why?

b) Which graph do you think is a better representation of the actual change in rural population? Why?

c) Use the graphs to interpolate what percent of the population was rural in 1916.

d) In what year was the population half rural and half urban?

e) Use the graph to extrapolate what percent of the population will be rural in 2011.

PRACTISE YOUR NEW SKILLS

1. Reba has joined a 13-week walking group. The graph below indicates her total steps per week. Use the graph to answer the following questions.

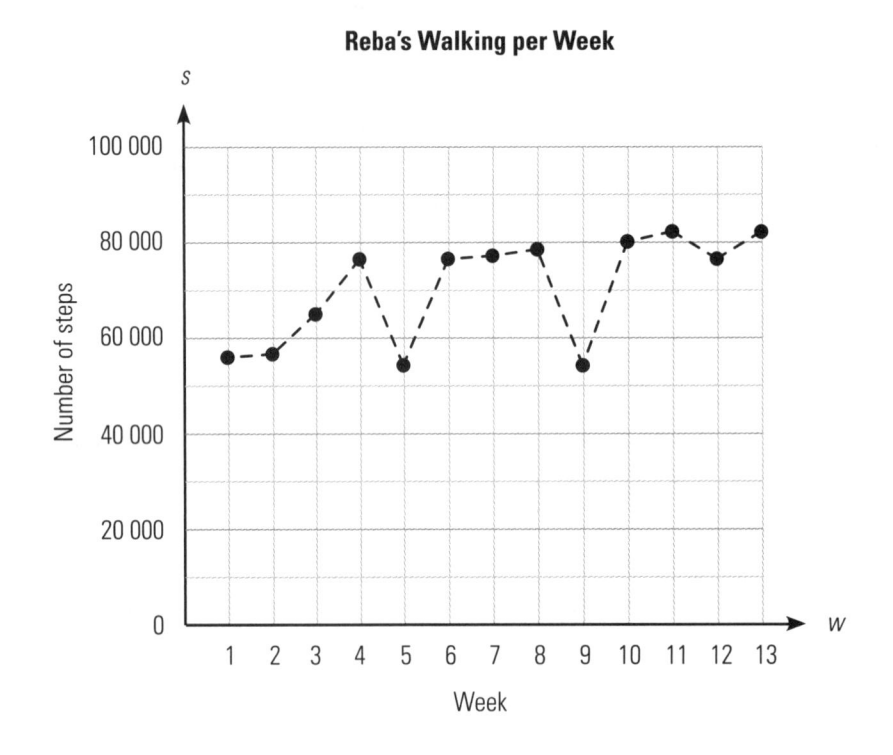

Reba's Walking per Week

(Graph: x-axis labeled Week (w) from 1 to 13; y-axis labeled Number of steps (s) from 0 to 100 000. Approximate data points: Week 1: 56 000; Week 2: 57 000; Week 3: 65 000; Week 4: 76 000; Week 5: 54 000; Week 6: 76 000; Week 7: 77 000; Week 8: 78 000; Week 9: 54 000; Week 10: 80 000; Week 11: 83 000; Week 12: 76 000; Week 13: 83 000.)

Walking can be a great way to get some exercise and spend time with friends.

a) Approximately how many steps did Reba walk the first week? The last week?

b) During what week(s) did she take the lowest number of steps? About how many steps did she take?

c) Is there a general trend in the number of steps she walked per week? If so, what is it?

2. The data below indicates the approximate area of forest burned in forest fires in Canada each year from 1999 to 2009. Display the data on a broken line graph and discuss any trends you see in the graph.

AREA OF FOREST BURNED IN CANADA, 1999–2009

Year	1999	2000	2001	2002	2003	2004	2005	2006	2007	2008	2009
No. of hectares burned (in millions)	1.6	0.6	0.6	2.9	1.7	3.3	1.7	2.8	1.6	1.7	0.8

3. The graph below shows the average house price in Vancouver in 2009, by month. Describe the trend in house prices in Vancouver during the year. During what month(s) were the prices highest?

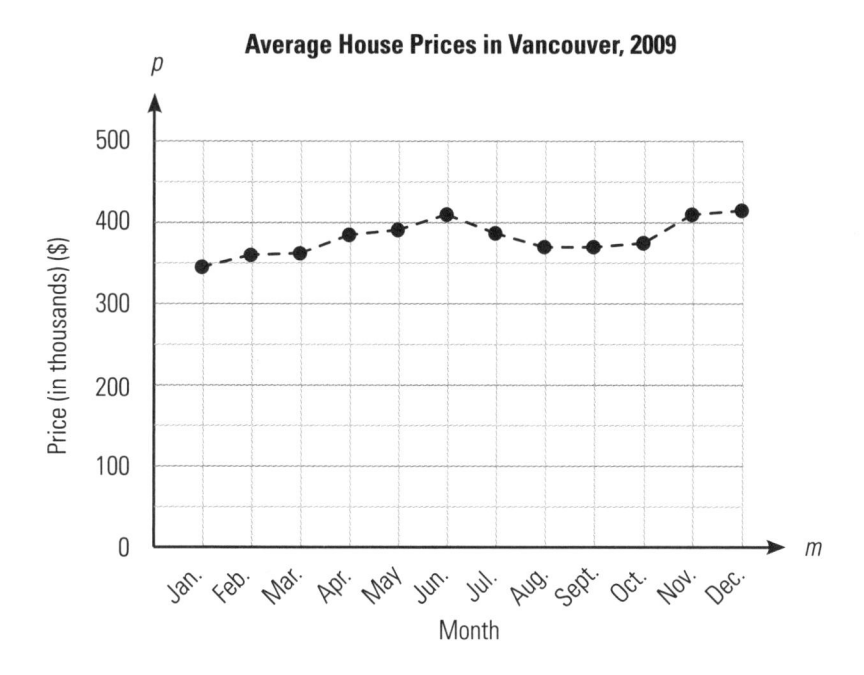

4. Use the multiple broken line graph provided to answer the following questions.

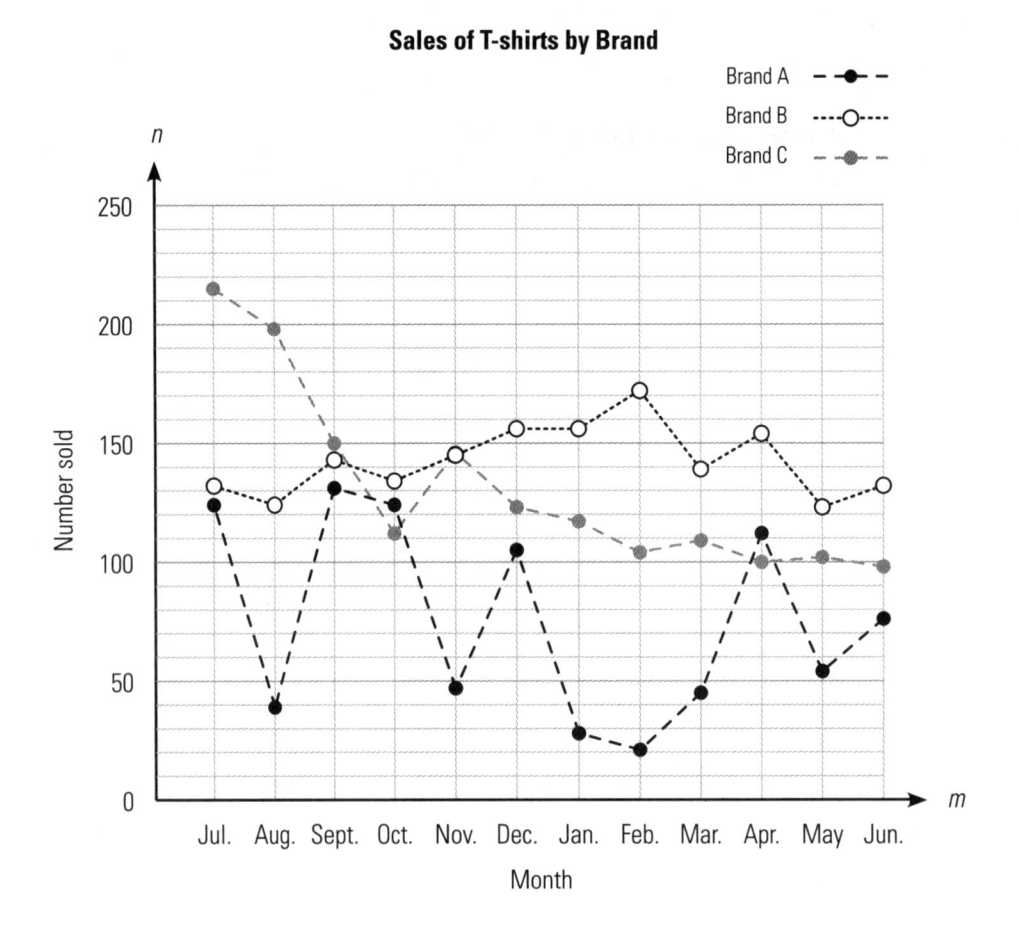

Sales of T-shirts by Brand

Brand A — ●——
Brand B ----○----
Brand C — ●——

a) What is the general trend for sales of each brand of T-shirt?

b) If you were to keep only two of the brands for sale, which two would you keep and why?

5. Each month the librarian does inventory to determine the number of different titles of different genres that are available in the library.

NUMBER OF BOOKS IN THE LIBRARY, BY GENRE

Month	Jan.	Feb.	Mar.	Apr.	May	Jun.	Jul.	Aug.
Science fiction	124	132	135	130	145	148	154	150
Historical fiction	128	154	156	150	153	160	162	162
Love stories	123	145	148	145	152	154	159	155

a) Use the data to draw a multiple line graph showing the number of science fiction, historical fiction, and love stories available each month over an 8-month period.

What types of books do you like to read? Do you visit the local library?

b) Explain any trends you see in the data. What might a drop in the number of titles available mean?

2.2 Bar Graphs

NEW SKILLS: WORKING WITH BAR GRAPHS

discrete data: data made up of distinct values, where intermediate values are not possible

A bar graph is another way to visually represent data. A bar graph is used to plot **discrete data** using rectangular bars, the lengths of which are proportional to the values represented. Discrete data is data that can only have certain distinct values; an example is the number of students in your class: the answer must be a whole number since you cannot have half a student in your class.

The bars on a bar graph can be either vertical or horizontal, and have spaces between them. Set the scale, label the axes, and give the graph a title the same way you would for a broken line graph.

As with broken line graphs, the scale and the starting point on the axes affect the way a graph is interpreted. By increasing or decreasing the scale, or by changing the starting point on an axis, you can make the viewer see the data a certain way.

For more details, see page 74 of *MathWorks 11*.

Example 1

The 2001 Canadian census data listed the following approximate populations of various cities, to the nearest thousand.

POPULATION OF CANADIAN CITIES, 2001							
City	Vancouver	Calgary	Victoria	Edmonton	Saskatoon	Winnipeg	Regina
Population (in thousands)	1987	951	312	938	197	671	193

Display the data on a bar graph.

SOLUTION

The data ranges from just under 200 to almost 2000, so increments of 100 would be appropriate for the vertical axis. Draw a bar with a height corresponding to the population.

You may want to arrange the bars according to height, because this gives a more visual representation of the ranking of the populations.

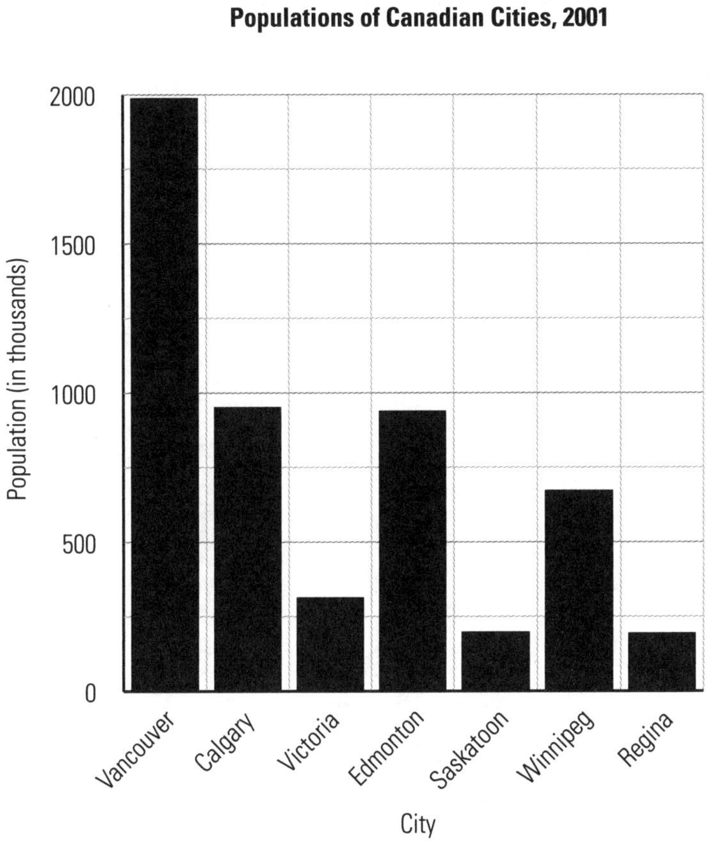
Populations of Canadian Cities, 2001
2000
1500
1000
500
0
Population (in thousands)
Vancouver
Calgary
Victoria
Edmonton
Saskatoon
Winnipeg
Regina
City

BUILD YOUR SKILLS

1. A company tracked how new software was obtained and installed on their computers. The results are given in the table below. Draw a bar graph to represent the data.

SOFTWARE INSTALLATIONS	
How software was obtained and installed	Percentage of total software installations
In-house IT department	58
In-house IT with help from provider	16
Outsourced to service provider	10
Outsourced to development partner	12
Other	4

2. The following graph shows Jamie's height from age 10 to age 18.

Jamie's Height

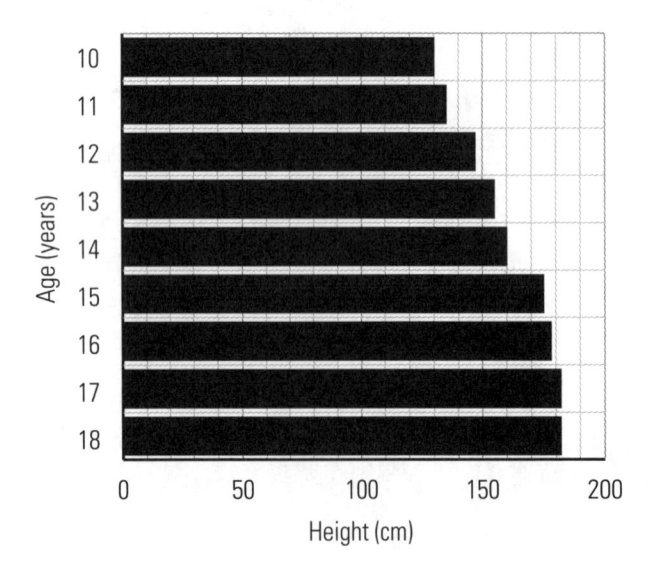

a) Suggest two ways to improve the way the data is presented.

b) Redraw the graph in a way that better represents the data.

3. Sabine is a staff supervisor at city fairgrounds. She made the graph below to show the number of employees working at the fair each month. Give two reasons why the graph may be misread.

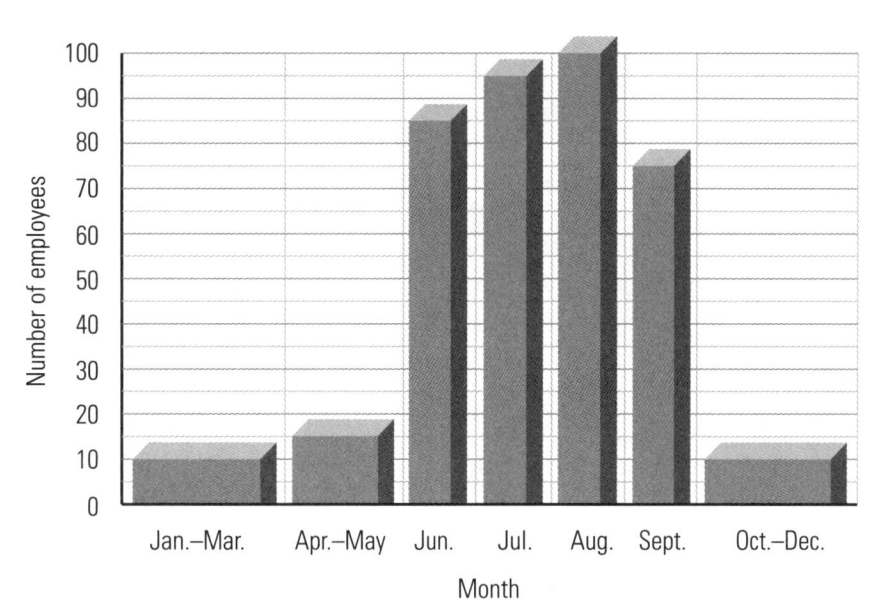

Employees Hired at Fair

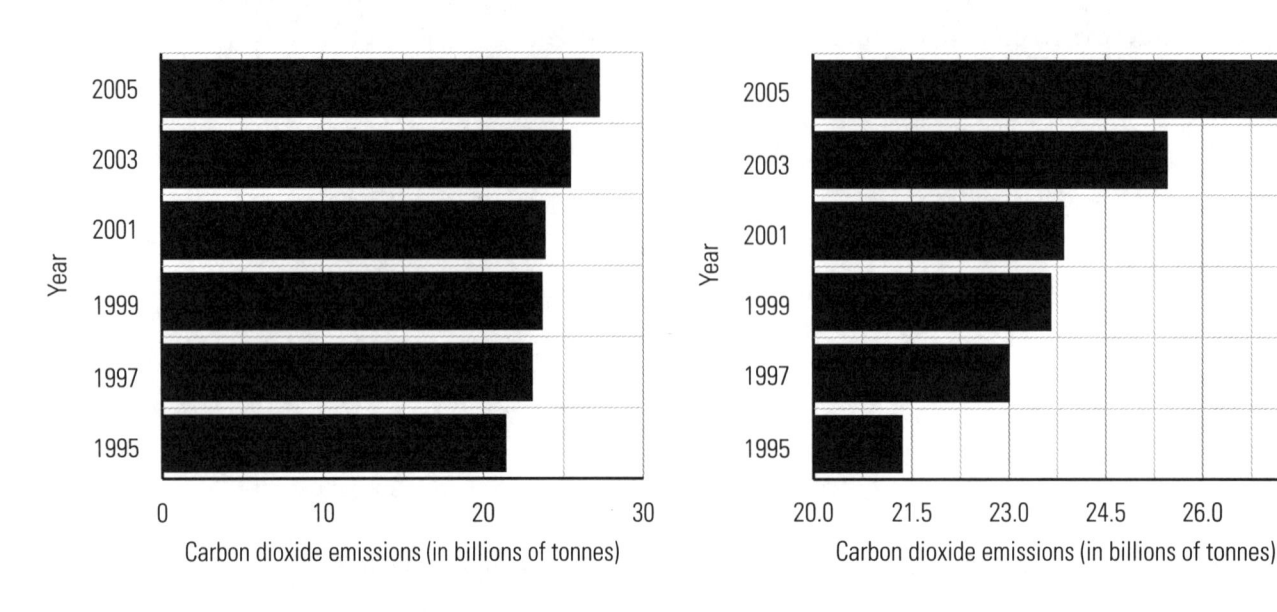

4. Carbon dioxide (CO$_2$) emissions contribute to climate change, and so they are closely monitored by governments and environmental groups. The following two graphs represent CO$_2$ emissions worldwide from 1995 to 2005.

Carbon Dioxide Emissions, by Year

Carbon Dioxide Emissions, by Year

a) Which graph is a better representation of worldwide CO$_2$ emissions? Why?

b) What were the emissions in 1999?

c) What were they in 2005?

d) Why might the more misleading graph be used to represent the data?

NEW SKILLS: WORKING WITH DIFFERENT REPRESENTATIONS OF DATA

Some data that can be represented using either a vertical bar graph or a horizontal bar graph can also be shown on a broken line graph. Each type of graph has its advantages for displaying certain kinds of data.

Example 2

The following table shows the approximate population of Moose Jaw, Saskatchewan, from 1980 to 2005.

POPULATION OF MOOSE JAW, SASKATCHEWAN, 1980–2005

Year	1980	1985	1990	1995	2000	2005
Population (in thousands)	33.5	34.3	33.4	32.8	32.0	32.0

a) Display the data on both a horizontal and a vertical bar graph.

b) Which graph is a better representation of the data? Why?

c) What is the trend in population size in Moose Jaw?

d) Draw a broken line graph of the data. Is the vertical bar graph or the broken line graph a better representation of the data?

e) Draw a broken line graph of the data so that the graph is misleading, making it appear that the population has declined significantly.

f) Draw a vertical bar graph using the same scales and starting points on the axes. Is it similarly misleading? Why or why not?

Mac the Moose is a fibreglass moose that stands next to the visitors' centre in Moose Jaw, SK. Mac is claimed to be the world's largest moose, at about 9.8 m tall.

SOLUTION

a) **Population of Moose Jaw, Saskatchewan, by Year**

Population of Moose Jaw, Saskatchewan, by Year

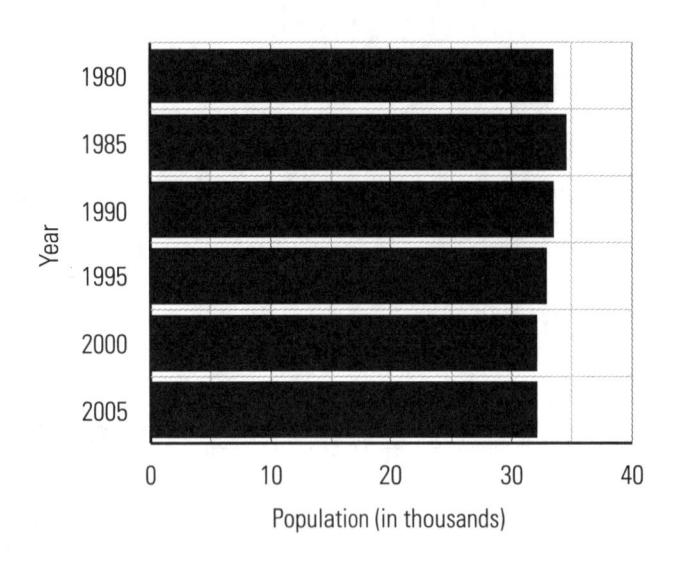

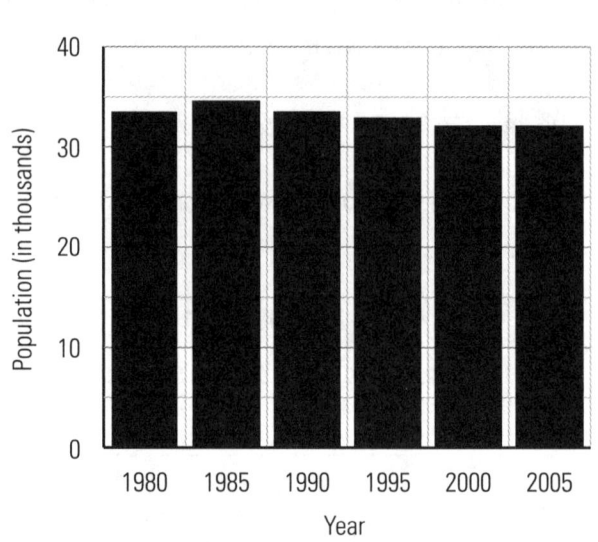

b) The vertical bar graph seems to be a better representation of the data because you can see the population trend more clearly as you read the graph from left to right.

c) The population trend shows a slight decline in population over the years.

d) **Population of Moose Jaw, Saskatchewan, by Year**

Both the broken line graph and the vertical bar graph are good representations of the data, but the broken line graph is better for showing a trend in the data.

e) **Population of Moose Jaw, Saskatchewan, by Year**

f) **Population of Moose Jaw, Saskatchewan, by Year**

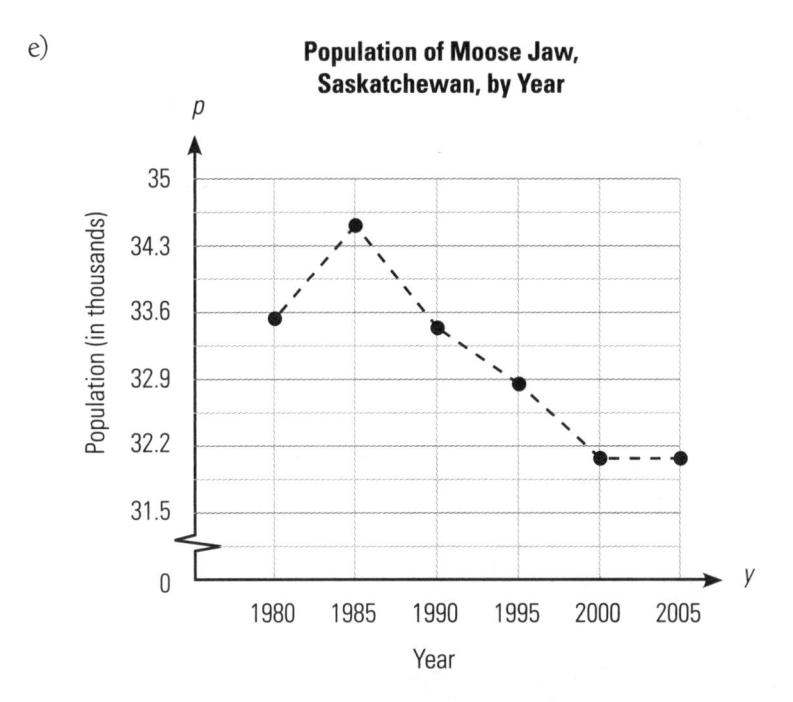

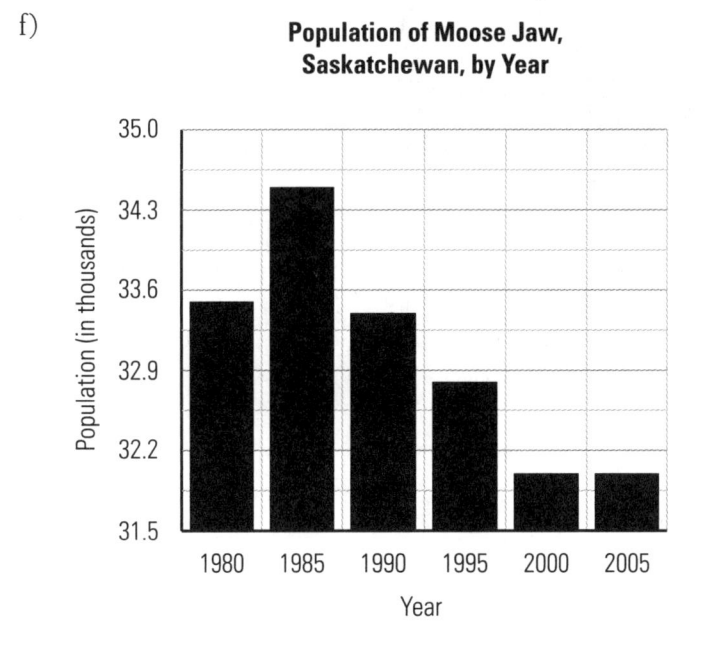

The bar graph does not seem to be quite as misleading as the broken line graph, because some of the difference appears to be absorbed in the width of the bars.

Canadian Forces 431 Air Demonstration Squadron, known as the Snowbirds, are Canada's flight demonstration team. The team is based out of Canadian Forces Base Moose Jaw, and performs at airshows worldwide.

BUILD YOUR SKILLS

5. Given the vertical bar graph below, draw a broken line graph depicting the same data. Which graph seems to be the better representation of the data? Why?

Will's Test Results

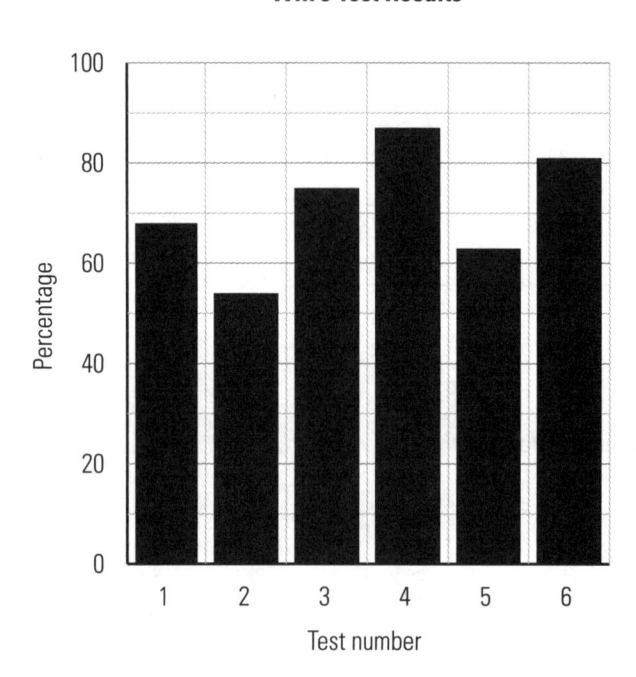

6. The table below shows the number of tickets sold per day until a rock concert is sold out.

NUMBER OF ROCK CONCERT TICKETS SOLD PER DAY										
Day	1	2	3	4	5	6	7	8	9	10
No. of tickets	2824	2531	1456	1687	1570	1280	796	578	329	105

a) What is the general trend in sales over the 10-day period?

b) Darlene used a graphing tool to draw a horizontal bar graph and a broken line graph of the data. Which graph is a better representation and why?

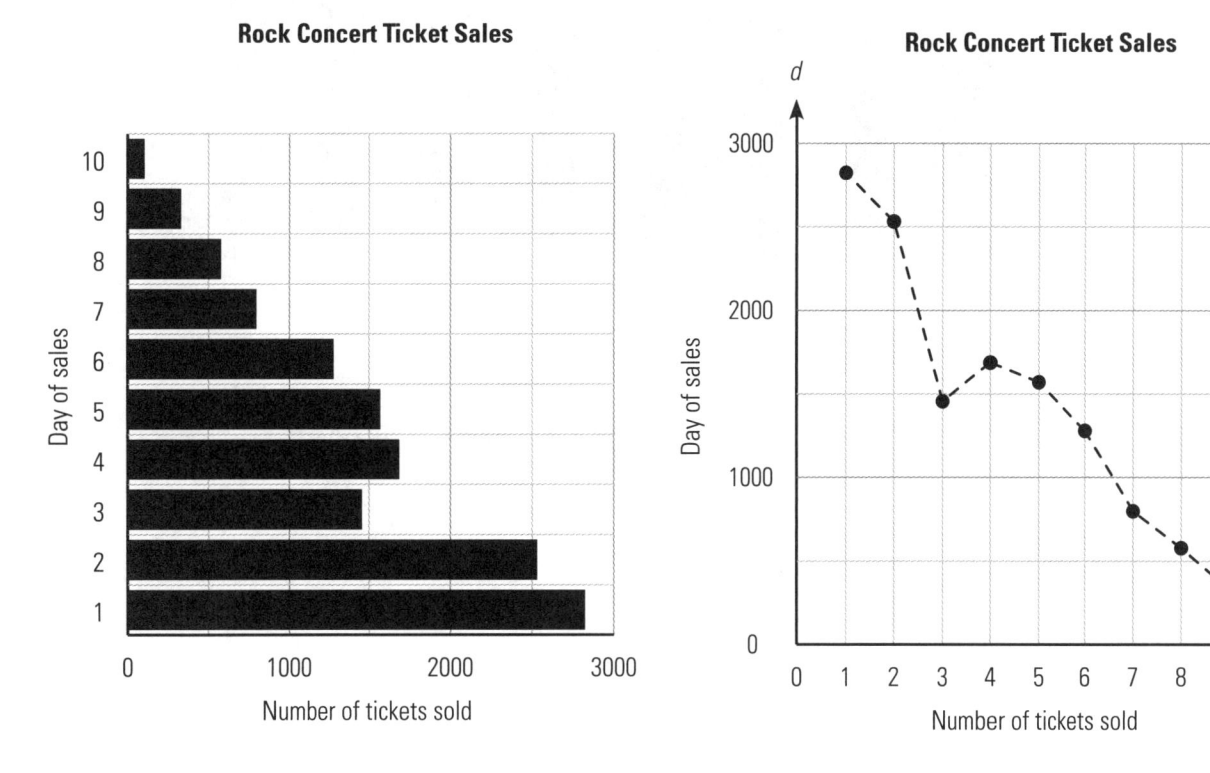

Example 3

Roger is a real estate agent in Red Deer, Alberta. The graph below compares the average house prices of new single-family homes and resale (not new) single-family homes.

Single-family House Prices in Red Deer, Alberta, 2002–2009

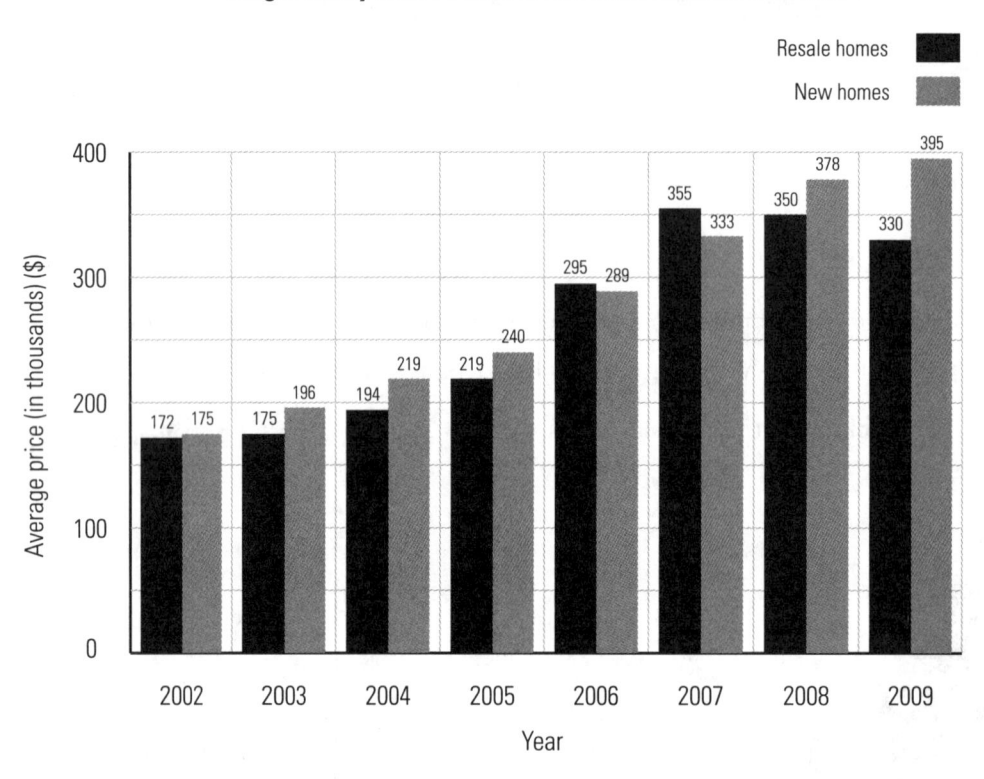

Year	Resale homes	New homes
2002	172	175
2003	175	196
2004	194	219
2005	219	240
2006	295	289
2007	355	333
2008	350	378
2009	330	395

Average price (in thousands) ($)

a) What was the average price of a new single-family home in 2005?

b) Between what years was there a drop in the price of resale single-family homes?

c) What is the general trend in the differences in prices (which cost more/less) of the two types of units? In which years was this not so?

SOLUTION

a) The cost was approximately $240 000.00.

b) Since the bar is lower in 2008 than in 2007, there was a drop in the prices.

c) Generally, new single-family homes sold for more than resale homes. In 2006 and 2007, resale homes sold for more than new homes.

BUILD YOUR SKILLS

7. The following table shows average weekly household expenses of all Canadian households with children compared to the expenses of households in the lowest income range in the country.

AVERAGE WEEKLY HOUSEHOLD EXPENSES, CANADA									
Item	Food & drink	Clothing	Heat & electricity	Health	Transportation	Communication	Recreation & culture	Education	Eating out
Lowest income households	104	44	124	2	70	22	78	6	56
All households with children	140	62	130	4	176	26	160	30	104

a) Draw a double bar graph to represent the data.

b) Explain the trends in spending of the lowest income families compared to all families.

8. In order for citizens of other countries to travel to Canada, they may be required to get a visa, which is a document that shows the person is authorized to enter the country. Sally works at Citizenship and Immigration Canada, and has gathered information on the number of visas applied for and the number approved over the course of one year.

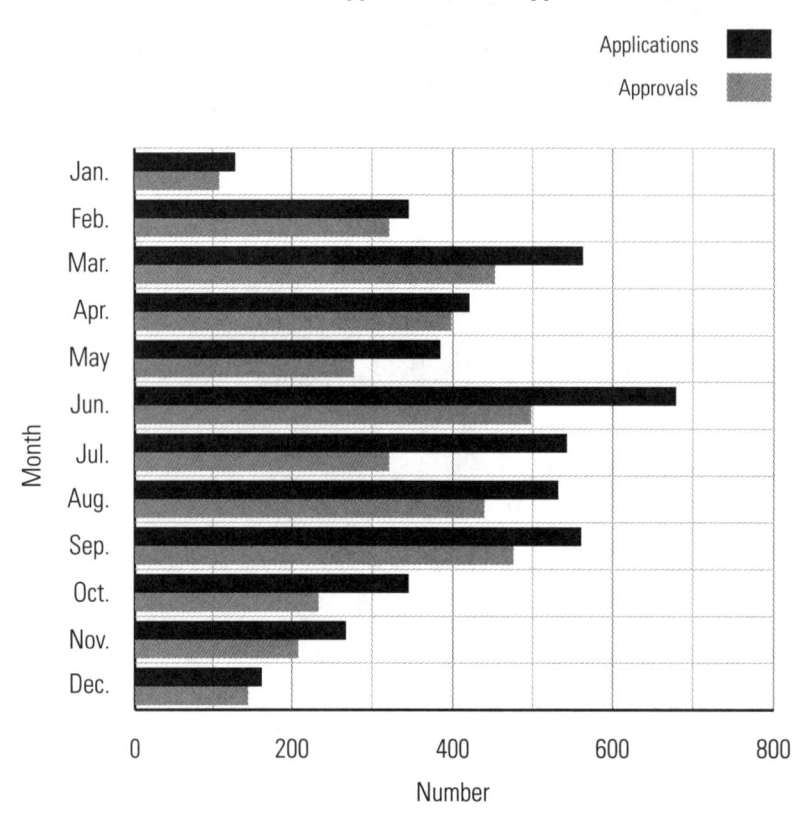

Visa Applications and Approvals

a) In which month was the most applications for visas received? How many visa applications were received that month? In which month were the fewest applications received? How many were received that month?

b) In which month was the greatest difference between the number of applications and the number of approvals? What was the approximate difference?

9. The following graph shows the high and low daily temperatures for one week in November in Pincher Creek, Alberta.

High and Low Daily Temperatures in Pincher Creek, AB

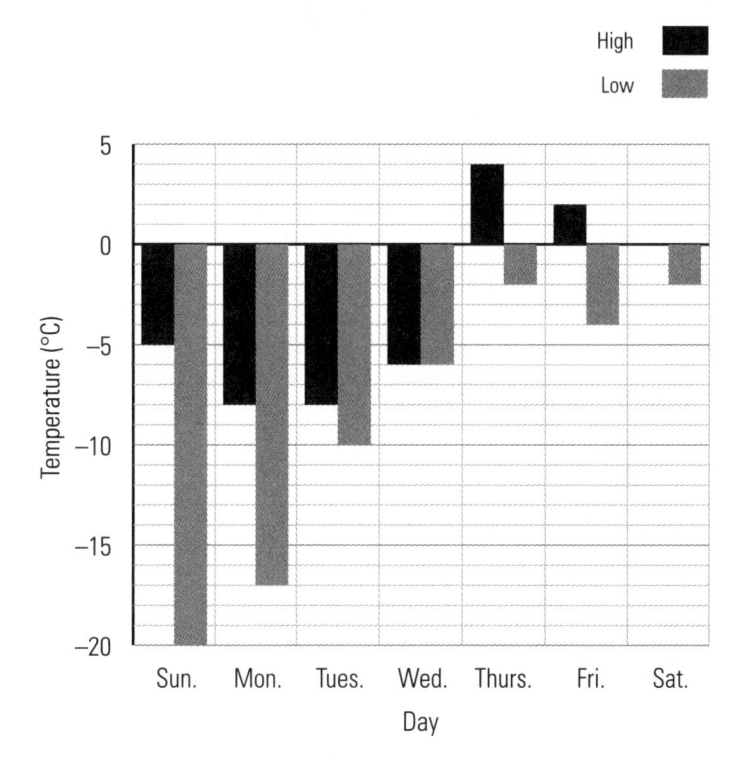

Pincher Creek, AB, is called the wind capital of Canada. Because of the strong winds that blow in the area, wind turbines have been installed to generate electricity.

a) Why are most of the bars going downward?

b) Why is there no black bar on Saturday?

c) What is significant about Wednesday's temperature?

d) What was the general trend in temperature during the week?

NEW SKILLS: WORKING WITH STACKED BAR GRAPHS

When comparing data, you can sometimes use a stacked bar graph. In this style of graph, each type of item is represented by a different colour, but instead of being drawn side by side, the bars are stacked on top of each other. It is important that the bars are stacked in the same order.

Example 4

For this example, use the data from Example 3 about Roger, the real estate agent from Red Deer, AB.

a) Draw a stacked bar graph showing the total sales of single-family houses in Red Deer from 2002 to 2009.

b) What is less obvious on the stacked graph than on the double bar graph?

SOLUTION

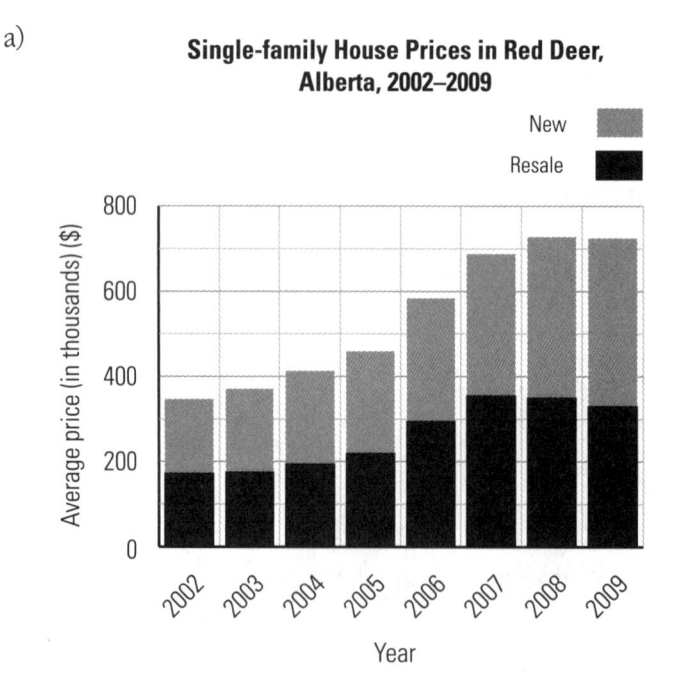

a)

Single-family House Prices in Red Deer, Alberta, 2002–2009

b) The trend in the value of new properties is less obvious on the stacked bar graph.

ALTERNATIVE SOLUTION

The graph could also have been drawn with the new sales on the bottom, and the resale houses stacked on top.

BUILD YOUR SKILLS

10. Trina did a survey of her school to find out students' favourite sports to watch on TV. The results are summarized below.

    SURVEY RESULTS: FAVOURITE SPORT TO WATCH ON TV

Sport	Football	Hockey	Basketball	Baseball	Golf
Boys	135	243	101	79	18
Girls	121	265	75	15	2

    a) Draw a double vertical bar graph and a stacked vertical bar graph to represent the data.

    b) How many people took the survey?

    c) What is the most popular sport to watch on TV?

    d) What is easier to see on the double bar graph than the stacked bar graph? When might the stacked bar graph be useful?

11. Consider the three multiple bar graphs in Build Your Skills questions 7, 8, and 9 above:

- Question #7: Average Weekly Household Expenses, Canada

- Question #8: Visa Applications and Approvals

- Question #9: High and Low Daily Temperatures in Pincher Creek, Alberta

Do any of the graphs show data that would be suitable for a stacked bar graph? Explain your answer.

PRACTISE YOUR NEW SKILLS

1. Petro is a trainer at the local gym. He recorded the following information about the number of people who used the equipment during the day. Graph the data on a horizontal bar graph.

NUMBER OF USERS OF FITNESS EQUIPMENT PER DAY				
Equipment	Stationary bike	Treadmill	Elliptical cross-trainer	Stairclimber
Number	142	167	85	149

Indoor fitness equipment allows people to exercise even during wet and cold weather.

2. A multiplex theatre has eight different-sized theatres. In order to determine which movie should be shown in which theatre, Mollie polled people on the street as to which movie they would attend. Her results are displayed in the graph below.

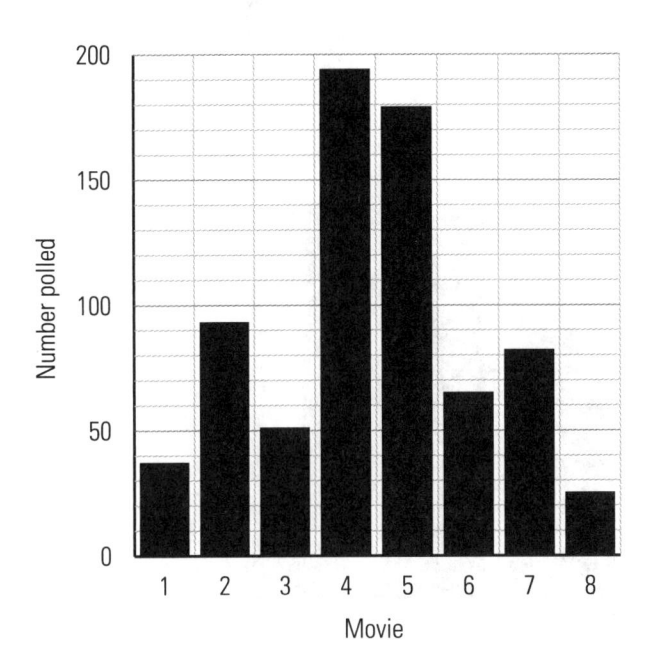

Movie Preferences

a) Which are the two most popular movies?

b) Which is least popular?

3. Use the graph below to discuss the general trend of students taking home economics classes at a high school in Brandon, MB, over a period of five years.

Students Taking Home Economic Classes, by Year

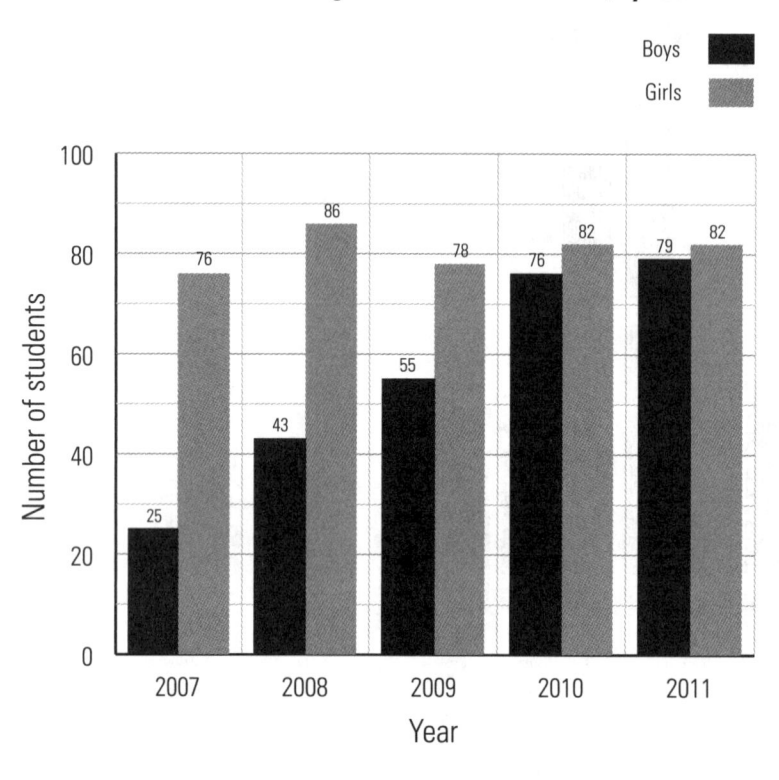

Year	Boys	Girls
2007	25	76
2008	43	86
2009	55	78
2010	76	82
2011	79	82

4. A real estate agent wants to compare the number of single-detached house and multiple-unit construction projects started in Abbotsford, BC, over a period of five years.

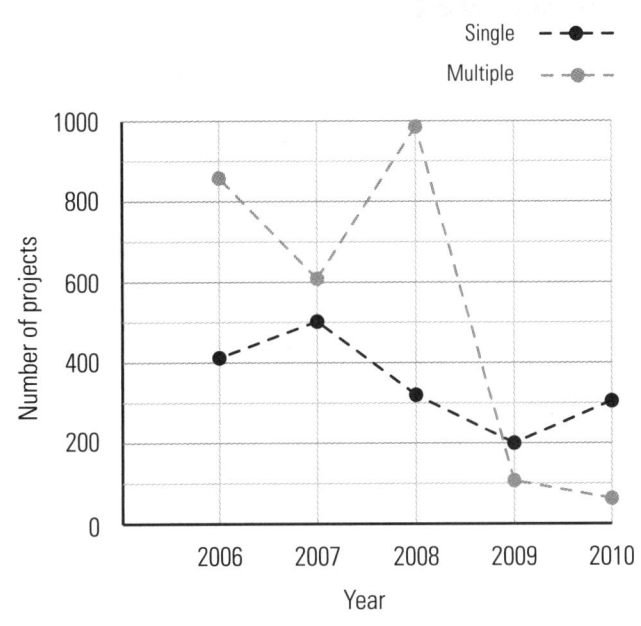

Housing Construction Projects Started in Abbotsford, BC, per Year

a) Use the graph to explain trends in housing projects in Abbotsford.

b) Use the data from the graph to draw a double bar graph comparing the number of housing projects. Which graph do you prefer for presenting the data? Why?

2.3 Histograms

NEW SKILLS: WORKING WITH HISTOGRAMS

A histogram is like a bar graph except that it is used to represent continuous data so that the bars are touching. The width of each bar represents a range of numbers.

For more details, see page 85 of *MathWorks 11*.

Example 1

The histogram below shows the number of airplanes scheduled to arrive at the Calgary International Airport on a particular day.

Number of Arrivals Scheduled, Calgary International Airport

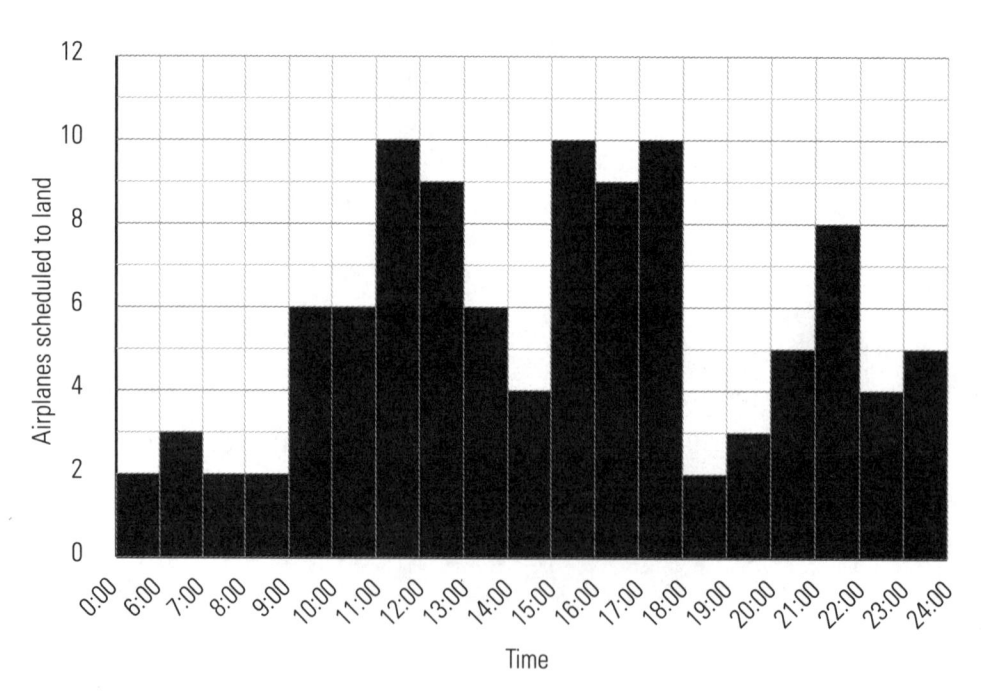

a) How many airplanes are scheduled to arrive between 2:00 pm and 3:00 pm?

b) What are the busiest times at the airport? How many airplanes are scheduled to arrive at these times?

c) What is the quietest time?

d) Are any airplanes scheduled to arrive between 4:00 am and 5:00 am?

SOLUTION

a) Four airplanes are scheduled to arrive between 2:00 pm and 3:00 pm (14:00–15:00).

b) The busiest times are between 11:00 and 12:00, between 15:00 and 16:00, and between 17:00 and 18:00. Ten airplanes are scheduled to arrive during each of these timeframes.

c) The quietest time at the airport is from midnight (24:00) to 6:00 am. Although it looks like 7:00 to 8:00 and 8:00 to 9:00 are just as quiet, with only two arrivals as well, the interval for midnight to 6:00 am is larger than the others.

d) The histogram shows that two planes arrived between midnight and 6:00 am, but you cannot be sure if one arrived at 4:00 am.

Airplane take-offs and landings must be carefully planned to ensure that they do not interfere with other airplanes' flight paths.

BUILD YOUR SKILLS

1. The histogram below shows the amount of money that households in one province spent on home renovations during the past year.

   Amount Spent on Home Renovations

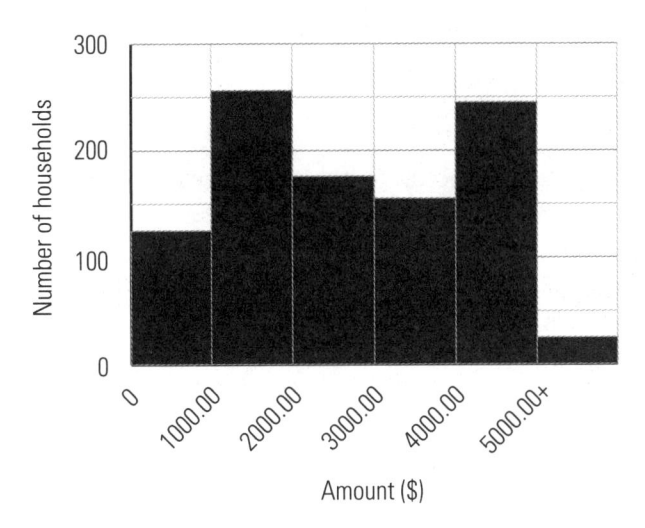

   a) How many households spent less than $1000.00 on renovations?

   b) What was the most common amount spent?

   c) What was the highest amount spent?

2. An internet service provider surveyed some of its customers across Canada to find out how much time people spend on the internet each week. The following histogram shows the results.

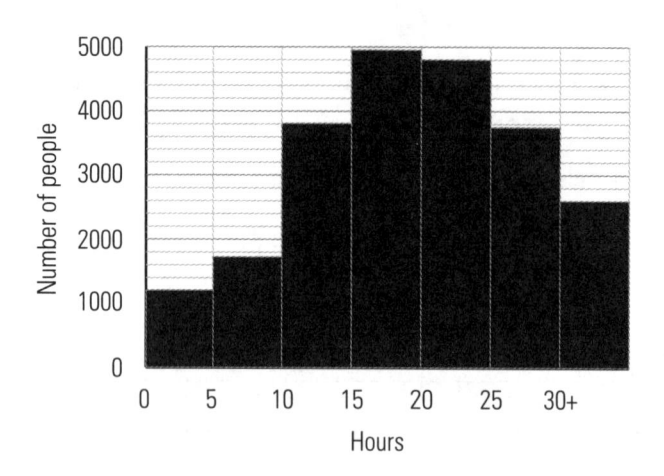

Number of Hours Spent on the Internet per Week

a) How many people spend between 10 and 15 hours on the internet each week?

b) How many people spend less than 15 hours on the internet each week?

c) How many people spend more than 30 hours on the internet each week?

d) Approximately how many people were surveyed?

Example 2

Arabella works as a server at a busy restaurant. She kept track of the amount of money she received in tips per table. Draw a histogram to represent the tips she received. What is more obvious from the histogram than in the table below?

Amount	Less than $2.00	$2.00–$3.99	$4.00–$5.99	$6.00–$7.99	$8.00–$9.99	Over $10.00
Number of tables	12	6	23	5	4	2

SOLUTION

To draw a histogram, put the intervals given for tip amounts on the horizontal axis. Choose a suitable scale for the vertical axis based on the number of tables. Here, since the maximum is 23, a suitable choice would be a scale of 1 or 2.

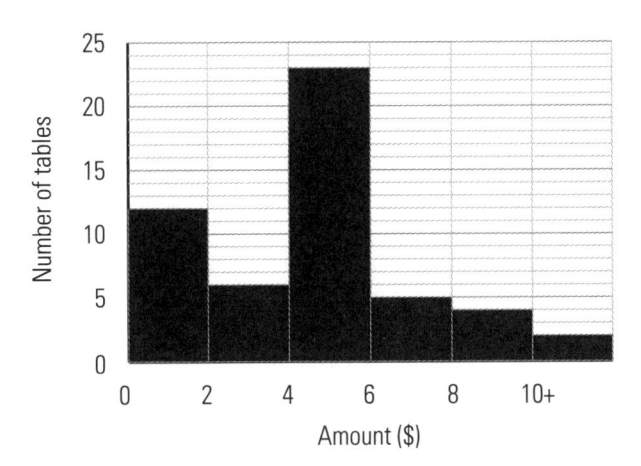

Amount Received in Tips

The variation in the number of people in each tip interval is more obvious from the graph than in the table.

BUILD YOUR SKILLS

3. An insurance company did a confidential survey of the ages of employees in a company, to estimate how many would be retiring in the coming years. The results are shown in the following table. Use the data to draw a histogram.

SURVEY RESULTS, AGES OF EMPLOYEES						
Age	Less than 25	25–34	35–44	45–54	55–64	65 and older
Number	1	6	8	16	24	6

4. a) Draw a histogram to represent the ages of people attending a theatre presentation.

| AGES OF AUDIENCE MEMBERS AT THEATRE PRESENTATION ||||||||
Age	<20	20–29	30–39	40–49	50–59	60–69	>70
Number of people	35	68	73	92	55	49	21

b) How many people under the age of 30 attended the presentation?

c) From the table, can you tell the age of the youngest audience member? Why or why not?

PRACTISE YOUR NEW SKILLS

1. The following histogram represents the scores of a math class on a recent test.

   Student Marks on Math Test

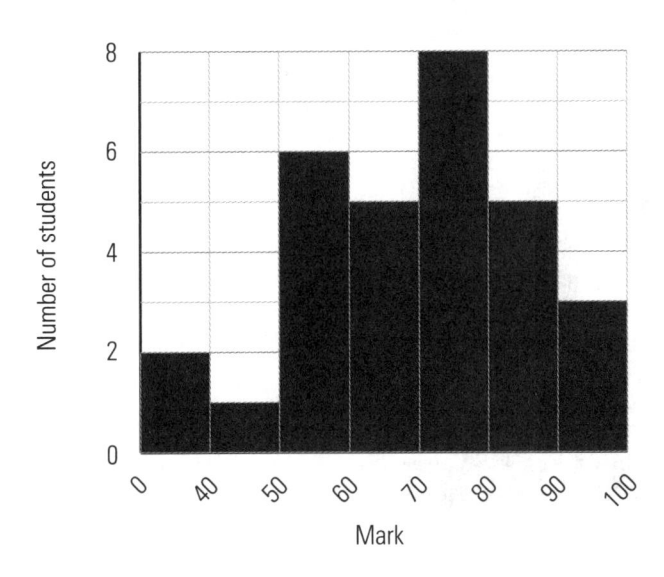

   a) How many students received a mark between 70% and 80%?

   b) How many students got below 60%?

   c) What was the highest mark received by a student?

2. The histogram below shows the salaries of the employees at Supersonic Businesses Inc.

Salaries of Employees at Supersonic Businesses Inc.

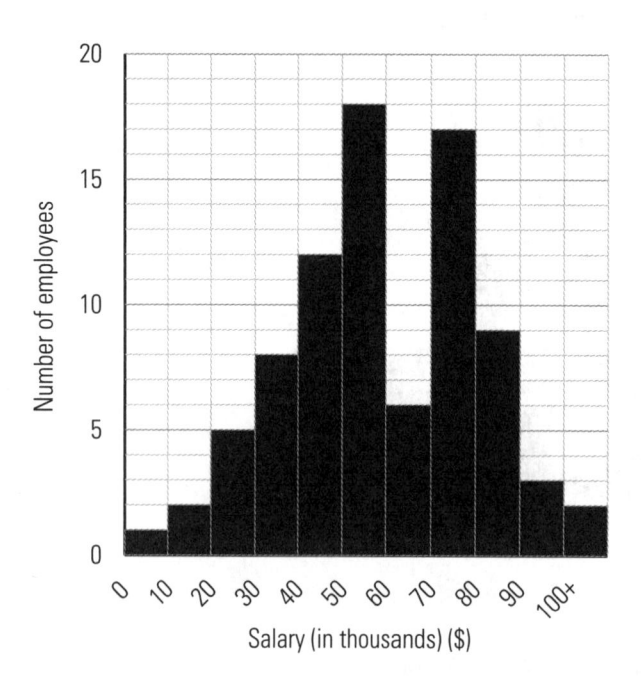

a) How many employees earn over $100 000.00?

b) How many employees earn between $30 000.00 and $50 000.00?

3. Rodney has recorded the housing sales over a period of time for his real estate company, Fixed Rate Real Estate. The data has been grouped based on the selling price.

FIXED RATE REAL ESTATE HOUSING SALES						
Selling price (in thousands) ($)	Less than 100	100–200	200–300	300–400	400–500	Over 500
Number of houses	5	2	7	12	5	3

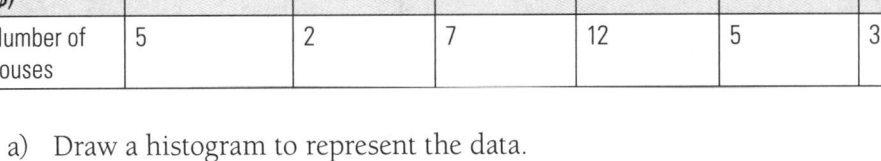

Real estate agents earn a commission on the houses they sell.

a) Draw a histogram to represent the data.

b) What was the lowest selling price?

c) How many houses sold for between $100 000.00 and $300 000.00?

4. Hurricanes are more likely to occur at certain times of the year than at others. The table below indicates the percentage of hurricanes that began at different times of the year.

HURRICANE OCCURRENCES, BY TIME OF YEAR

Dates	Mar. 21–Jun. 20	Jun. 21–Jul. 20	Jul. 21–Aug. 20	Aug. 21–Sep. 20	Sep. 21–Oct. 20	Oct. 21–Nov. 20
Percentage of hurricane occurrences	5	7	18	35	27	8

a) Draw a histogram to represent the data.

b) During what time of the year are hurricanes unlikely to occur?

c) At what time of year is a hurricane most likely to occur?

2.4 Circle Graphs

NEW SKILLS: WORKING WITH CIRCLE GRAPHS

A circle graph is used to display how a whole is divided. The sectors of the circle represent parts of the data.

For more details, see page 99 of *MathWorks 11*.

Example 1

The following circle graph shows how people in Maxine's office building get to work. There are 350 people working in the building.

Transportation Methods of Employees

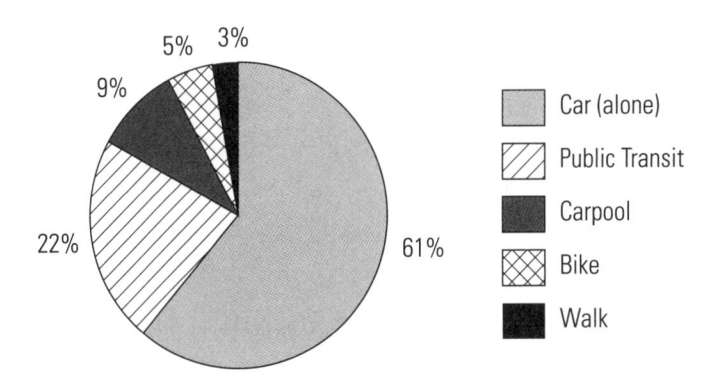

- Car (alone): 61%
- Public Transit: 22%
- Carpool: 9%
- Bike: 5%
- Walk: 3%

a) What percentage of the people walk to work? How many people does this represent?

b) What percentage of people come to work in a car? How many people is this?

c) Consider those who carpool, walk, or bike. Is this more or less than the number who take public transport? How many more or less?

SOLUTION

a) The graph shows that 3% of the people walk to work. Calculate 3% of 350.

   0.03 × 350 = 10.5

   11 people walk to work.

How do you get to school or work? Bicycling is a popular method of commuting.

b) You will need to consider the people who drive alone, and also those who carpool: 61% come by car alone and 9% carpool, so 70% come to work by car. Calculate 70% of 350.

0.70 × 350 = 245

245 people come to work by car.

c) The graph shows that 9% carpool, 3% walk, and 5% bike, for a total of 17%. This is less than the number who take public transport (22%).

Calculate 17% of 350.

0.17 × 350 = 59.5

60 people carpool, walk, or bike to work.

Calculate 22% of 350.

0.22 × 350 = 77

77 people use public transit to get to work.

Calculate the difference between the number who use public transit and the number who carpool, walk, or bike to work.

77 − 60 = 17

There are 17 fewer people who carpool, walk, or bike to work than take public transit.

BUILD YOUR SKILLS

1. The circle graph below shows the results of a student survey: 171 students were asked their favourite colour.

   Favourite Colours

   Blue 25%, Purple 17%, Pink 15%, Green 14%, Red 12%, Orange 11%, Black 4%, White 2%

   a) How many students chose green as their favourite colour?

   b) What is the most popular colour? Approximately how many students chose it?

2. The circle graph below indicates the percentage of his income that Frank spends on different items.

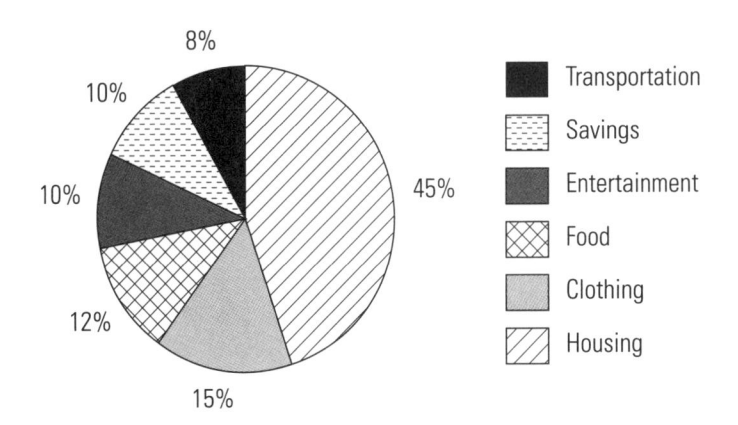

   Expenditures

   Transportation 8%, Savings 10%, Entertainment 10%, Food 12%, Clothing 15%, Housing 45%

   a) On what two items does he spend the same amount?

b) If he puts $250.00 per month into savings, what is his total income?

c) Draw a bar graph depicting the same information. Which graph gives you a better picture of his expenditures? Why?

3. The circle graph below shows a typical household's water use.

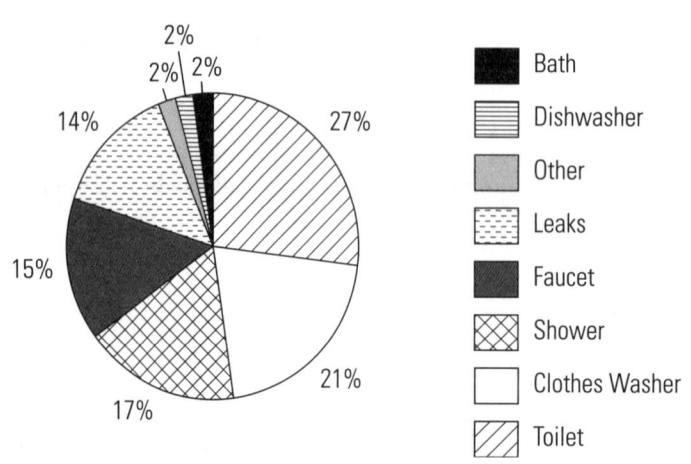

Household Water Use

- Bath: 2%
- Dishwasher: 2%
- Other: 2%
- Leaks: 14%
- Faucet: 15%
- Shower: 17%
- Clothes Washer: 21%
- Toilet: 27%

a) What is the total percentage of water used for the faucet, shower, and bath?

b) What percentage is used by the dishwasher and the clothes washer?

c) Which two uses together account for about half of the water used per day?

Example 2

Jasmine surveyed students at her college to find out how they commute to school. The results are shown in the table below. Create a circle graph of the data.

SURVEY RESULTS: MODE OF TRANSPORTATION TO SCHOOL						
Means of travel	Car (alone)	Carpool	Motorbike	Bus	Bicycle	Walk
Number of people	75	20	5	75	10	15

SOLUTION

Step 1: To draw a circle graph, first calculate what proportion of the total data is represented by each category.

Calculate the total number of people surveyed.

$75 + 20 + 5 + 75 + 10 + 15 = 200$

Car (alone) and Bus: 75 people each

$$\frac{75}{200} = 0.375$$

Carpool: 20 people

$$\frac{20}{200} = 0.1$$

Motorbike: 5 people

$$\frac{5}{200} = 0.025$$

Bicycle: 10 people

$$\frac{10}{200} = 0.05$$

Walking: 15 people

$$\frac{15}{200} = 0.075$$

Step 2: Next, calculate how many degrees of the 360 degrees of a circle are represented by each category.

Car (alone): $0.375 \times 360° = 135°$

Carpool: $0.1 \times 360° = 36°$

Motorbike: $0.025 \times 360° = 9°$

Bus: $0.375 \times 360° = 135°$

Bicycle: $0.05 \times 360° = 18°$

Walking: $0.075 \times 360° = 27°$

Step 3: Draw a circle and a radius. Use your protractor to measure the degrees of the first section. Label the sector.

Measure the next section from one edge of the first. Continue until you have marked and labelled each sector.

Survey Results: Mode of Transportation to School

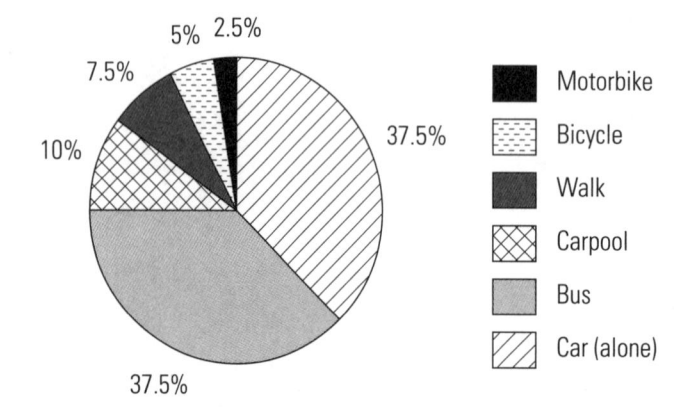

BUILD YOUR SKILLS

4. Patty surveyed students at her school to find out what kind of pets they have. The following table shows the survey results.

SURVEY RESULTS: TYPE OF PET			
Pet	Dog	Cat	Rodent (gerbil/rat/mouse)
Number of students	39	44	21

a) Draw a circle graph to represent the data.

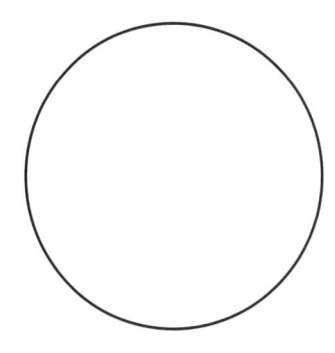

b) Gerard says that the graph does not accurately display the data as there were 24 students who do not have pets and that this should be recorded. If this data is included, what difference will it make to the size of the sectors? Draw a circle graph to include the sector of students who do not have pets.

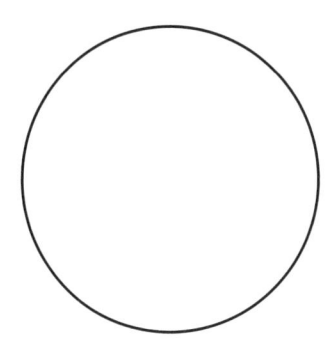

5. A school had a fundraiser to help raise money for international disaster relief. The table below shows the amounts raised through different activities. Display the information on a circle graph.

SCHOOL FUNDRAISING FOR INTERNATIONAL DISASTER RELIEF						
Means of fundraising	Parental donations	Chocolate bar sales	Hot lunches	Concert proceeds	Classroom donations
Amount raised	$750.00	$325.00	$375.00	$150.00	$100.00

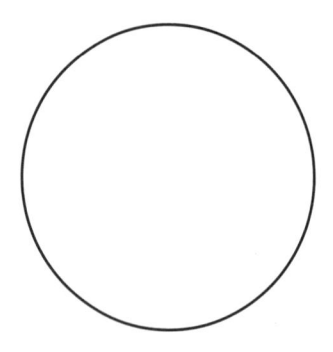

6. Marjorie is a stockperson at a drugstore. She tracks sales of the different brands of hairspray sold at the store. The table below indicates the number of containers of each brand that sold in the past month.

HAIRSPRAY SALES IN ONE MONTH							
Hairspray brand	A	B	C	D	E	F
Number of containers	68	45	127	93	76	12

a) Draw a circle graph to display the data.

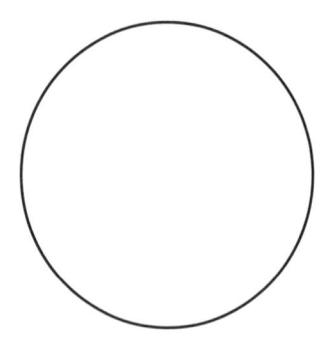

b) Display the data on one other type of suitable graph.

PRACTISE YOUR NEW SKILLS

1. Before a school dance, the organizing committee did a survey of students to find out their music preferences. The graph below shows the number of students who prefer each type of music.

    Survey Results: Music Preferences

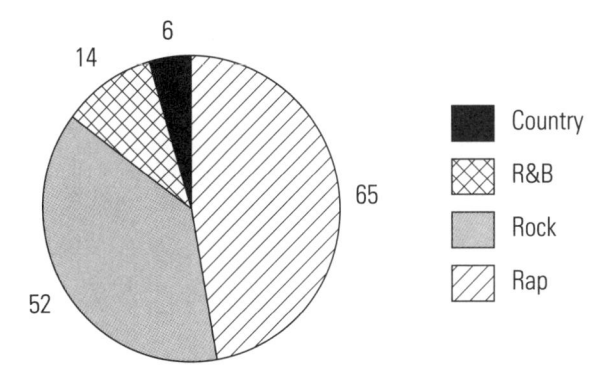

    - Country: 6
    - R&B: 14
    - Rock: 52
    - Rap: 65

    a) How many people were surveyed?

    b) What percentage of the people prefer rock music?

    c) Calculate the number of degrees in the circle that represent those who prefer R&B music.

2. Greg works as a tour guide. He tracks how tourists heard about the tours.

    - 60% took the tour as part of a travel package;
    - 15% had the tour recommended by the local tourism office;
    - 10% came based on the recommendation of a friend; and
    - the remainder were walk-ins.

    Draw a circle graph to display the data. Show all calculations.

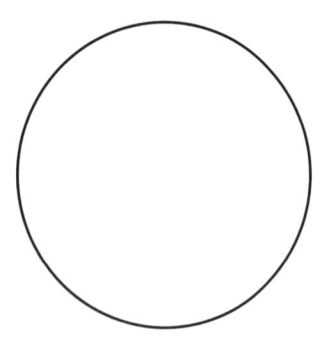

3. Given the bar graph below, create a circle graph that displays the same information.

    Number of Books in Mary's Home Library

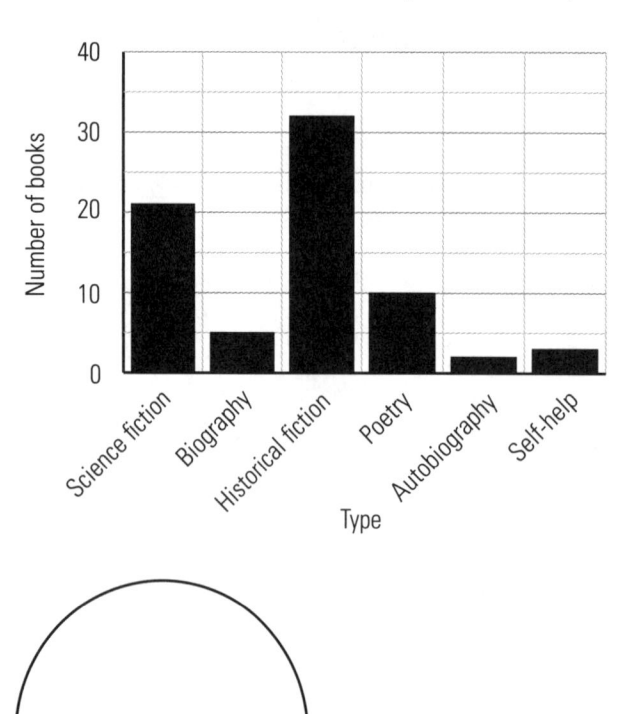

CHAPTER TEST

1. The profits in thousands of dollars for a company over a 10-year period are listed in the table below.

   COMPANY PROFITS, 2001–2010

Year	2001	2002	2003	2004	2005	2006	2007	2008	2009	2010
Profit	6	8	25	5	8	12	15	13	15	14

   a) Graph the data on a broken line graph.

   b) During which year was the profit highest?

   c) Is there a general trend in the data? If so, what is it? Are there any exceptions to the trend?

2. Tomas owns a boat shop and is tracking the sales of different brands of outboard motors. The table below shows the number of motors Tomas has ordered and the number of sales.

Type	Brand A	Brand B	Brand C	Brand D
Number bought	25	32	15	34
Number sold	21	22	14	32

a) Use the data to draw a double bar graph showing the relationship between number of motors ordered and the number sold.

b) Which brand has the smallest difference between the number bought and the number sold? What is the difference?

c) Which brand has the largest difference between the number bought and the number sold? What is the difference?

3. Honoria manages a movie rental store and is considering expanding the store's floor space. She is preparing a graph to show the trend in the number of video rentals each month for the past year.

Month	Jan.	Feb.	Mar.	Apr.	May	Jun.	Jul.	Aug.	Sep.	Oct.	Nov.	Dec.
Number	7267	7754	6987	8956	4199	5589	5826	5432	6125	8978	6674	7932

a) Graph the data from the above table on a suitable style of graph and explain your choice.

b) Which month had the most movie rentals? Which had the least?

c) Is there a general trend in the data? If so, what is it? Are there any exceptions to the trend?

4. Leroy has a net monthly income of $3000.00. A breakdown of his monthly expenses is shown in the following circle graph.

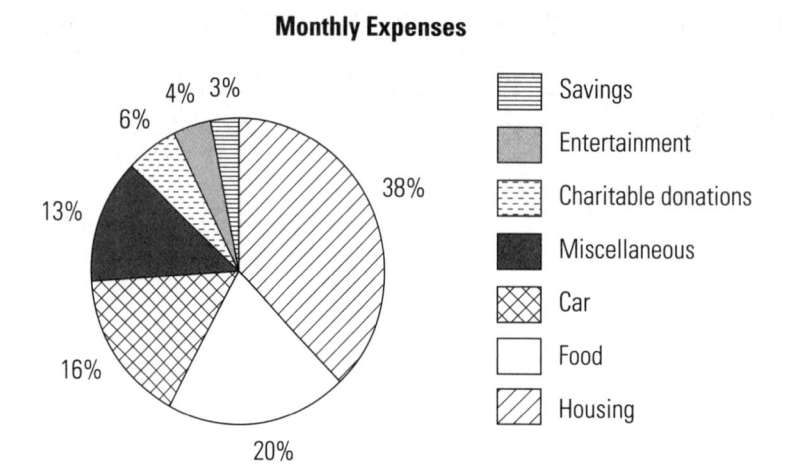

Monthly Expenses

- Savings: 3%
- Entertainment: 4%
- Charitable donations: 6%
- Miscellaneous: 13%
- Car: 16%
- Food: 20%
- Housing: 38%

How much does Leroy spend on each category each month?

5. A survey was taken of high school students to find out how much volunteer work they do each month. The survey results are shown in the table.

SURVEY RESULTS: NUMBER OF HOURS SPENT PER MONTH DOING VOLUNTEER WORK					
Hours	$0 \leq h < 2$	$2 \leq h < 5$	$5 \leq h < 10$	$10 \leq h < 15$	$15 +$
Number of respondents	56	34	15	21	9

a) Draw a histogram to represent the data.

b) How many respondents volunteer less than 5 hours per month?

c) What percentage of respondents volunteers at least 5 hours per month?

Chapter 3

Surface Area, Volume, and Capacity

How much water do you think this water tank can hold? What would you need to know to calculate the exact amount?

3.1 Surface Area of Prisms

REVIEW: WORKING WITH AREAS OF TWO-DIMENSIONAL FIGURES

In this chapter, you will need to know how to calculate the area of various two-dimensional figures, including squares, rectangles, parallelograms, triangles, and circles. The following diagrams show how to calculate the areas of each of these shapes.

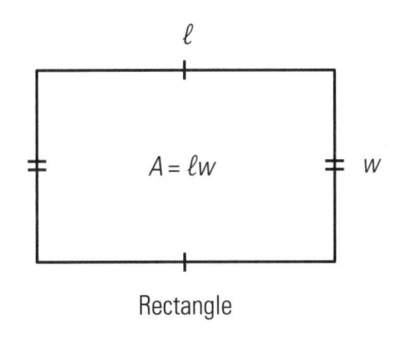

Chapter 3 Surface Area, Volume, and Capacity

Rectangle
$A = \ell w$

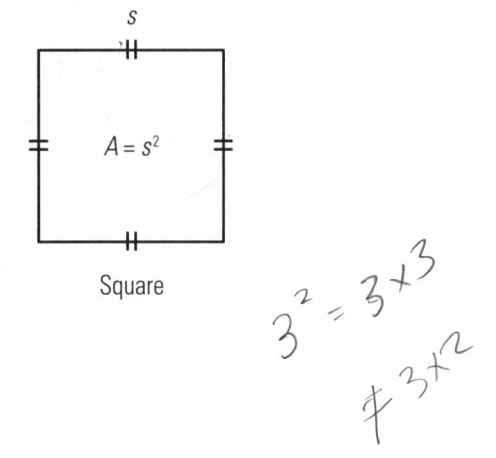

Square
$A = s^2$

$3^2 = 3 \times 3$
$\neq 3 \times 2$

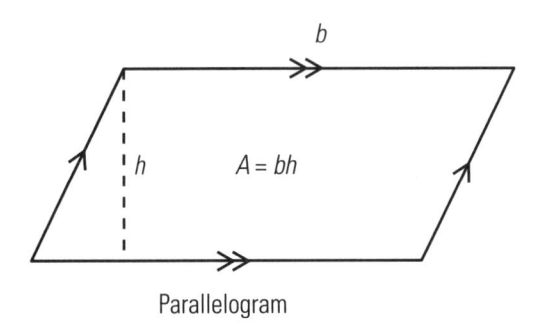

Parallelogram
$A = bh$

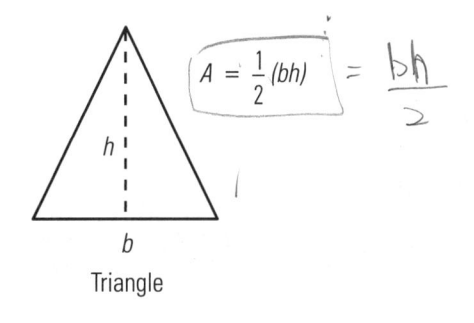

Triangle
$A = \frac{1}{2}(bh) = \frac{bh}{2}$

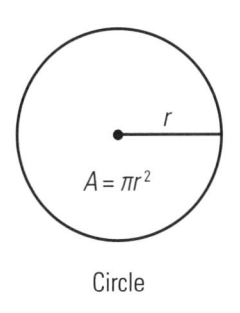

Circle
$A = \pi r^2$

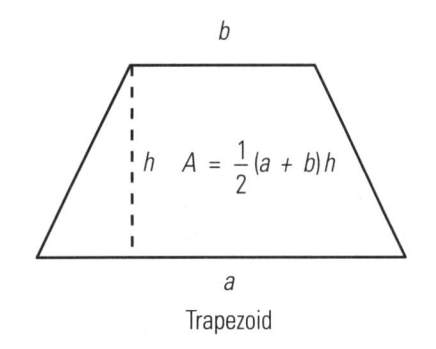

Trapezoid
$A = \frac{1}{2}(a+b)h$

Example 1

Calculate the area of each figure.

a) [rectangle: 6.8 cm by 4.5 cm]

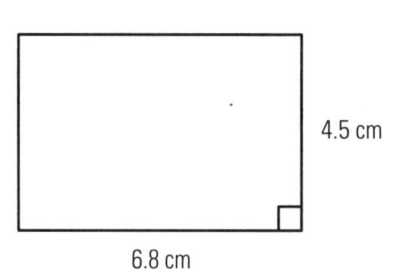

b) [triangle: base 12.8 cm, height 7.8 cm]

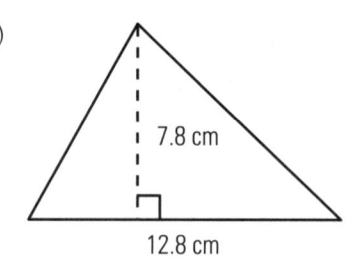

c) [parallelogram: base 3.1 m, height 2.1 m]

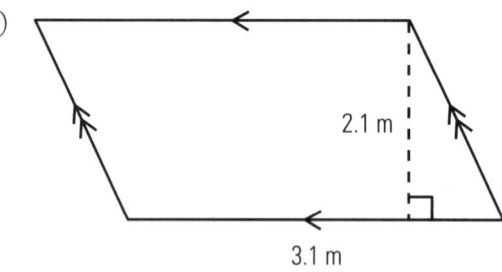

SOLUTION

a) Use the formula for calculating the area of a rectangle.

$A = \ell w$

$A = 6.8 \times 4.5$

$A = 30.6 \text{ cm}^2$

b) Calculate the area of the triangle.

$A = \frac{1}{2}bh$

$A = \frac{1}{2} \times 12.8 \times 7.8$

$A = 49.92 \text{ cm}^2$

c) Calculate the area of the parallelogram.

$A = bh$

$A = 3.1 \times 2.1$

$A = 6.51 \text{ m}^2$

> Remember that, for any figure, the height is always perpendicular (at right angles) to the base.

Chapter 3 Surface Area, Volume, and Capacity   **127**

you can use your formula sheet.
show all your work!

BUILD YOUR SKILLS

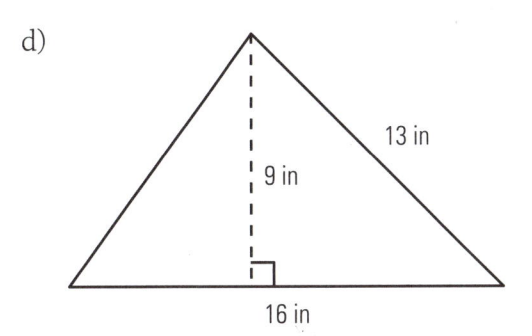

1. For each picture, name the shape and calculate the area.

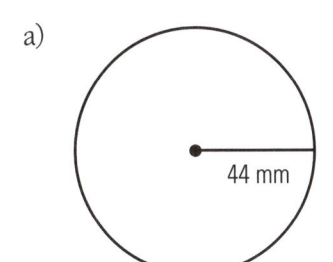

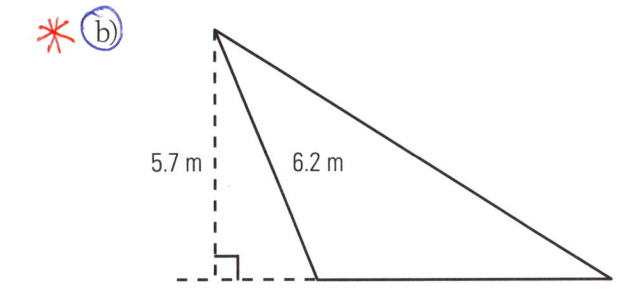

   a) (circle with radius 44 mm)

   b) (triangle with height 5.7 m, side 6.2 m, base 9.3 m)

   $$A = \frac{hb}{2}$$

   $$A = \frac{(5.7)(9.3)}{2}$$

   $$A = 26.5 \text{ m}^2$$

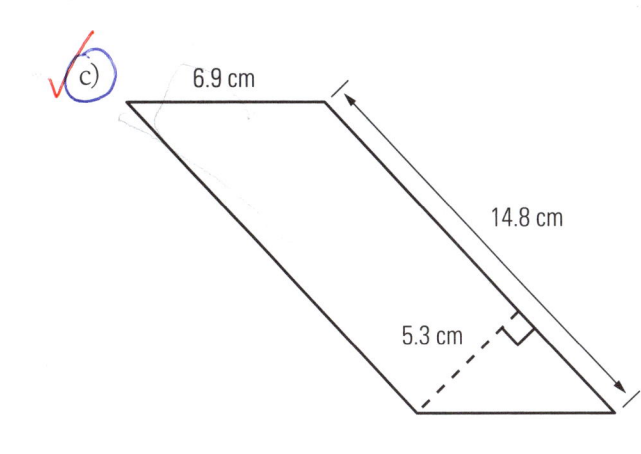

   c) (parallelogram with sides 6.9 cm, 14.8 cm, height 5.3 cm) = Parallelogram

   $$A = bH$$
   $$A = (14.8 \text{ cm})(5.3 \text{ cm})$$
   $$A = 78.44 \text{ cm}^2 \checkmark$$

   d) (triangle with height 9 in, side 13 in, base 16 in)

2. For each picture, name the shape and calculate the area.

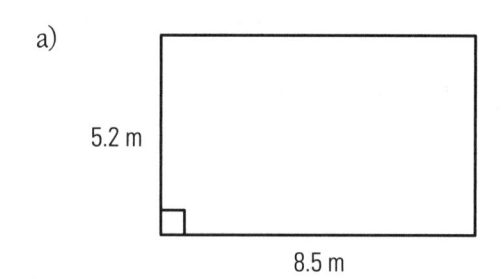

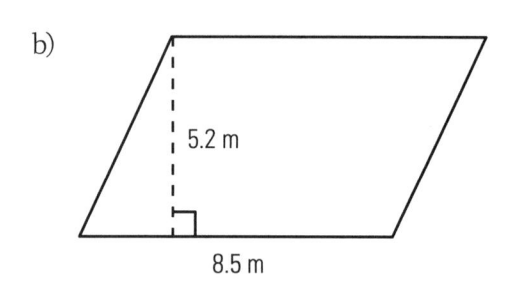

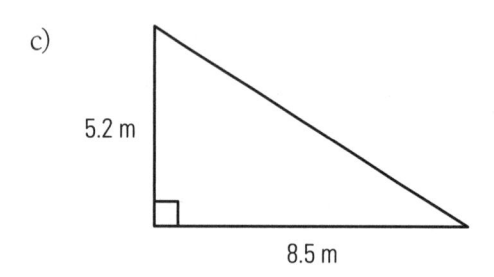

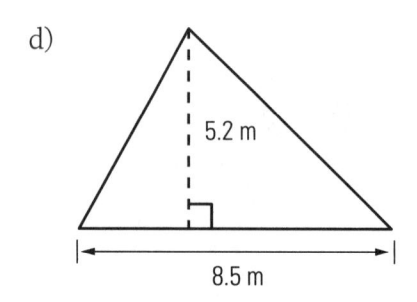

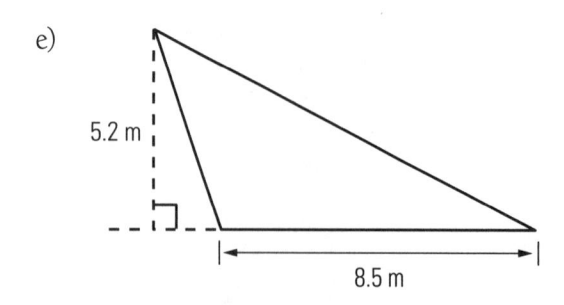

   a) 5.2 m, 8.5 m

   b) 5.2 m, 8.5 m

   c) 5.2 m, 8.5 m

   d) 5.2 m, 8.5 m

   e) 5.2 m, 8.5 m

   f) What do you notice about the area calculations?

Example 2

Find the area of the following figure.

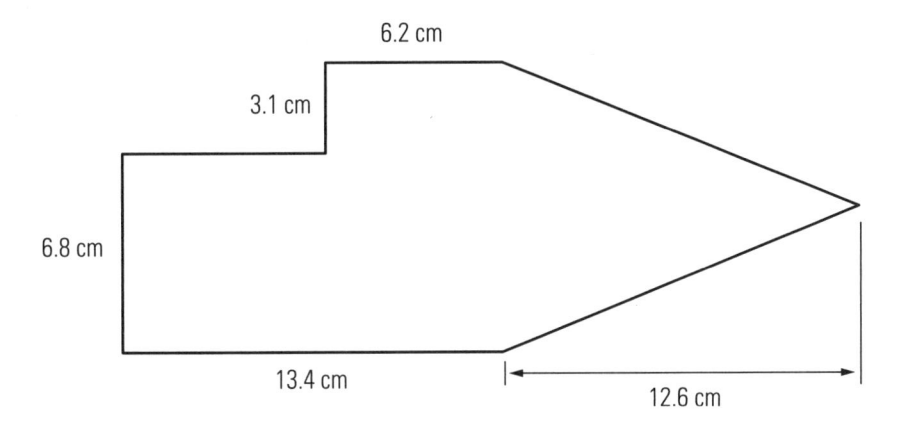

SOLUTION

To calculate the area, you will need to divide the figure into regular shapes. This figure can be divided into a triangle and two rectangles. The dimensions will be as indicated. Find the area of each part and add them together.

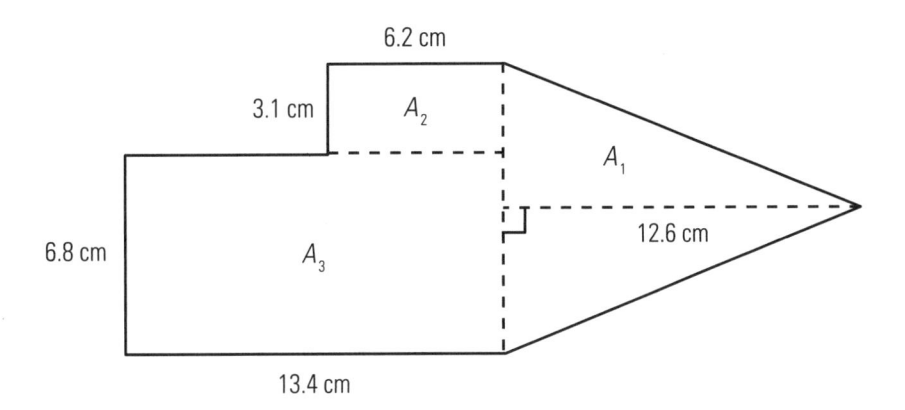

Start by calculating the area of the triangle.

$A_1 = \frac{1}{2} bh$

$A_1 = \frac{1}{2} \times 9.9 \times 12.6$

$A_1 = 62.37 \text{ cm}^2$

> Label the area calculations with subscript numbers (A_1, A_2, A_3) to help you keep track of the shapes.

Next, calculate the area of the smaller rectangle.

$A_2 = \ell w$

$A_2 = 6.2 \times 3.1$

$A_2 = 19.22$ cm²

Calculate the area of the second rectangle.

$A_3 = \ell w$

$A_3 = 13.4 \times 6.8$

$A_3 = 91.12$ cm²

Add the areas of the shapes to calculate the total area.

$A_{total} = A_1 + A_2 + A_3$

$A_{total} = 62.37 + 19.22 + 91.12$

$A_{total} = 172.71$ cm²

The total area is 172.71 cm².

ALTERNATIVE SOLUTION

The figure could have been divided into different regular shapes.

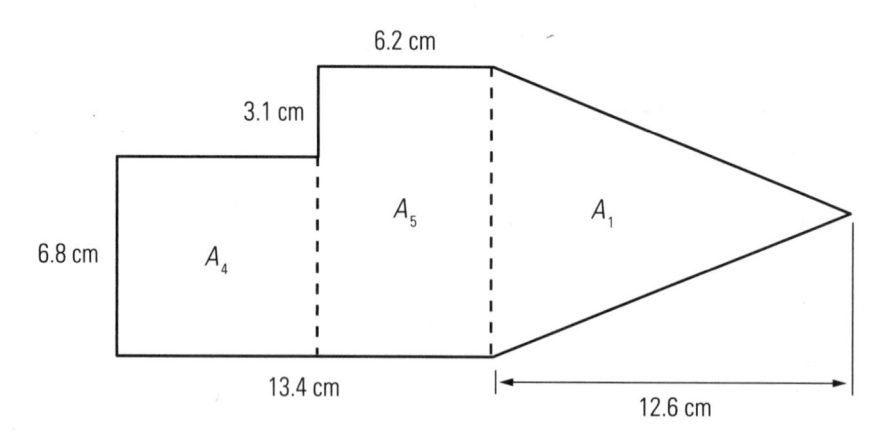

You would calculate the area of the triangle, A_1, as above. You would then find the areas of the two rectangles, A_4 and A_5.

Chapter 3 Surface Area, Volume, and Capacity

BUILD YOUR SKILLS

3. Find the areas of the following figures.

   a)

   A of TOP
   $A = l \times w$
   $A = 8 \times 14$
   $A = 112\ in$

   A of ▢
   $A = l \times w$
   $A = 5 \times 6.5$
   $A = 32.5\ in$

   $112\ in^2 + 32.5\ in$
   $A = 144.5\ in$

   (dimensions shown: 8 in, 7 in, 6.5 in, 5 in)

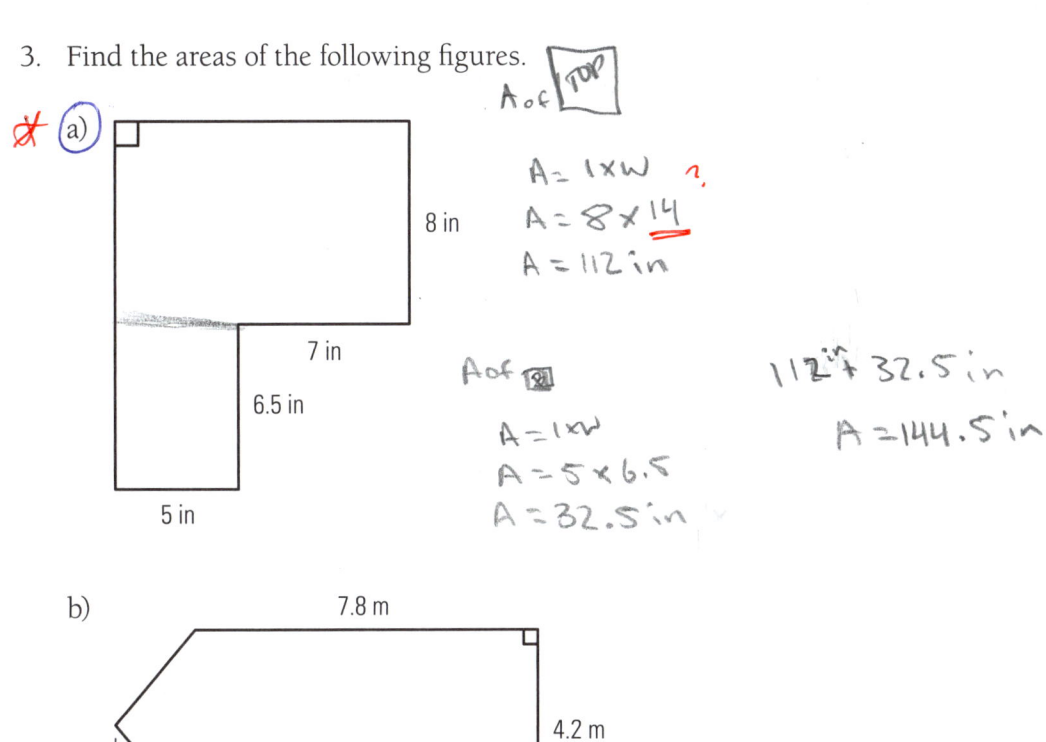

   A carpet installer needs to know how to calculate the surface area of irregularly shaped rooms, in order to know how much carpet will be needed.

   b) (dimensions shown: 7.8 m, 4.2 m, 9.6 m)

4. Show four different ways you could divide the figure below to calculate its area. Show all measurements. Choose one method to calculate the area.

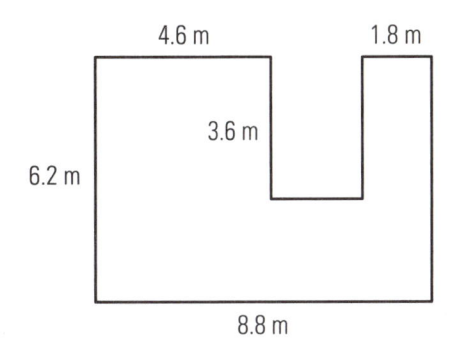

   (dimensions shown: 4.6 m, 1.8 m, 3.6 m, 6.2 m, 8.8 m)

NEW SKILLS: WORKING WITH THE SURFACE AREA OF PRISMS

prism: a 3-D shape with ends that are congruent, parallel polygons and sides that are parallelograms

base: one of the parallel faces of a prism

lateral face: a face that connects the bases of a prism

A **prism** is a three-dimensional object with:

- ends, called **bases**, that are congruent and parallel, and
- sides, called **lateral faces,** that are parallelograms.

The prism is a right prism if the sides are perpendicular to the bases. The lateral faces will be rectangles.

If the lateral faces are not perpendicular to the base, it is an oblique prism and the sides will be parallelograms.

A prism is named by the shape of its base and whether it is right or oblique.

For more details, see page 118 of *MathWorks 11*.

Example 3

Name the following prisms.

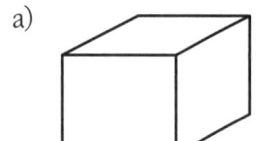

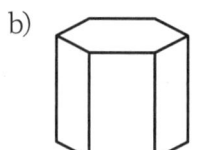

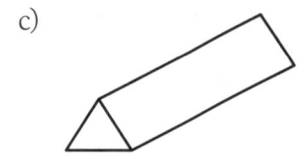

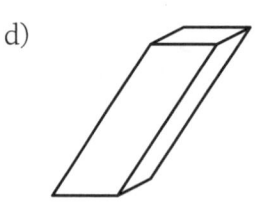

a)

b)

c)

d)

SOLUTION

a) This is a right rectangular prism. The base is a rectangle and the lateral faces are perpendicular to it.

b) This is a right hexagonal prism. The base is a hexagon and the lateral faces are perpendicular to it.

c) This is a right triangular prism. The base is a triangle and the lateral faces are perpendicular to it.

d) This is an oblique rectangular prism. The base is a rectangle and the lateral faces are not perpendicular to it.

BUILD YOUR SKILLS

5. Name the following prisms.

   a)

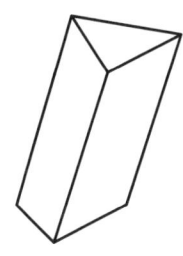

   b)

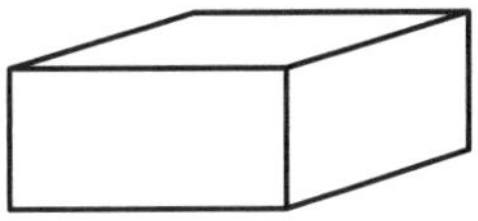

   c)

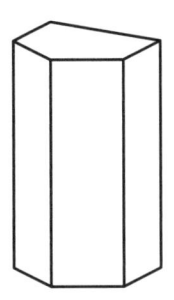

   d)

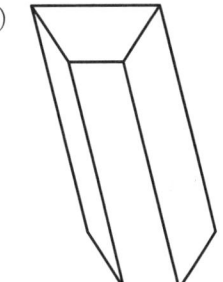

   e)

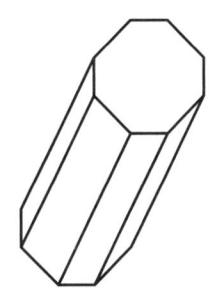

   f)

Prism	Shape of base	Right or oblique	Shape of lateral faces	Name of prism
a)				
b)				
c)				
d)				
e)				
f)				

NEW SKILLS: WORKING WITH NETS

net: 2-D pattern that can be folded to make a 3-D shape

surface area: the area covered by the outside surfaces of a three-dimensional shape

A **net** is a two-dimensional pattern that can be folded to form a three-dimensional shape. Think of a pizza box: it is made up of one piece of cardboard, folded into the shape of a right rectangular prism.

The **surface area** of a prism is the area that it would take up if it were laid out flat, as in its net.

For more details, see page 117 of *MathWorks 11*.

Example 4

If this right pentagonal prism were made from one piece of cardboard, what would the piece of cardboard look like?

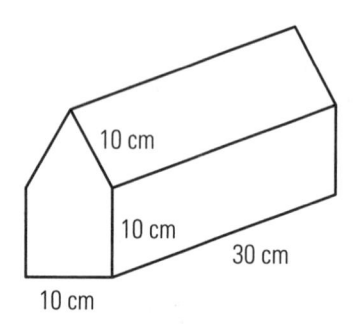

SOLUTION

The net of the prism would look like the following diagram.

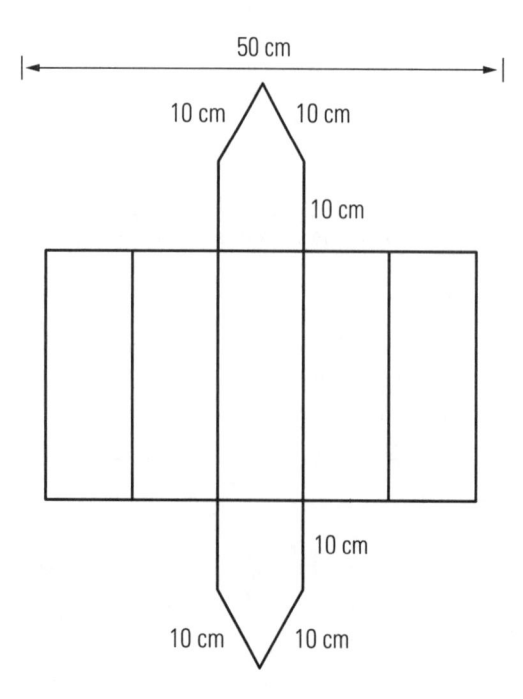

BUILD YOUR SKILLS

6. Draw nets for the following prisms, and label the dimensions of each side.

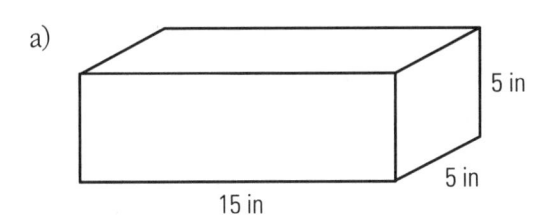

   a) [Rectangular prism: 15 in × 5 in × 5 in]

   Can you imagine what the net of this box might look like?

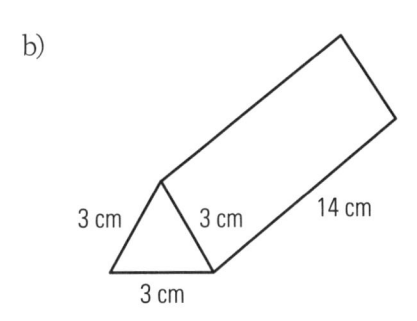

   b) [Triangular prism: triangular face with sides 3 cm, 3 cm, 3 cm; length 14 cm]

7. Ralph says that diagram A is the net of a right octagonal prism. Manon disagrees. She says that diagram B is the correct net for a right octagonal prism. Who is correct? Justify your answer.

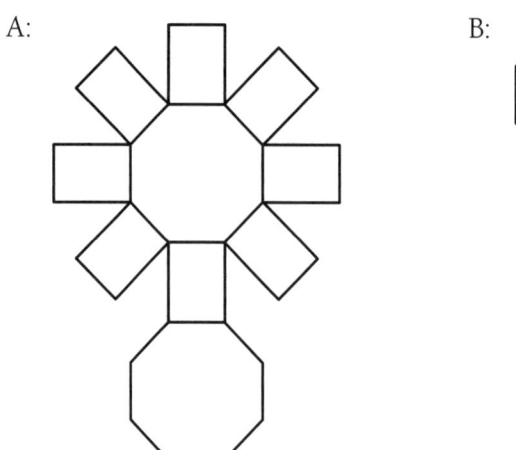

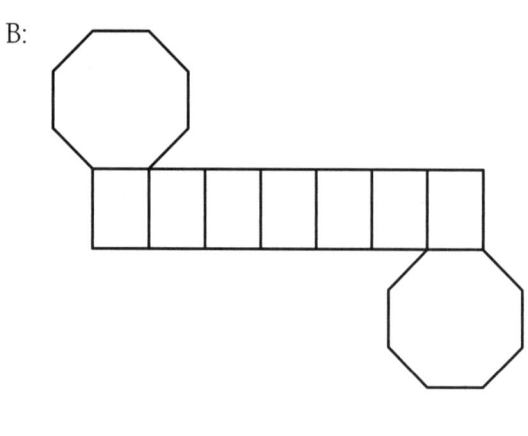

A:

B:

Example 5

Find the surface area of the right rectangular prism given below.

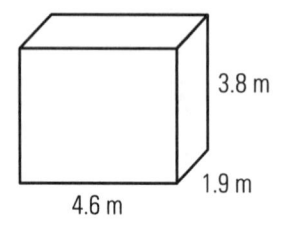

3.8 m
1.9 m
4.6 m

SOLUTION

Draw a net of the prism.

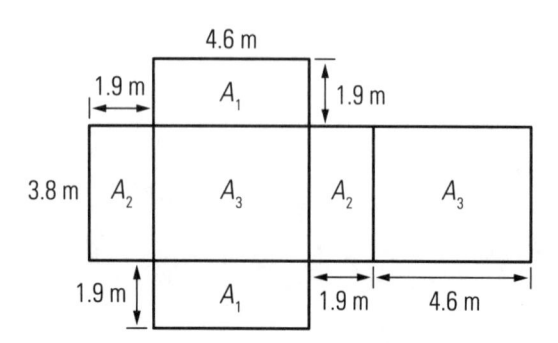

Calculate the area of each of the parts of the net.

There are two rectangles that are 1.9 m by 4.6 m (labelled as A_1).

$A_1 = \ell w$

$A_1 = 1.9 \times 4.6$

$A_1 = 8.74$ m^2

There are two rectangles that are 1.9 m by 3.8 m (labelled as A_2).

$A_2 = \ell w$

$A_2 = 1.9 \times 3.8$

$A_2 = 7.22$ m^2

There are two rectangles that are 4.6 m by 3.8 m (labelled as A_3).

$A_3 = \ell w$

$A_3 = 4.6 \times 3.8$

$A_3 = 17.48$ m^2

Calculate the total surface area.

$SA = 2(A_1) + 2(A_2) + 2(A_3)$

$SA = 2(8.74) + 2(7.22) + 2(17.48)$

$SA = 17.48 + 14.44 + 34.96$

$SA = 66.9$ m^2

The surface area of the prism is 66.9 m^2.

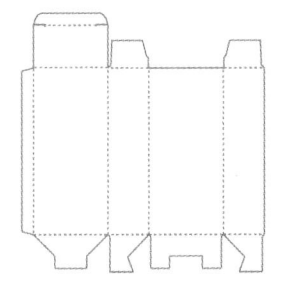

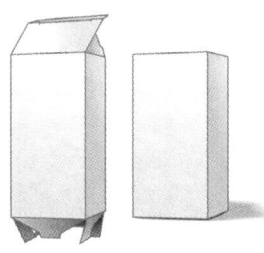

Nets are sometimes used in assembly instructions, as shown in this illustration for a box manufacturer.

BUILD YOUR SKILLS

8. For each diagram, draw a net and use it to calculate surface area.

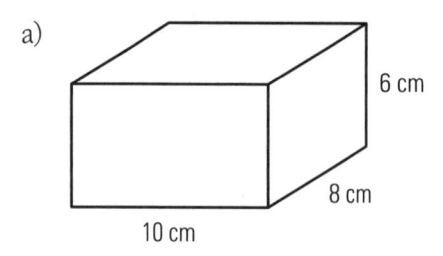

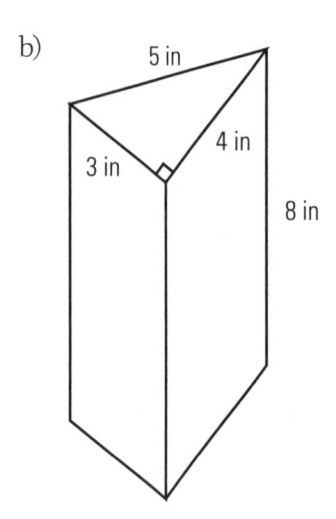

   a) 10 cm × 8 cm × 6 cm rectangular prism

   b) Triangular prism with right triangle base (3 in, 4 in, 5 in) and length 8 in

c)

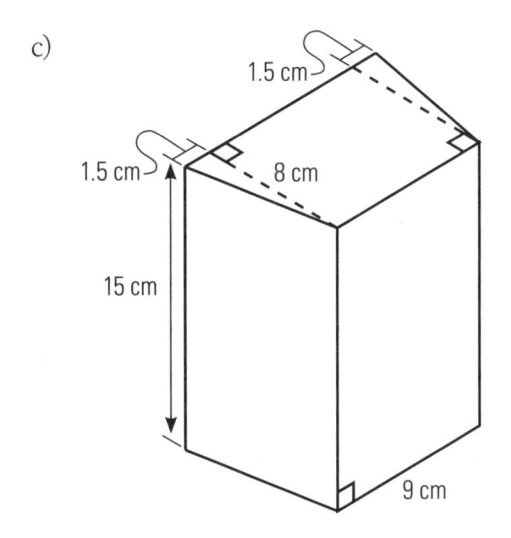

1.5 cm
1.5 cm
8 cm
15 cm
9 cm

Example 6

Find the surface area of this figure.

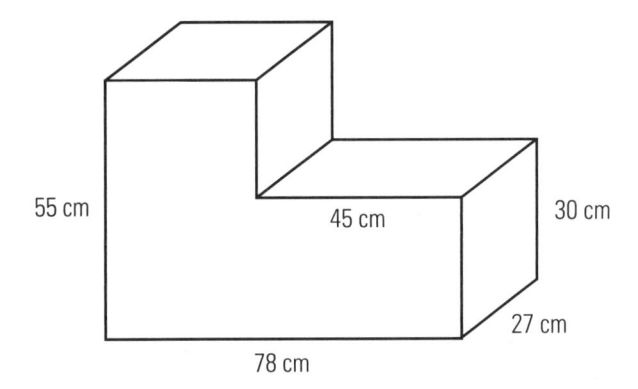

55 cm
45 cm
30 cm
27 cm
78 cm

SOLUTION

Divide the figure into parts.

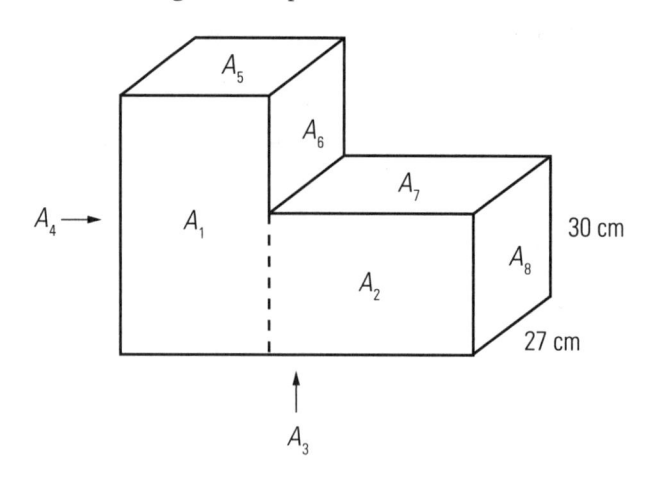

$A_1 = \ell w$
$A_1 = (78 - 45) \times 55$
$A_1 = 1815 \text{ cm}^2$

$A_5 = \ell w$
$A_5 = (78 - 45) \times 27$
$A_5 = 891 \text{ cm}^2$

$A_2 = \ell w$
$A_2 = 45 \times 30$
$A_2 = 1350 \text{ cm}^2$

$A_6 = \ell w$
$A_6 = (55 - 30) \times 27$
$A_6 = 675 \text{ cm}^2$

$A_3 = \ell w$
$A_3 = 78 \times 27$
$A_3 = 2106 \text{ cm}^2$

$A_7 = \ell w$
$A_7 = 45 \times 27$
$A_7 = 1215 \text{ cm}^2$

$A_4 = \ell w$
$A_4 = 55 \times 27$
$A_4 = 1485 \text{ cm}^2$

$A_8 = \ell w$
$A_8 = 30 \times 27$
$A_8 = 810 \text{ cm}^2$

Calculate the total surface area.

$SA = 2(A_1) + 2(A_2) + A_3 + A_4 + A_5 + A_6 + A_7 + A_8$

$SA = 2(1815) + 2(1350) + 2106 + 1485 + 891 + 675 + 1215 + 810$

$SA = 13\ 512 \text{ cm}^2$

ALTERNATIVE SOLUTION

If you look carefully at the diagram, you will discover that you don't need to calculate the area of each individual surface.

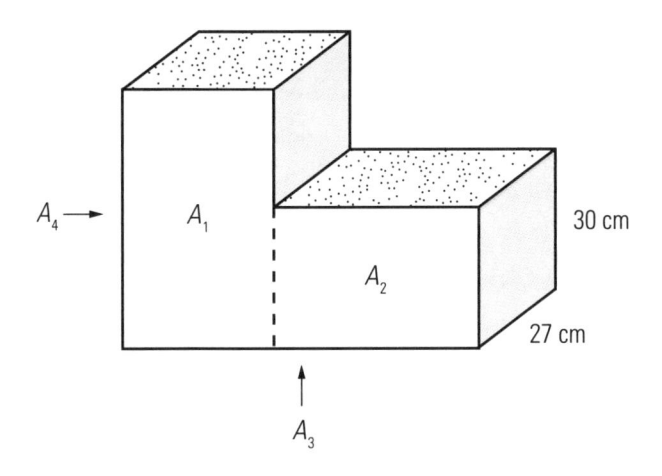

The shaded portions are equal in area to the left side of the figure (the end that you can't see, A_4). The polka-dotted parts are equal in area to the bottom of the figure, A_3. You will need to divide the front and back into two rectangles as indicated.

Calculate the areas of the different parts as in the solution above, but you only need to calculate parts A_1, A_2, A_3, and A_4.

$A_1 = 1815 \text{ cm}^2$

$A_2 = 1350 \text{ cm}^2$

$A_3 = 2106 \text{ cm}^2$

$A_4 = 1485 \text{ cm}^2$

Calculate the total surface area.

$SA = 2(A_1) + 2(A_2) + 2(A_3) + 2(A_4)$

$SA = 2(1815) + 2(1350) + 2(2106) + 2(1485)$

$SA = 3630 + 2700 + 4212 + 2970$

$SA = 13\ 512 \text{ cm}^2$

The total surface area is $13\ 512 \text{ cm}^2$.

BUILD YOUR SKILLS

9. Calculate the surface area of the figure below.

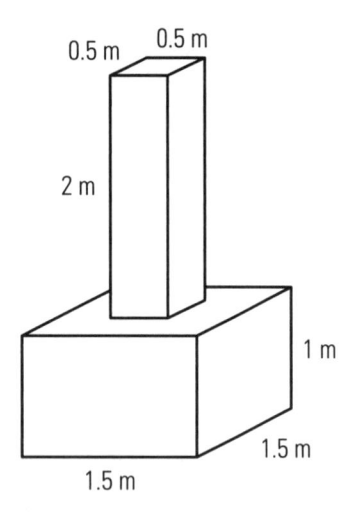

   0.5 m   0.5 m

   2 m

   1 m

   1.5 m

   1.5 m

10. Find the surface area of the figure below.

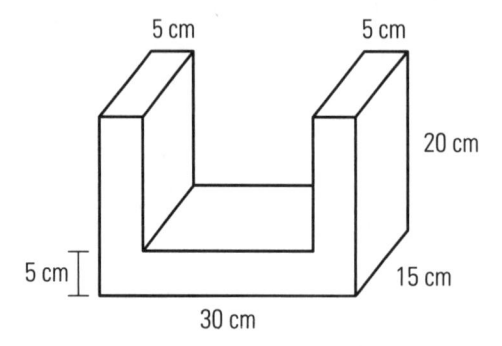

    5 cm   5 cm

    20 cm

    5 cm

    15 cm

    30 cm

Example 7

Kareem has been hired to paint the walls and ceiling of a living room in a house. The room is 22.5 feet long, 13.5 feet wide, and 8.5 feet high. There is one window that is 10.5 feet by 6 feet, two windows that are 3.5 feet by 2.5 feet, and two doors that are 2.5 feet by 8 feet.

a) What surface area must he paint?

b) One gallon of paint covers approximately 255 sq. ft. How many gallons will he have to buy?

c) If paint costs $55.40 per gallon and he wants to make a profit of about $225.00, how much should he charge to paint the room?

It is important to accurately calculate the surface area to be painted, so that you can make sure you buy enough paint to complete the project.

SOLUTION

a) Find the total surface area of the walls and ceiling and subtract the areas of the windows and doors.

The ceiling is 22.5 feet by 13.5 feet.

$A_1 = \ell w$

$A_1 = 22.5 \times 13.5$

$A_1 = 303.75$ sq. ft.

There are two walls that are 22.5 feet by 8.5 feet.

$A_2 = \ell w$

$A_2 = 22.5 \times 8.5$

$A_2 = 191.25$ sq. ft.

There are two walls that are 13.5 feet by 8.5 feet.

$A_3 = \ell w$

$A_3 = 13.5 \times 8.5$

$A_3 = 114.75$ sq. ft.

Calculate the total surface area of the walls.

$SA_1 = A_1 + 2(A_2) + 2(A_3)$

$SA_1 = 303.75 + 2(191.25) + 2(114.75)$

$SA_1 = 303.75 + 382.5 + 229.5$

$SA_1 = 915.75$ sq. ft.

There is one window that is 10.5 feet by 6 feet.

$A_4 = \ell w$

$A_4 = 10.5 \times 6$

$A_4 = 63$ sq. ft.

There are two windows that are 3.5 feet by 2.5 feet.

$A_5 = \ell w$

$A_5 = 3.5 \times 2.5$

$A_5 = 8.75$ sq. ft.

There are two doors that are 2.5 feet by 8 feet.

$A_6 = \ell w$

$A_6 = 2.5 \times 8$

$A_6 = 20$ sq. ft.

Calculate the surface area that does not need painting.

$SA_2 = A_4 + 2(A_5) + 2(A_6)$

$SA_2 = 63 + 2(8.75) + 2(20)$

$SA_2 = 63 + 17.5 + 40$

$SA_2 = 120.5$ sq. ft.

Calculate the area to be painted.

$SA_{paint} = SA_1 - SA_2$

$SA_{paint} = 915.75 - 120.5$

$SA_{paint} = 795.25$ sq. ft.

The area to be painted is 795.25 square feet.

b) Each can of paint covers approximately 255 square feet, and Kareem has 795.25 square feet to cover. Divide the total surface area by the area per can.

795.25 ÷ 255 ≈ 3.1 gallons

Kareem will need to buy 4 gallons of paint.

c) Multiply the number of gallons by the cost per gallon.

4 × $55.40 = $221.60

If Kareem wants to make a profit of about $225.00, add this amount to the cost of the paint.

$221.60 + $225.00 = $446.60

Kareem will need to charge about $446.60 to paint the room. He might round this up to $450.00.

BUILD YOUR SKILLS

11. Aamir is building a storage chest in the shape of a rectangular prism. The chest will be 90 cm long, 70 cm deep, and 60 cm high.

    a) What will be the outer surface area of the box?

    b) Aamir needs to buy 20% more wood than the surface area, to account for wastage during cutting. What area of wood will he need to buy?

12. Shar is installing an L-shaped heating duct in a house. If the duct has the measurements shown in the diagram below, what will be the total surface area of the duct? The ends of the duct are open.

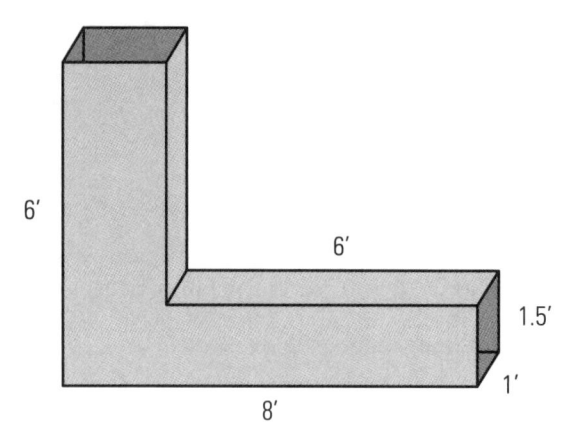

PRACTISE YOUR NEW SKILLS

1. Sketch the nets of the prisms and use them to determine their surface areas.

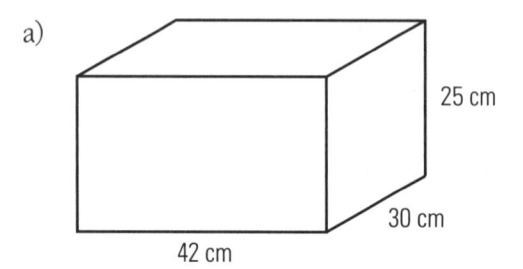

   a)

b)

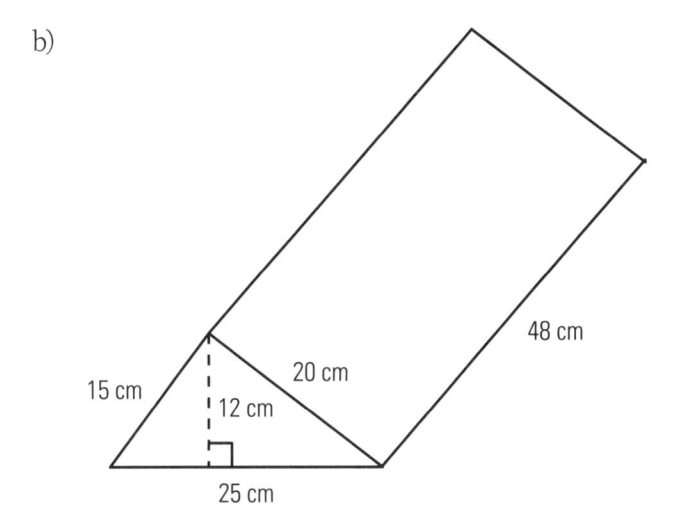

15 cm
20 cm
12 cm
25 cm
48 cm

2. Hoeth is building a feed trough for his cattle. The trough is to be triangular with a length of 12 feet, a height 1.5 feet, and a width of 4 feet. How much wood is required to build it?

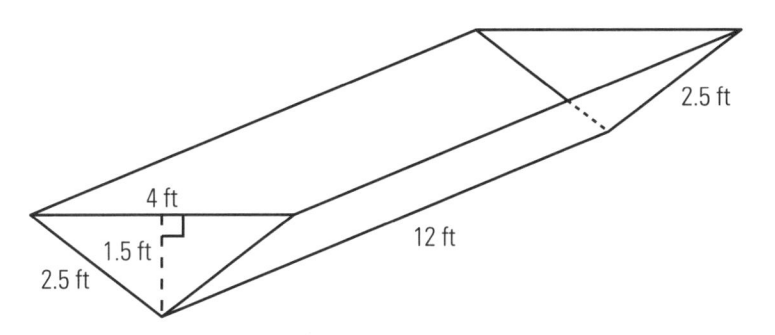

4 ft
1.5 ft
2.5 ft
12 ft
2.5 ft

Modern cattle troughs are often made out of durable plastics or metal.

3. Aaron is going to construct a fish tank that is 1.2 m long, 0.6 m wide, and 0.4 m high. How much glass will he need to make it? (Note: There will be no glass on the top.)

4. A grain elevator is a tower containing a bucket elevator, which scoops up grain and deposits it into a storage facility.

Calculate the surface area of the grain elevator shown here. (Assume that the front face of the grain elevator is vertically symmetrical.)

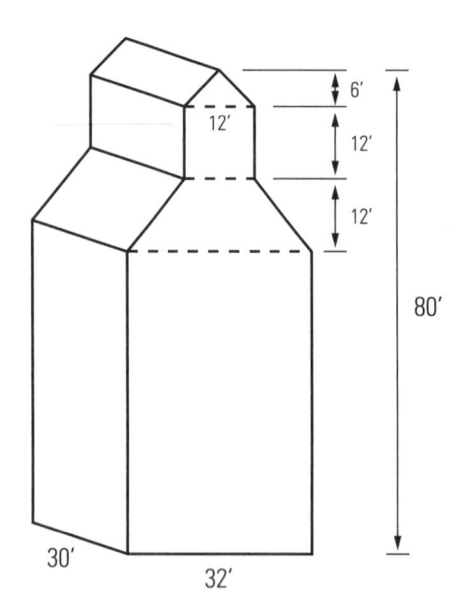

Grain elevators were traditionally build of wood, but they are being replaced by more modern ones made of steel or concrete. Some of the old wooden structures are being preserved as heritage sites.

Surface Area of Pyramids, Cylinders, Spheres, & Cones

3.2

REVIEW: WORKING WITH CIRCLES

In this section, you will need to calculate the circumference and the area of circles.

Example 1

Find the area of the following figure.

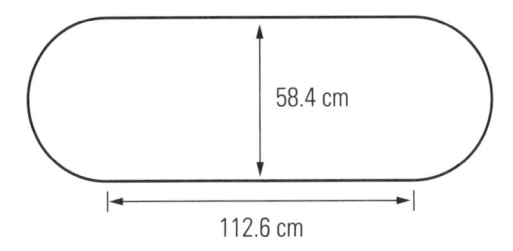

58.4 cm

112.6 cm

SOLUTION

This can be divided into parts: a rectangle 112.6 cm long and 58.4 cm wide, and two semicircles, each with a diameter of 58.4 cm. The two semicircles will make a full circle.

Calculate the area of the rectangle and the circle.

$A_r = \ell w$ $A_c = \pi r^2$

$A_r = 112.6 \times 58.4$ $A_c = \pi(58.4 \div 2)^2$

$A_r = 657.84 \text{ cm}^2$ $A_c = \pi(29.2)^2$

$A_c \approx 2678.65 \text{ cm}^2$

$A = A_r + A_c$

$A = 657.84 + 2678.65$

$A \approx 3336.5 \text{ cm}^2$

The area is 3336.5 cm².

> Use the π button on your calculator to calculate the area and circumference. Round your answer to same degree of accuracy (number of decimal places) as are given in the question.

BUILD YOUR SKILLS

1. Calculate the area of the following figure.

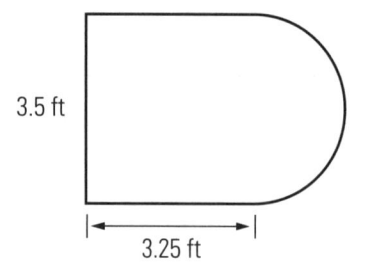

   3.5 ft

   3.25 ft

2. Calculate the area of the following figure.

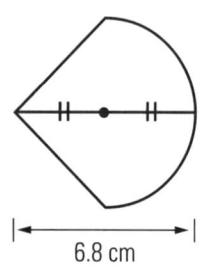

   6.8 cm

3. Calculate the area of the following figure.

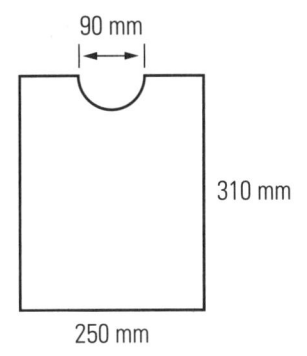

90 mm
310 mm
250 mm

NEW SKILLS: WORKING WITH THE SURFACE AREA OF CYLINDER

A cylinder is like a prism but it has circular bases. To find the surface area, you have to find the area of the two circles and the area between them. If you draw a net of a cylinder, you will find that it is made up of a rectangle and two circles. The length of the rectangle will be the circumference of the circle, and the width will be the height of the cylinder.

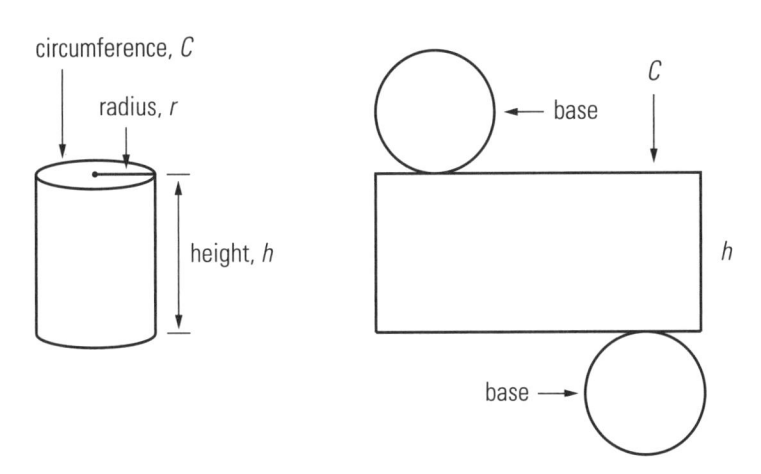

For more details, see page 127 of *MathWorks 11*.

Example 2

Find the surface area of a cylinder that has a radius of 90 mm and a height of 300 mm.

SOLUTION

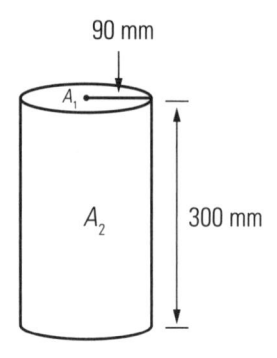

First find the area of the circular base of the cylinder.

$A_1 = \pi r^2$

$A_1 = \pi(90)^2$

$A_1 \approx 25\ 446.9$ mm²

Next, find the circumference of the cylinder.

$C = 2\pi r$

$C = 2\pi(90)$

$C \approx 565.5$ mm

Find the area of the lateral face.

$A_2 = C \times h$

$A_2 = 565.5 \times 300$

$A_2 \approx 169\ 646.0$ mm²

Calculate the total surface area.

$SA = 2(A_1) + A_2$

$SA = 2(25\ 446.9) + 169\ 646.0$

$SA = 220\ 539.8$ mm²

The total surface area is 220 539.8 mm².

BUILD YOUR SKILLS

4. Find the surface area of a cylindrical tank that has a radius of 1.5 m and a height of 5 m.

5. Find the surface area of a pipe that has a diameter of 4.5 cm and is 18.8 cm long.

How would you calculate how much icing was needed to cover this cake?

6. Find the surface area of the figure below. The upper cylinder is centred on the lower one.

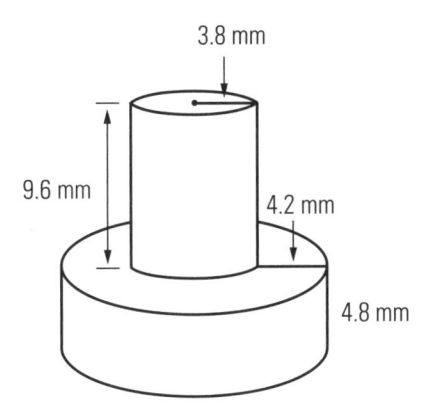

3.8 mm
9.6 mm
4.2 mm
4.8 mm

NEW SKILLS: WORKING WITH THE SURFACE AREA OF PYRAMIDS

A pyramid is a three-dimensional object with a polygonal base and lateral sides that are triangles. The triangles meet at a point, called the apex. In a right pyramid, the apex is aligned above the centre of the base.

The net of a pyramid will consist of the base plus as many triangles as there are sides to the base.

For more details, see page 127 of *MathWorks 11*.

Example 3

Find the surface area of the square-based pyramid below.

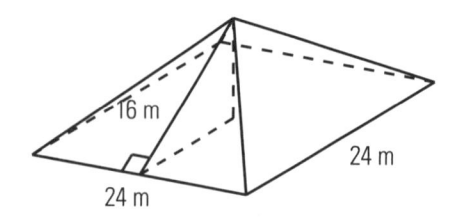

SOLUTION

The pyramid has a square base that is 24 m by 24 m. The four sides are congruent triangles with a base of 24 m and a height of 16 m.

Calculate the area of the base.

$A_1 = s^2$

$A_1 = 24^2$

$A_1 = 576 \text{ m}^2$

Calculate the area of one of the side triangles.

$A_2 = \frac{1}{2}(bh)$

$A_2 = \frac{1}{2} \times 24 \times 16$

$A_2 = 192 \text{ m}^2$

Calculate the total surface area.

$SA = A_1 + 4(A_2)$

$SA = 576 + 4(192)$

$SA = 1344 \text{ m}^2$

The surface area of the pyramid is 1344 m².

BUILD YOUR SKILLS

7. Find the surface area of the square-based pyramid below.

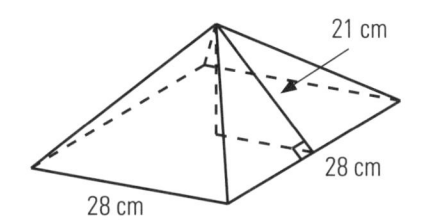

8. A pentagonal-based pyramid is sitting on a table. If the sides of the pentagon are 18 cm and the slant height of the triangles is 28 cm, what is the exposed area of the pyramid?

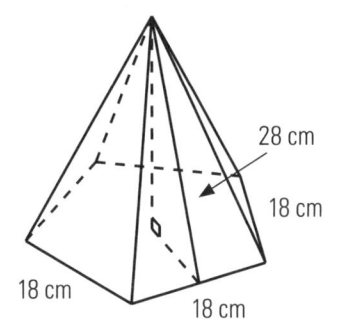

9. An octagonal-based pyramid has a slant height of 18.7 cm and each side of the octagon measures 12.6 cm. What is the lateral surface area of the pyramid?

Example 4

You must first find the slant height of the pyramid using the Pythagorean theorem.

Find the surface area of the square-based pyramid.

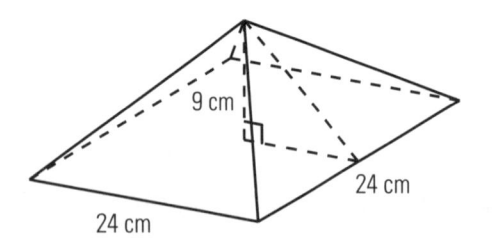

SOLUTION

To find the height of the triangles that form the lateral faces—or the slant height of the pyramid—you must use a triangle as indicated below.

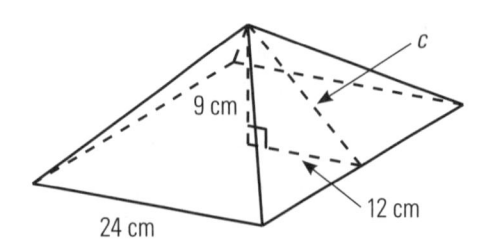

The two sides of the triangle will be 9 cm and 12 cm (half the length of a side of the square), and the hypotenuse of this triangle will be slant height of the pyramid.

$$a^2 + b^2 = c^2$$
$$9^2 + 12^2 = c^2$$
$$81 + 144 = c^2$$
$$225 = c^2$$
$$\sqrt{225} = c$$
$$15 = c$$

The surface area of the pyramid is the area of the square base plus the area of the four triangles.

$$A_{square} = s^2$$

$$A_{square} = 24^2$$

$$A_{square} = 576 \text{ cm}^2$$

$$A_{triangle} = \tfrac{1}{2}bh$$

$$A_{triangle} = \tfrac{1}{2} \times 24 \times 15$$

$$A_{triangle} = 180 \text{ cm}^2$$

$$SA = A_{square} + 4(A_{triangle})$$

$$SA = 576 + 4(180)$$

$$SA = 1296 \text{ cm}^2$$

The surface area of the pyramid is 1296 cm².

The courtyard of the Louvre Museum in Paris, France, features a large glass pyramid designed by architect I.M. Pei. The Louvre is home to many famous works of art, including the *Mona Lisa* and the *Venus de Milo*.

BUILD YOUR SKILLS

10. Find the total surface area of a square pyramid with a base of 12 cm by 12 cm and a height of 8 cm.

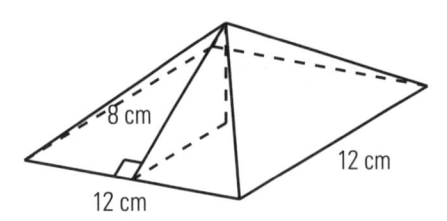

11. A triangular pyramid has faces that are all equilateral triangles. Each side length is 16 cm. What is the surface area of the pyramid?

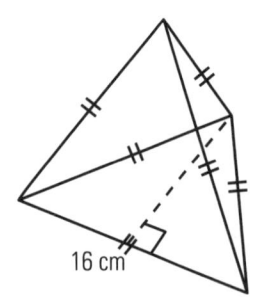

12. If the surface area of the sides of a square-based pyramid is 680 cm² and the side lengths of the square are 16 cm, what is the height of the pyramid?

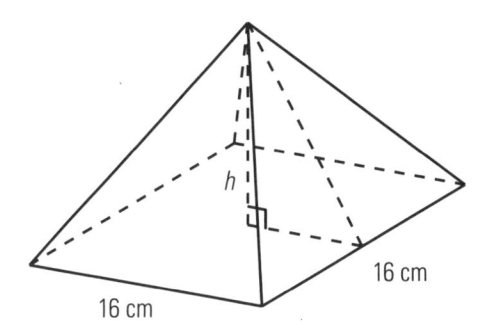

NEW SKILLS: WORKING WITH THE SURFACE AREA OF CONES

A cone is like a pyramid, but it has a circular base. The net of a cone is a sector of a large circle, and the circular base of the cone.

The surface area of the lateral area of the cone (the area not including the base) can be calculated using this formula, where r is the radius of the circular base and s is the slant height of the lateral face:

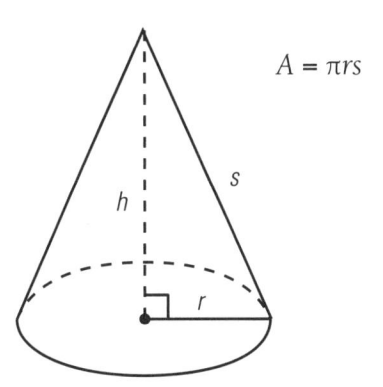

$$A = \pi r s$$

Example 5

Find the surface area of a cone that has a radius of 12 feet and a slant height of 15 feet.

SOLUTION

Calculate the area of the circular base.

$A_1 = \pi r^2$

$A_1 = \pi (12)^2$

$A_1 \approx 452.39$ sq. ft.

Calculate the area of the lateral surface.

$A_2 = \pi rs$

$A_2 = \pi (12)(15)$

$A_2 \approx 565.49$ sq. ft.

Calculate the total surface area.

$SA = A_1 + A_2$

$SA = 452.39 + 565.49$

$SA \approx 1017.9$ sq. ft.

The surface area of the cone is about 1017.9 sq. ft.

ALTERNATIVE SOLUTION

If you are calculating the total surface area of a cone, you can combine the equations for the base and the lateral surface.

$SA = \pi rs + \pi r^2$

$SA = \pi r(s + r)$

Use this formula to calculate the surface area.

BUILD YOUR SKILLS

13. Find the surface area of a cone that has a slant height of 82 cm and a radius of 28 cm.

14. Find the surface area of a cone with a diameter of 13.6 cm and a slant height of 9.8 cm.

Example 6

Find the surface area of the cone.

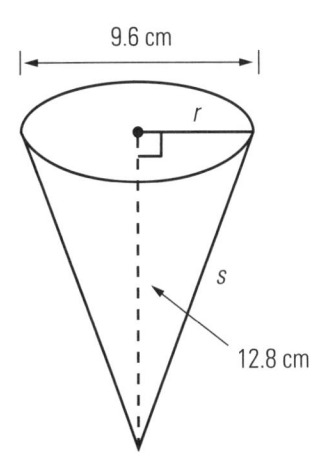

SOLUTION

The slant height is not given, so you will first need to calculate it using the Pythagorean theorem. Since the diameter of the cone is 9.6 cm, the radius is 4.8 cm.

$$a^2 + b^2 = c^2$$
$$h^2 + r^2 = s^2$$
$$(12.8)^2 + (4.8)^2 = s^2$$
$$163.84 + 23.04 = s^2$$
$$186.88 = s^2$$
$$\sqrt{186.88} = s$$
$$13.67 \approx s$$

The slant height is approximately 13.67 cm.

Since you are calculating the total surface area, you can use the combined formula used in Example 6.

$SA = \pi r(s + r)$

$SA = \pi(4.8)(13.67 + 4.8)$

$SA \approx 278.5$ cm²

The surface area is approximately 278.5 cm².

BUILD YOUR SKILLS

15. Find the total surface area of a cone with a radius of 16 inches and a height of 20 inches.

16. Find the surface area of a cone with a radius of 45.7 mm and a height of 39.7 mm.

17. Find the lateral surface area of a cone whose height is 32 cm and whose diameter is 28 cm.

NEW SKILLS: WORKING WITH THE SURFACE AREA OF SPHERES

A sphere is like a ball. All points on the sphere are equidistant (of equal distance) from the centre. It is not possible to draw a net of a sphere. The formula for a sphere's surface area depends only on the radius and π. The formula for the surface area of a sphere is:

$SA = 4\pi r^2$

For more details, see page 127 of *MathWorks 11*.

Example 7

A ball has a surface area of approximately 9900 cm². What is its radius?

SOLUTION

You are given the surface area and need to find the radius. Use the formula for surface area.

$$SA = 4\pi r^2$$
$$9900 = 4\pi r^2$$
$$\frac{9900}{4\pi} = \frac{4\pi r^2}{4\pi}$$
$$\frac{9900}{4\pi} = r^2$$
$$\sqrt{\frac{9900}{4\pi}} = r$$
$$28.07 \approx r$$

The radius is approximately 28.1 cm.

BUILD YOUR SKILLS

18. Find the surface area of a sphere with a radius of 1.3 m.

19. Find the surface area of a sphere with a diameter of 24.8 mm.

A hemisphere is half of a sphere.

20. Find the surface area of a hemisphere with a radius of 18.5 cm.

Example 8

Find the surface area of the composite figure.

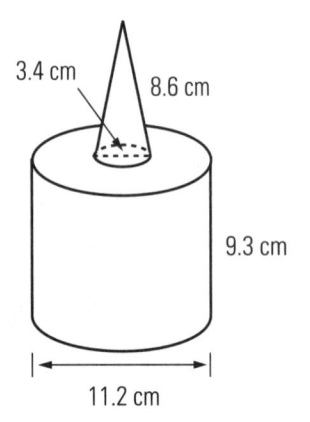

3.4 cm
8.6 cm
9.3 cm
11.2 cm

SOLUTION

The component parts of the surface area of the figure will be the lateral area of the cone plus the surface area of the cylinder minus the circular area of the cone.

Calculate the lateral area of the cone. The diameter is 3.4 cm, so the radius is 1.7 cm.

$A_1 = \pi r s$

$A_1 = \pi(1.7)(8.6)$

$A_1 \approx 45.93$ cm^2

Calculate the surface area of the top and bottom of the cylinder. The diameter is 11.2 cm, so the radius is 5.6 cm.

$A_2 = \pi r^2$

$A_2 = \pi(5.6)^2$

$A_2 \approx 98.52$ cm^2

Calculate the surface area of the side of the cylinder.

$A_3 = C \times h$

$A_3 = 2\pi r \times h$

$A_3 = 2\pi(5.6)(9.3)$

$A_3 \approx 327.23$ cm^2

Calculate the area of the base of the cone.

$A_4 = \pi r^2$

$A_4 = \pi(1.7)^2$

$A_4 \approx 9.08$ cm^2

Calculate the total surface area of the figure.

SA = surface area of cylinder + surface area of cone – area of base of cone

$SA = 2(A_2) + A_3 + A_1 - A_4$

$SA = 2(98.52) + 327.23 + 45.93 - 9.08$

$SA \approx 561.1$ cm^2

The surface area is approximately 561.1 cm^2.

BUILD YOUR SKILLS

21. Find the surface area the following figure.

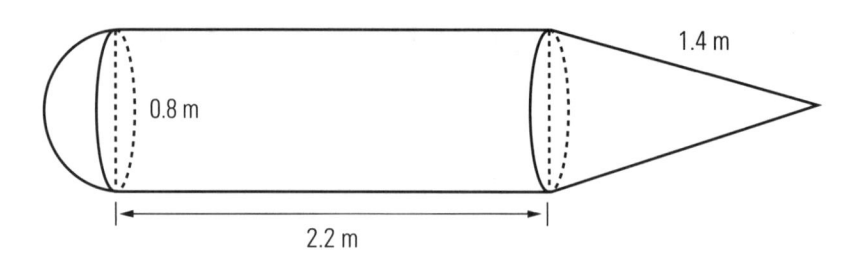

22. Three cylinders with radii of 4 feet, 3 feet, and 2 feet are stacked one on top of the other. Each has a height of 2 feet. What is the total exposed surface area?

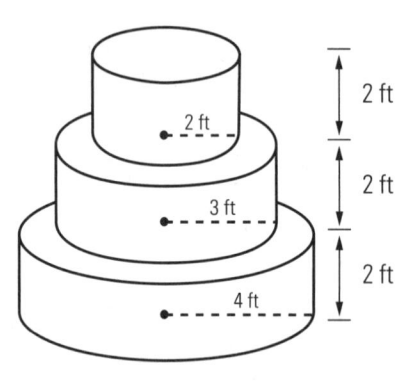

23. Find the surface area of the cone topped by the hemisphere shown in the following diagram.

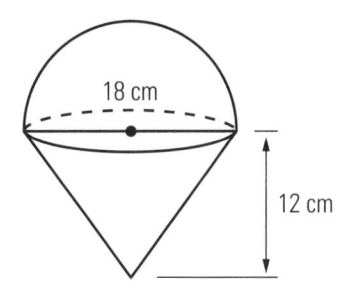

PRACTISE YOUR NEW SKILLS

1. Bob is a metal worker and is making round cake pans. How much metal will he use in making a 9-inch round cake tin that is $1\frac{1}{2}$ inches tall?

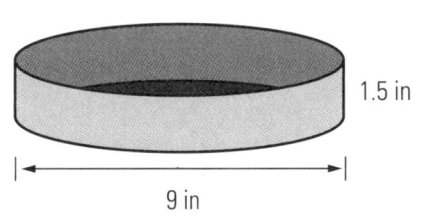

What if the cake pan had a hole in the middle? How would you calculate how much metal was needed?

2. How many square centimetres of paper are needed to produce 50 conical cups like the one below?

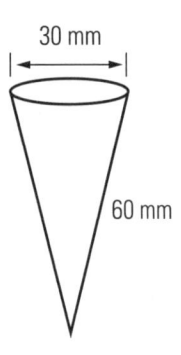

30 mm
60 mm

3. How much corrugated steel will be needed to cover a Quonset hut (a kind of building that is half a cylinder) that is 20 feet wide by 48 feet long if both the front and the back are covered, except for a door that is 8 feet tall by 7 feet wide?

8 ft 7 ft 48 ft
20 ft

Quonset huts are made of corrugated steel. They are popular because they are easy to assemble and are very durable. They are often used as sheds or garages.

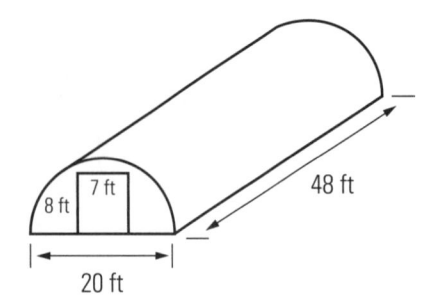

4. Find the lateral surface area of the hexagonal pyramid below.

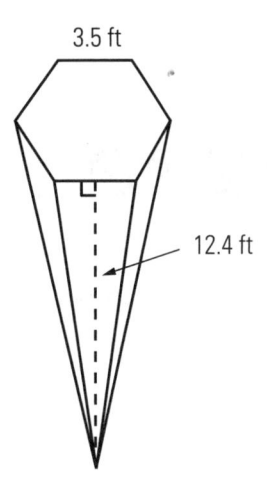

3.5 ft

12.4 ft

5. Calculate the surface area of a cone that has a radius of 12 feet and a slant height of 15 feet.

6. A tennis ball has a diameter of 6.7 cm. What is its surface area?

3.3 Volume and Capacity of Prisms and Cylinders

NEW SKILLS: VOLUME AND CAPACITY OF RECTANGULAR PRISMS

volume: the measure of the space a three-dimensional object occupies

capacity: the amount a three-dimensional object can hold

The **volume** of an object is a measure of the amount of space it occupies. The **capacity** of an object is a measure of how much it can hold. Hollow objects (like a cardboard box) have volume and capacity, while solid objects (like a cement brick) have only volume.

Volume is measures in cubed units, such as m³. Capacity is measured in units such as litres or gallons.

Volume and capacity are closely related. In the metric system a volume of 1000 cm³ is equivalent to a capacity of 1 L.

The volume of both a prism and a cylinder are found by multiplying the area of the base by the height of the object.

$V = A_{base} \times h$

The formula is the same even if the prism/cylinder is oblique. Just remember that the height is always the perpendicular distance between the two bases.

For more details, see page 138 of *MathWorks 11*.

Example 1

A rectangular prism that has a base that is 15 cm by 12 cm and a height of 20 cm.

a) Draw a diagram and calculate the volume of the prism.

b) Calculate the capacity of the first prism.

SOLUTION

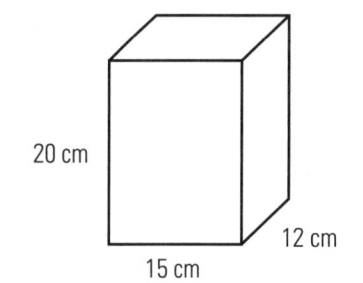

a)

20 cm, 15 cm, 12 cm

Use the formula for volume.

$V = A_{base} \times h$

$V = \ell w h$

$V = 15 \times 12 \times 20$

$V = 3600 \text{ cm}^3$

b) Since 1 L equals 1000 cm³, divide the volume by 1000.

$3600 \div 1000 = 3.6 \text{ L}$

The prisms each have a capacity of 3.6 L.

BUILD YOUR SKILLS

1. Find the volume and capacity of the following rectangular prisms.

    a) The base is 15.7 cm by 18.8 cm and the height is 12.5 cm.

    b) The base is a square with sides of 2.75 m, and the height is 4.5 m.

    c) The base is $1\frac{1}{2}$ inches by $3\frac{3}{4}$ inches, and the height is $2\frac{1}{4}$ inches.

Example 2

A rectangular prism has a square base with side lengths of 7 cm. Its volume is 392 cm³. Calculate the height of the prism.

SOLUTION

Use the formula for volume and solve for h.

$$V = \ell w h$$
$$392 = 7 \times 7 \times h$$
$$392 = 49h$$
$$\frac{392}{49} = h$$
$$8 = h$$

The height of the rectangular prism is 8 cm.

BUILD YOUR SKILLS

2. A rectangular prism has a base of 5.2 m by 7.8 m. Its volume is 142 m³. What is the height of the prism?

3. One rectangular prism has dimensions of 18 cm by 12 cm by 32 cm. A second prism has a base that is 14 cm by 20 cm. Approximately what must its height be if it has the same volume as the first prism?

4. Patrice is in charge of the excavation for the foundation of a building. If a hole must be dug that is 35 m by 25 m by 12 m, how many trips will be required to remove the dirt if a trailer can carry only 15 cubic metres of dirt?

Excavators are used to remove dirt and rocks when constructing foundations.

Example 3

Calculate the volume and capacity of the composite prism.

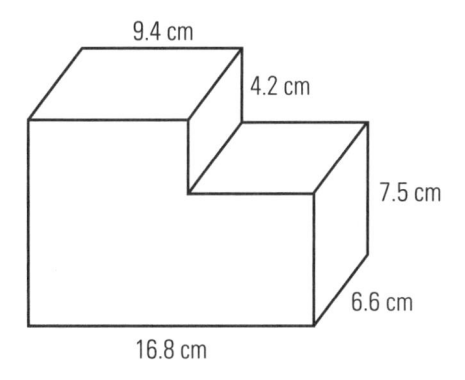

9.4 cm
4.2 cm
7.5 cm
6.6 cm
16.8 cm

SOLUTION

The volume of this composite prism can be found by dividing it into two rectangular prisms.

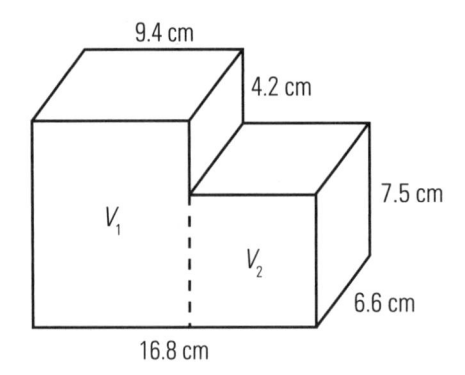

$V_1 = \ell wh$ $\qquad\qquad$ $V_2 = \ell wh$

$V_1 = 9.4 \times 6.6 \times (4.2 + 7.5)$ $\qquad$ $V_2 = (16.8 - 9.4) \times 6.6 \times 7.5$

$V_1 = 9.4 \times 6.6 \times 11.7$ $\qquad\qquad$ $V_2 = 7.4 \times 6.6 \times 7.5$

$V_1 \approx 725.9 \text{ cm}^3$ $\qquad\qquad\qquad$ $V_2 \approx 366.3 \text{ cm}^3$

Calculate the total volume.

$V_{total} = V_1 + V_2$

$V_{total} = 725.9 + 366.3$

$V_{total} = 1092.2 \text{ cm}^3$

The total volume is 1092.2 cm³.

Divide by 1000 to calculate capacity.

1092.2 ÷ 1000 = 1.0922 L

Its capacity is about 1.1 L.

BUILD YOUR SKILLS

5. a) The volume of the figure in Example 3 could have been calculated by dividing the composite prism into two different prisms than the ones used in the solution given. Draw a diagram to indicate this. Label it with its dimensions.

b) The volume could also have been calculated by subtraction. Draw a diagram to indicate how you could do this. Label the diagram with its dimensions.

6. Find the volume of this figure.

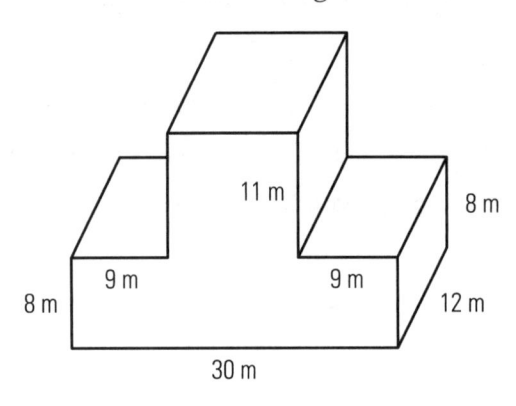

   11 m
   8 m
   9 m
   9 m
   8 m
   12 m
   30 m

7. The capacity of this composite prism is 1.8 litres. Determine its depth, w.

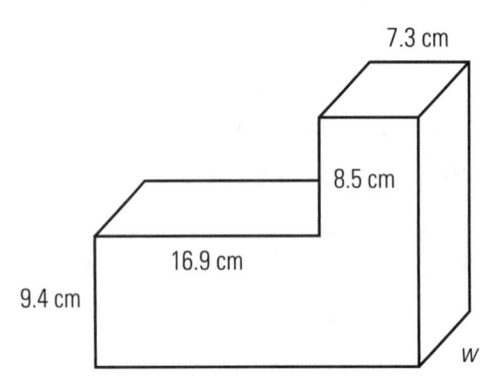

   7.3 cm
   8.5 cm
   16.9 cm
   9.4 cm
   w

NEW SKILLS: WORKING WITH THE VOLUME OF CYLINDERS

The volume of a prism is calculated using the following formula.

$V = A_{base} \times h$

The area of a the base of a cylinder can be calculated as:

$A = \pi r^2$

If you combine these two formulas, the formula for the volume of a cylinder is as follows.

$V = \pi r^2 h$

Example 4

A can of tomato sauce has a radius of 3.8 cm and a height of 10.2 cm.

a) What is the volume of the can?

b) How much tomato sauce (in litres) does the can hold?

SOLUTION

a) Start by calculating the volume of the can.

$V = \pi r^2 h$

$V = \pi (3.8)^2 (10.2)$

$V \approx 462.7 \text{ cm}^3$

b) 1000 cm³ equals 1 L, so divide the volume by 1000.

462.7 ÷ 1000 = 0.4627 L

The can holds about 0.5 L of tomato sauce.

Delicious home-made sauce recipes are sometimes kept as secret family recipes, passed down through generations.

BUILD YOUR SKILLS

8. Calculate the volume and capacity of a cylinder with a diameter of 15 cm and a height of 36 cm.

9. Calculate the volume and capacity of the stacked cylinders below. Each cylinder has a height of 20 cm.

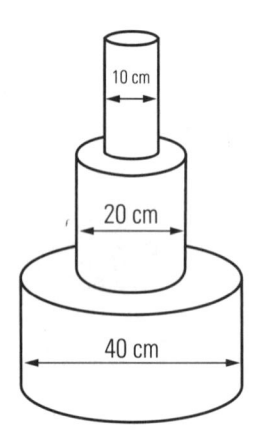

10. A large tin can has a capacity of 3.24 L. If the can has a diameter of 15.56 cm. What is the height of the can?

Chapter 3 Surface Area, Volume, and Capacity **179**

PRACTISE YOUR NEW SKILLS

1. Calculate the volume of each figure.

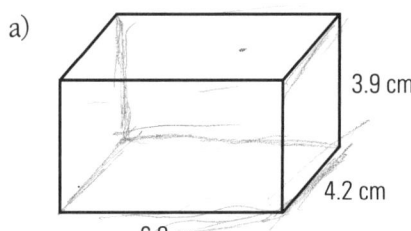

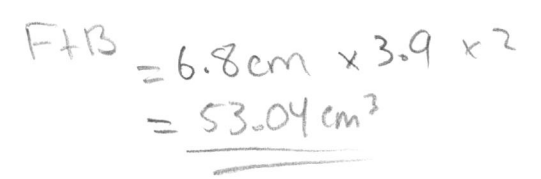

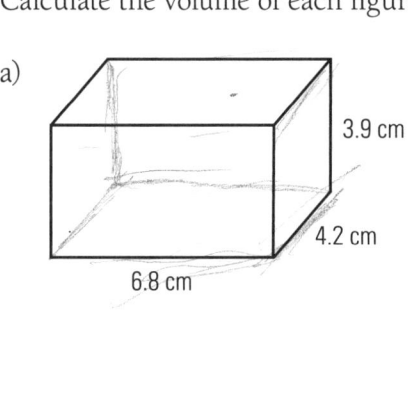

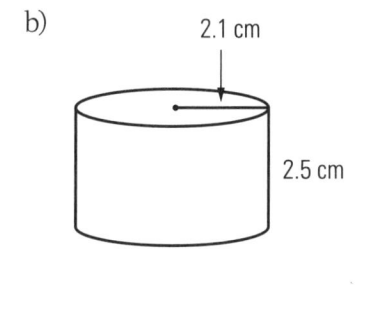

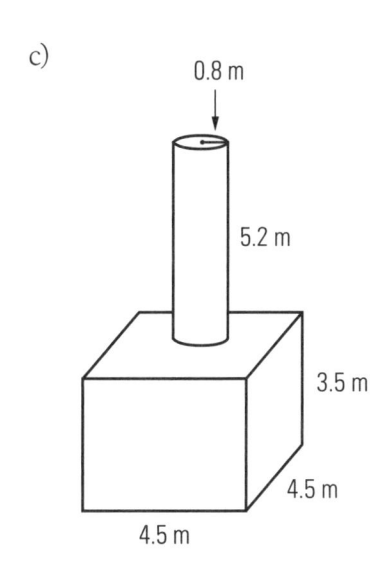

   a) [rectangular prism: 6.8 cm × 4.2 cm × 3.9 cm]

   T+b
   = 6.8 cm × 4.2 cm × 2
   = 57.12 cm³

   S+S
   = 4.2 × 3.9 × 2
   = 32.76 cm³

   F+B
   = 6.8 cm × 3.9 × 2
   = 53.04 cm³

   Add: 57.12 cm³ + 32.76 cm³ + 53.04 cm³
   = 142.92 cm³

   b) [cylinder: radius 2.1 cm, height 2.5 cm]

   c) [cylinder on top of cube: cylinder diameter 0.8 m, height 5.2 m; cube 4.5 m × 4.5 m × 3.5 m]

2. Which of these figures has the larger capacity? Show your work.

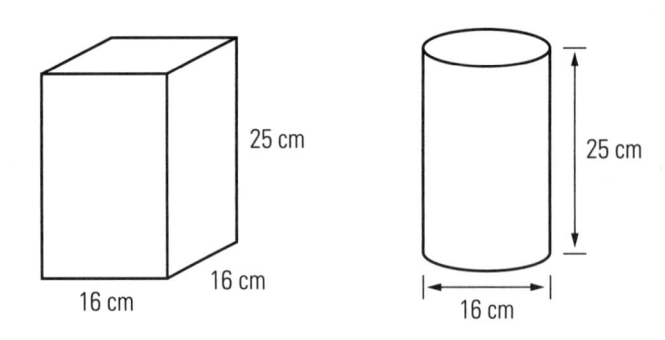

3. A silo has a diameter of 24 feet and is filled to a height of 70 feet. What is the volume of grain stored in it?

4. Graydon is laying a cement patio. It is to be 6 m long by 4.5 m wide, and 15 cm deep.

   a) Calculate the volume of concrete needed to fill the patio area.

   b) If concrete weighs approximately 2400 kg per cubic metre, how much will the patio concrete weigh?

5. A fish tank in the shape of a rectangular prism contains 15 L of water. If the base of the tank is 30 cm by 20 cm, what is the depth of the water?

6. A large cylindrical fuel storage tank has a capacity of 20 000 L. If it has a diameter of 2.4 m, what is the height of the tank?

3.4 Volume and Capacity of Spheres, Cones, and Pyramids

NEW SKILLS: WORKING WITH VOLUME AND CAPACITY OF SPHERES

The volume of a sphere is calculated using the following formula.

$$V_{sphere} = \frac{4}{3}\pi r^3$$

The capacity of a spherical container can be calculated the same as for a prism or cylinder. Start by calculating the volume, then convert to a unit of capacity. Remember that 1000 cm³ equals 1 L.

You will also need to know how to convert between cubic metres and cubic centimetres. A box with dimensions of 1 m by 1 m by 1 m would have a volume of 1 m³.

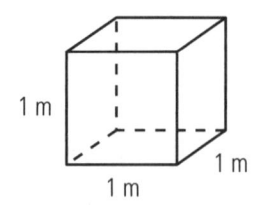

Convert the box's dimensions to centimetres.

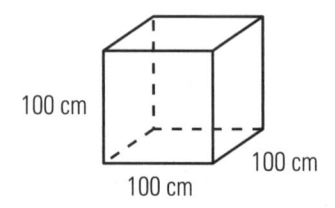

1 m = 100 cm

Calculate the volume.

$V = \ell wh$

$V = 100 \times 100 \times 100$

$V = 1\,000\,000$ cm³

Therefore, 1 m³ is equal to 1 000 000 cm³.

For more details, see page 148 of *MathWorks 11*.

Example 1

A spherical exercise ball has a diameter of 1.2 m.

a) What is its volume?

b) What is its capacity?

SOLUTION

a) Use the formula for the volume of a sphere. The radius is half the diameter, so the radius is 0.6 m.

$$V = \frac{4}{3}\pi r^3$$

$$V = \frac{4}{3} \times \pi \times (0.6)^3$$

$$V \approx 0.904\,779 \text{ m}^3$$

The volume of the sphere is about 0.9 m³.

b) Convert the volume in cubic metres to cubic centimetres.

1 m³ = 1 000 000 cm³

0.904 778 7 × 1 000 000 = 904 779 cm³

Convert to litres.

1000 cm³ = 1 L

904 779 ÷ 1000 ≈ 905 L

The capacity is approximately 905 L.

An exercise ball can be a great way to work out your abdominal muscles.

BUILD YOUR SKILLS

1. Find the volume of each sphere.

   a) A sphere with a radius of 8.5 cm.

b) A sphere with a diameter of 78 cm.

2. A sphere with a radius of 46 cm is centred inside a sphere with a radius of 76 cm.

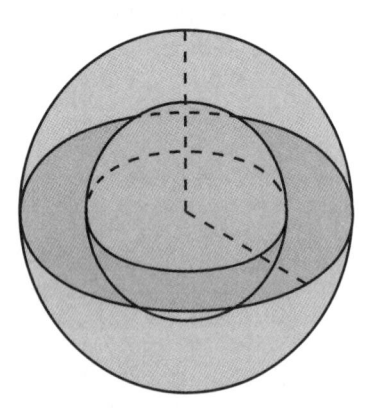

a) What is the volume of the space between the two spheres?

b) What is the capacity?

NEW SKILLS: WORKING WITH VOLUME AND CAPACITY OF PYRAMIDS

The volume of a pyramid is directly related to the volume of a prism with the same base and height. The volume is calculated using the following formula.

$$V = \frac{1}{3} \times A_{base} \times h$$

For a rectangular pyramid this can be written as:

$$V = \frac{1}{3} \ell w h$$

Example 2

Calculate the volume and capacity of this pyramid.

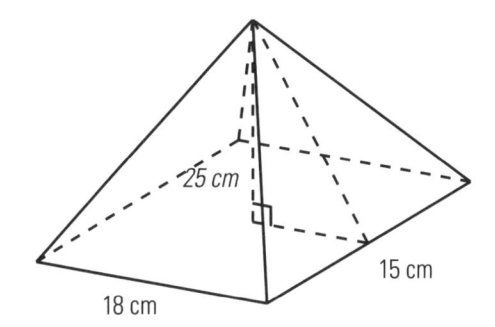

SOLUTION

Use the formula for calculating the volume of a pyramid.

$$V = \frac{1}{3} \ell w h$$

$$V = \frac{1}{3} \times 15 \times 25 \times 18$$

$$V = 2250 \text{ cm}^3$$

The volume of the pyramid is 2250 cm³.

Convert the volume to units of capacity.

2250 ÷ 1000 = 2.25 L

The capacity of the pyramid is 2.25 L.

BUILD YOUR SKILLS

3. Find the volume of each pyramid.

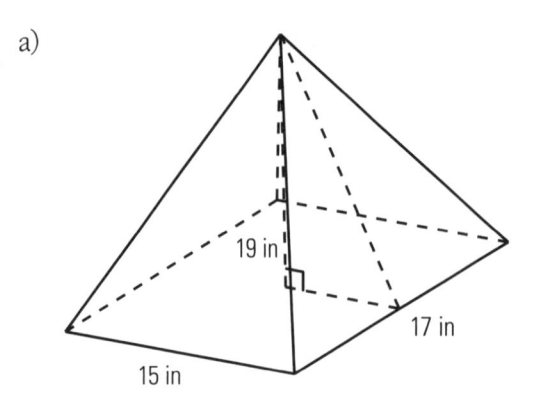

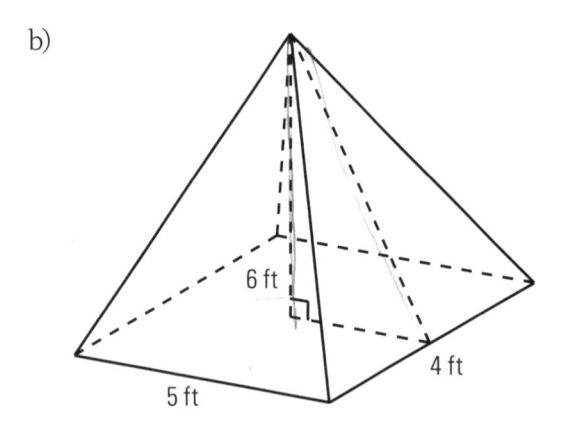

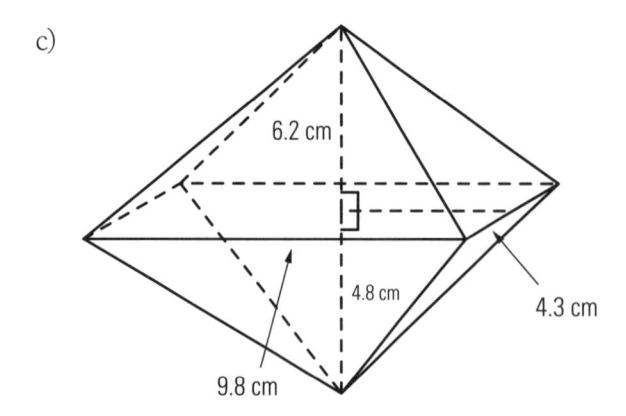

a)

19 in
17 in
15 in

b)

6 ft
4 ft
5 ft

c)

6.2 cm
4.8 cm
4.3 cm
9.8 cm

4. What are the volume and capacity of the following figure? The height to the peak is 15 ft.

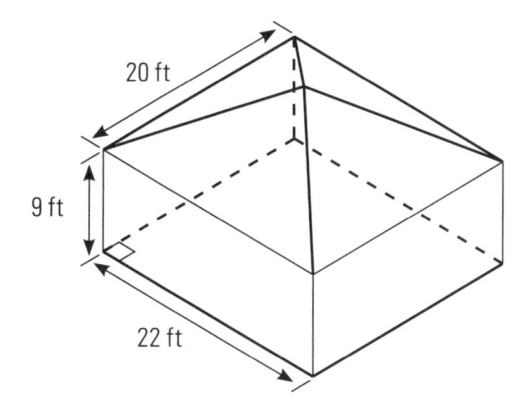

20 ft
9 ft
22 ft

5. Calculate the volume of this prism and pyramid. What is the difference in volume?

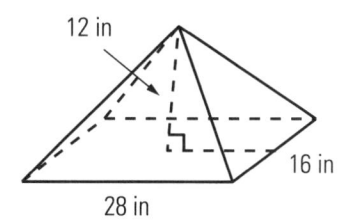

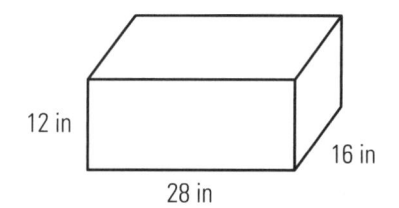

12 in
16 in
28 in

12 in
16 in
28 in

Example 3

Calculate the volume of this pyramid.

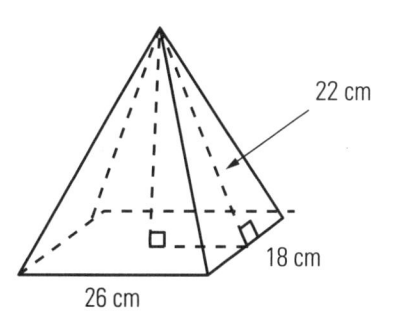

22 cm
18 cm
26 cm

SOLUTION

You are given the slant height of the pyramid, but not the actual height. Calculate the height using the Pythagorean theorem.

The base of the triangle will be half the width of the pyramid.

26 cm ÷ 2 = 13 cm

$$a^2 + b^2 = c^2$$
$$13^2 + b^2 = 22^2$$
$$b^2 = 22^2 - 13^2$$
$$b = \sqrt{22^2 - 13^2}$$
$$b = \sqrt{484 - 169}$$
$$b = \sqrt{315}$$
$$b \approx 17.7 \text{ cm}$$

Use this height to calculate the volume.

$$V = \frac{1}{3} \ell w h$$
$$V = \frac{1}{3} \times 26 \times 18 \times 17.7$$
$$V \approx 2761.2 \text{ cm}^3$$

The volume of the pyramid is about 2761.2 cm3.

If you knew the side lengths and height of this sand pyramid, could you estimate how much sand was used to make it?

BUILD YOUR SKILLS

6. Calculate the volume of each of these pyramids.

a) 25 mm, 35 mm, 35 mm

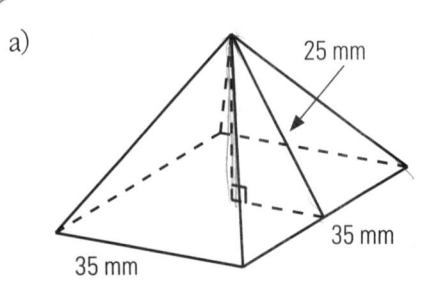

b)

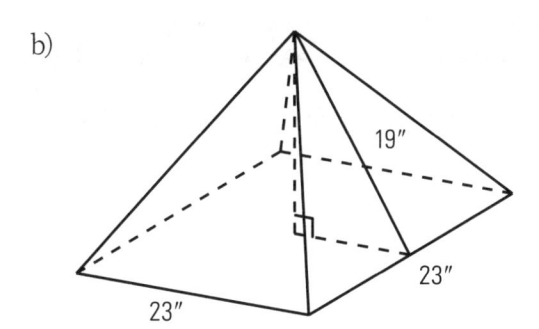

19"
23"
23"

c)

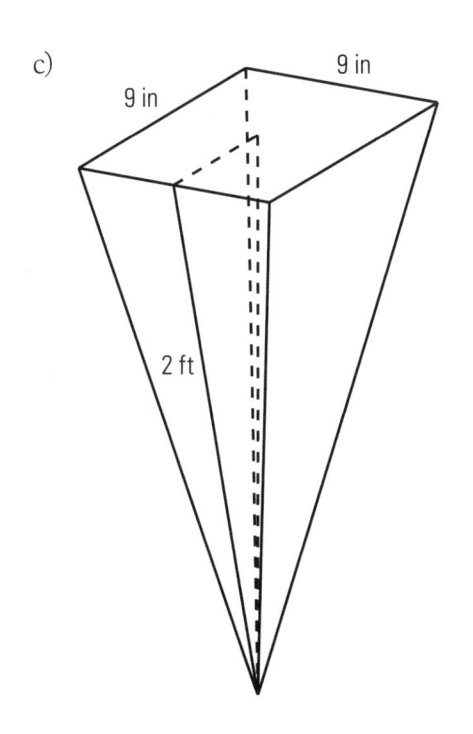

9 in
9 in
2 ft

d)

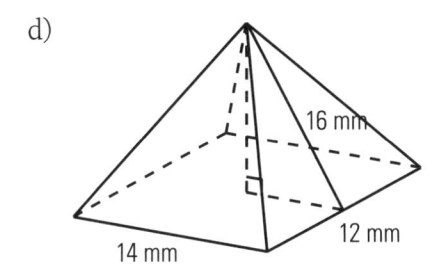

16 mm
14 mm
12 mm

NEW SKILLS: WORKING WITH THE VOLUME AND CAPACITY OF CONES

The volume of a cone is equal to $\frac{1}{3}$ of the volume of a cylinder with the same base and height. As with pyramids, the volume is calculated using the following formula.

$$V = \frac{1}{3} \times A_{base} \times h$$

Since the base is a circle, the formula can be rewritten as:

$$V = \frac{1}{3} \pi r^2 h$$

Example 4

A paper cup in the shape of a cone has a radius of 3.2 cm and a height of 6 cm. How much water can the cup hold?

SOLUTION

Calculate the volume of the cone.

$$V = \frac{1}{3} \times A_{base} \times \text{height}$$

$$V = \frac{1}{3} \times \pi r^2 \times h$$

$$V = \frac{1}{3} \pi (3.2)^2 (6)$$

$$V \approx 64.3 \text{ cm}^3$$

Convert the volume to units of capacity.

1000 cm³ = 1 L or 1000 mL

64.3 cm³ equals 64.3 mL. The cup can hold 64.3 mL of water.

BUILD YOUR SKILLS

7. Find the volume of each of the following figures.

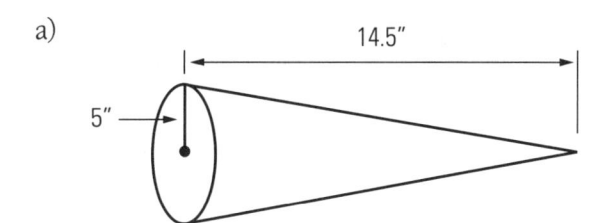

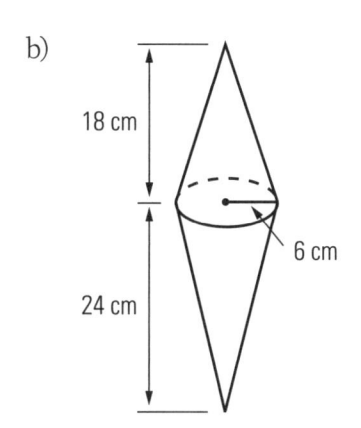

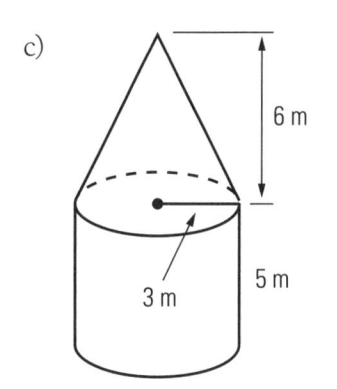

   a)

   [Cone with diameter 5" and length 14.5"]

   b)

   [Double cone: top cone height 18 cm, bottom cone height 24 cm, radius 6 cm]

   c)

   [Cylinder with cone on top: radius 3 m, slant height 5 m, cone height 6 m]

8. A cone has a radius of 12 mm and a volume of 4071.5 mm³. What is its height?

9. A cone has a slant height of 15 cm and a radius of 8 cm. Determine its volume.

PRACTISE YOUR NEW SKILLS

1. Find the volume of each of the following figures.

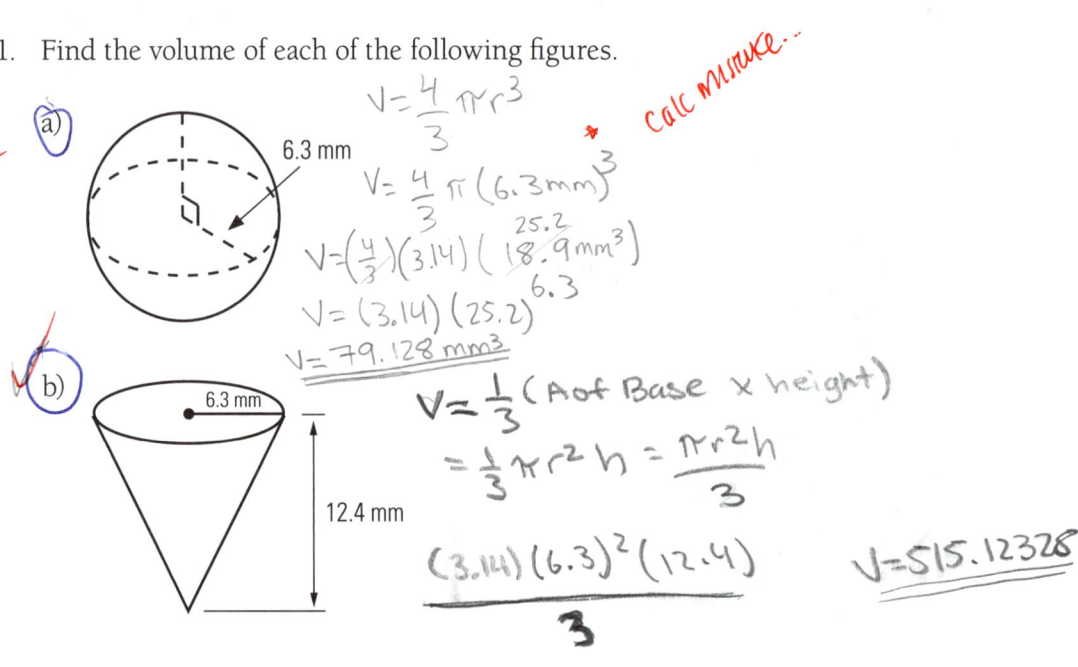

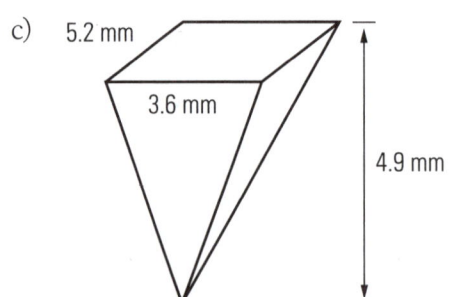

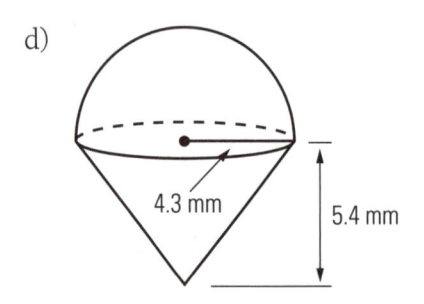

   a) *(sphere, 6.3 mm radius)*

   Student work:
   Answer Key says 1047 mm³

   $V = \dfrac{4}{3}\pi r^3$

   $V = \dfrac{4}{3}\pi (6.3\,mm)^3$

   $V = \left(\dfrac{4}{3}\right)(3.14)(18.9\,mm^3)$ — 25.2, 6.3 *(calc mistake)*

   $V = (3.14)(25.2)$

   $V = 79.128\,mm^3$

   b) *(cone, radius 6.3 mm, height 12.4 mm)*

   $V = \dfrac{1}{3}(A\text{ of Base} \times \text{height})$

   $= \dfrac{1}{3}\pi r^2 h = \dfrac{\pi r^2 h}{3}$

   $\dfrac{(3.14)(6.3)^2(12.4)}{3}$ $V = 515.12328$

   c) *(triangular pyramid: 5.2 mm, 3.6 mm, 4.9 mm)*

   d) *(hemisphere on cone: radius 4.3 mm, cone height 5.4 mm)*

2. What is the capacity in US gallons of a spherical water tower with a diameter of 31.2 feet? 1 cubic foot equals 7.48 US gallons.

3. A square-based pyramid with a base with sides of 14 cm, and its height is 45 cm. A cone has a diameter of 14 cm and also has a height of 45 cm.

   a) What is the difference in volume between the two figures?

   b) What is the difference in capacity?

4. When grain is poured from a hopper onto the ground, it forms a cone-shaped pile. The diameter of the base is approximately 4.5 m and the height is 1.2 m. How many cubic metres of grain are in the pile?

5. Three metal spheres are dropped into a jug of water and sink to the bottom. If the spheres are 3.4 cm, 2.8 cm, and 4.6 cm in radius, what volume of water do they displace?

CHAPTER TEST

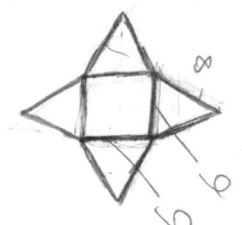

1. Draw the net of each figure and calculate its surface area.

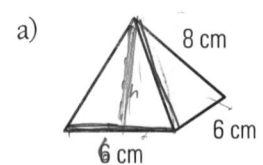

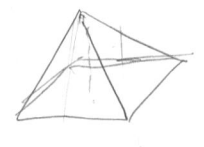

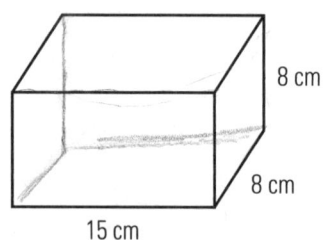

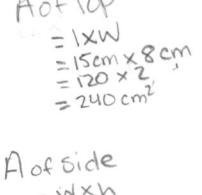

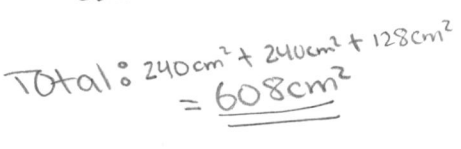

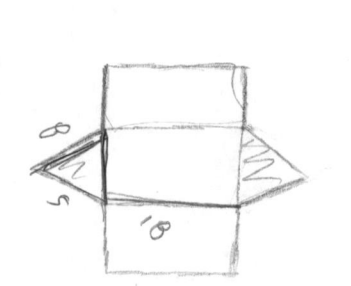

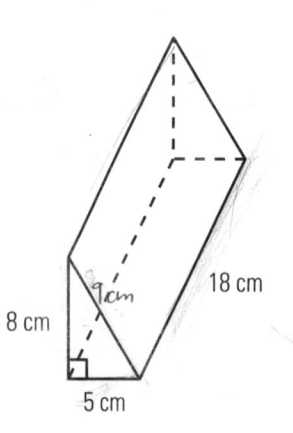

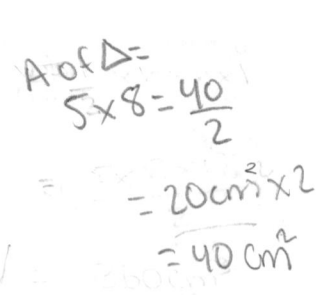

   a) [pyramid: 8 cm, 6 cm, 6 cm]

   b) [rectangular box: 15 cm × 8 cm × 8 cm]

   A of TOP
   = l × w
   = 15 cm × 8 cm
   = 120 × 2
   = 240 cm²

   A of Side
   = w × h
   = 8 cm × 8 cm
   = 64 × 2
   = 128 cm²

   A of front
   = l × h
   = 15 cm × 8 cm
   = 120 × 2
   = 240 cm²

   Total: 240 cm² + 240 cm² + 128 cm²
   = 608 cm²

   c) [triangular prism: 8 cm, 5 cm, 9 cm, 18 cm]

   A of △ = 5 × 8 = 40/2
   = 20 cm² × 2
   = 40 cm²

   A of ▭

2. Calculate surface area and the volume of a box that is 3 m by 2 m by 7.5 m.

3. A cylindrical tin can has a radius of 4.5 cm and a height of 5 cm.

   a) What is the surface area of the can?

   b) What is its volume?

   c) What is the can's capacity?

4. A ball has a radius of 56 mm.

   a) Calculate the surface area.

   b) What is the volume of the sphere?

5. Calculate the total surface area and volume of the following figure.

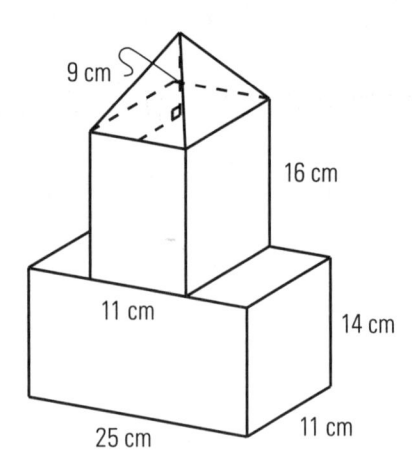

[Figure: composite shape with a rectangular prism base (25 cm × 11 cm × 14 cm) topped by a square prism (11 cm × 11 cm × 16 cm) with a square pyramid on top (slant height 9 cm)]

6. A pile of gravel is conical in shape. If the diameter is approximately 6.8 m and the height is 2.8 m, what is the volume of gravel in the pile?

7. The roof of a building is shaped like a square pyramid, with a base of 18 m by 18 m. If the slant height of the roof is 12 m and roofing costs $5.75/m², how much will it cost for roofing material?

Chapter 4

Trigonometry of Right Triangles

Surveyors use theodolites to measure angles in the field. These angles can be used to solve problems involving trigonometric ratios.

4.1 Solving for Angles, Lengths, and Distances

REVIEW: WORKING WITH TRIGONOMETRIC RATIOS

In this chapter, you will be working with trigonometric ratios to solve problems. The trigonometric ratios of sine (abbreviated as sin), cosine (cos), and tangent (tan) are based on the lengths of the sides of a right triangle.

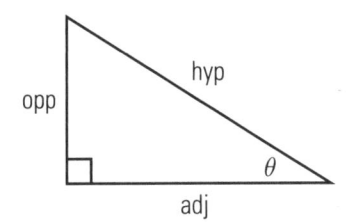

The sides are labelled as opposite (opp) angle θ, adjacent (adj) to angle θ, and as the hypotenuse (hyp).

The ratios are defined as:

$$\sin \theta = \frac{\text{opp}}{\text{hyp}}$$

$$\cos \theta = \frac{\text{adj}}{\text{hyp}}$$

$$\tan \theta = \frac{\text{opp}}{\text{adj}}$$

Your calculator will give you the ratios if you know the size of the angles.

If you know the value of the ratio, but you don't know the size of the angle, you can use the inverse of the ratios ($\sin^{-1}$, $\cos^{-1}$, and $\tan^{-1}$) to calculate the size of the angle.

You may also have to use the Pythagorean theorem ($a^2 + b^2 = c^2$) when working with right triangles.

Example 1

Solve the triangles.

> Solving a triangle means finding all the missing parts.

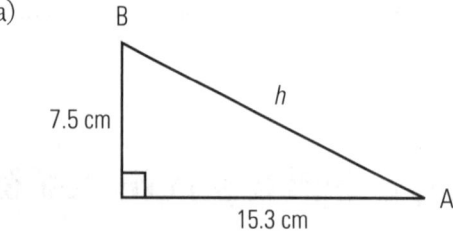

a)

b)

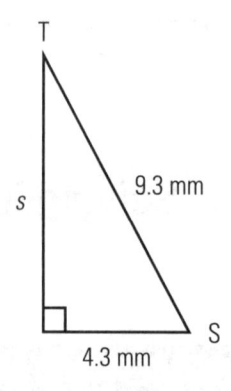

SOLUTION

a) First, find the value of the hypotenuse, h, using the Pythagorean theorem.

$$h^2 = a^2 + b^2$$

$$h^2 = (15.3)^2 + (7.5)^2$$

$$h = \sqrt{(15.3)^2 + (7.5)^2}$$

$$h = \sqrt{234.09 + 56.25}$$

$$h \approx 23.2 \text{ cm}$$

Find the value of ∠A using the tangent function.

$$\tan A = \frac{15.3}{17.5}$$

$$A = \tan^{-1}\left(\frac{15.3}{17.5}\right)$$

$$A \approx 41.2°$$

Since the sum of the two acute angles of a right triangle is 90°, you can calculate ∠B.

∠B = 90° − 41.2°

∠B = 48.8°

The hypotenuse is about 23.2 cm, and the acute angles are about 41.2° and 48.8°.

> Do not use the sine or cosine function here, because the value you calculated for the hypotenuse is an approximation. Using sine or cosine will result in rounding errors.

b) Find the missing side, s, using the Pythagorean theorem.

$$s^2 + t^2 = h^2$$

$$s^2 + (4.3)^2 = (9.3)^2$$

$$s^2 = (9.3)^2 - (4.3)^2$$

$$s = \sqrt{(9.3)^2 - (4.3)^2}$$

$$s = \sqrt{86.49 - 18.49}$$

$$s \approx 8.2 \text{ mm}$$

Calculate ∠S using the cosine ratio.

$$\cos S = \frac{4.3}{9.3}$$

$$S = \cos^{-1}\left(\frac{4.3}{9.3}\right)$$

$$S \approx 62.5°$$

Find ∠T by subtraction.

90° − 62.5° = 27.5°

Side s is approximately 8.2 mm, and the acute angles are approximately 62.5° and 27.5°.

The Pythagorean theorem can be used to calculate the length of the diagonal of a picture frame.

BUILD YOUR SKILLS

1. Find the value of the indicated trigonometric ratio to 4 decimal places, and calculate angle θ to one decimal place.

a) 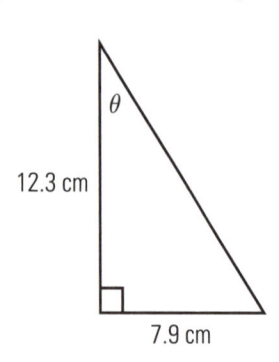 12.3 cm, 7.9 cm   tan θ

$$\text{Tan } \theta = \frac{opp}{adj} = \frac{7.9}{12.3}$$

$$\text{Tan } \theta = 0.642276...$$
$$= 0.6423$$

$$\theta = \text{Tan}^{-1}(0.6423), \text{ Calculator}$$

$$\theta = 32.71263...$$
$$\underline{\underline{\theta = 32.7°}}$$

b) 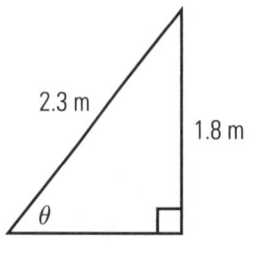 2.3 m, 1.8 m   sin θ

$$\theta = 0.7826 = \underline{\underline{51.5°}}$$

c) 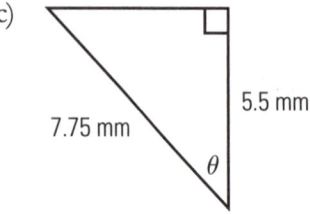 7.75 mm, 5.5 mm   cos θ

$$\theta = 0.7097 = \underline{\underline{44.8°}}$$

2. Find the height, h, of the triangle to one decimal place.

19.8 cm, h, 10.6 cm

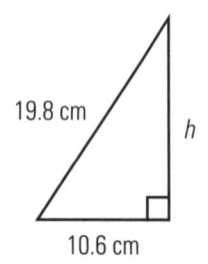

$$\underline{\underline{16.7 \text{ cm}}}$$

NEW SKILLS: TRIGONOMETRIC RATIOS IN COMPLEX SITUATIONS

In this section, you will use trigonometric ratios to solve problems in contexts that require multiple steps and in real-life scenarios.

Example 2

Solve for QS, ST, and RT.

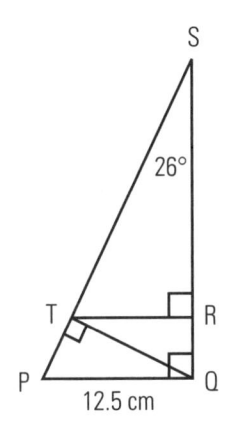

SOLUTION

Using $\triangle$PQS and the tangent ratio, you can solve for QS.

$$\tan \theta = \frac{\text{opp}}{\text{adj}}$$

$$\tan \theta = \frac{PQ}{QS}$$

$$\tan 26° = \frac{12.5}{QS}$$

$$QS \times \tan 26° = \frac{12.5}{QS} \times QS$$

$$QS \times \tan 26° = 12.5$$

$$QS = \frac{12.5}{\tan 26°}$$

$$QS \approx 25.6 \text{ cm}$$

Next, use ΔQST and the cosine ratio to solve for ST.

$$\cos\theta = \frac{adj}{hyp}$$

$$\cos 26° = \frac{ST}{QS}$$

$$\cos 26° = \frac{ST}{25.6}$$

$$25.6\cos 26° = ST$$

$$23.0 \text{ cm} \approx ST$$

Finally, you can use ΔRST and the sine ratio to solve for RT.

$$\sin\theta = \frac{opp}{hyp}$$

$$\sin 26° = \frac{RT}{ST}$$

$$\sin 26° = \frac{RT}{23.0}$$

$$23.0\sin 26° = RT$$

$$10.1 \text{ cm} \approx RT$$

BUILD YOUR SKILLS

3. What is the length of x?   *35.6 cm*

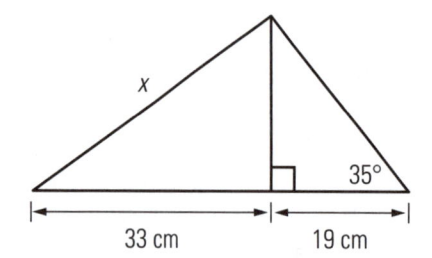

4. Calculate the measure of angle θ.

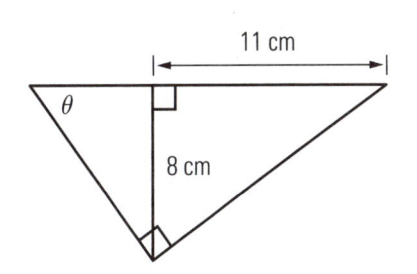

11 cm
θ
8 cm

54°

Construction workers need architects to create blueprints with very accurate measurements and angles.

5. Find each of the indicated sides.

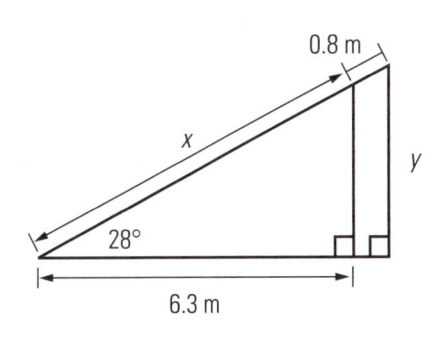

0.8 m
x
y
28°
6.3 m

x = 7.1 m
z = 3.7 m

Example 3

A piece of plywood is cut into the shape shown. Calculate the dimensions of the plywood.

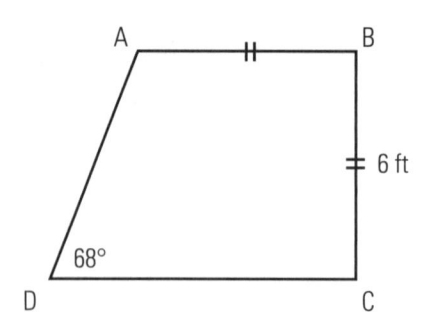

SOLUTION

The piece of plywood can be divided into a square and a right triangle.

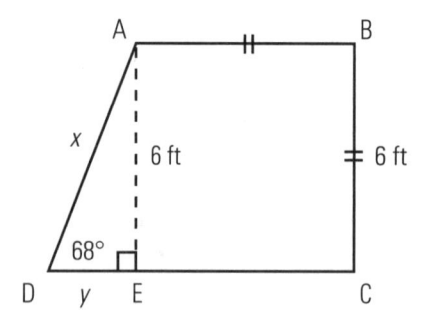

Use the sine ratio to find x.

$$\sin \theta = \frac{\text{opp}}{\text{hyp}}$$

$$\sin 68° = \frac{AE}{x}$$

$$\sin 68° = \frac{6}{x}$$

$$x \sin 68° = \frac{6}{x} \times x$$

$$x \sin 68° = 6$$

$$x = \frac{6}{\sin 68°}$$

$$x \approx 6.5 \text{ ft}$$

Next, use the tangent ratio to find y.

$$\tan \theta = \frac{\text{opp}}{\text{adj}}$$

$$\tan 68° = \frac{6}{y}$$

$$y \tan 68° = \frac{6}{y} \times y$$

$$y \tan 68° = 6$$

$$y = \frac{6}{\tan 68°}$$

$$y \approx 2.4 \text{ ft}$$

Calculate the length of DC.

DC = y + EC

DC = 2.4 + 6

DC = 8.4 ft

The lengths AB and BC are each 6 feet. The length AD is about 6.5 feet, and DC is about 8.4 feet.

Carpenters need to be able to measure angles carefully to do their job properly.

BUILD YOUR SKILLS

6. Find the angle of offset between the two pipes. How long is the travel pipe?

40.2°, 19.5 cm

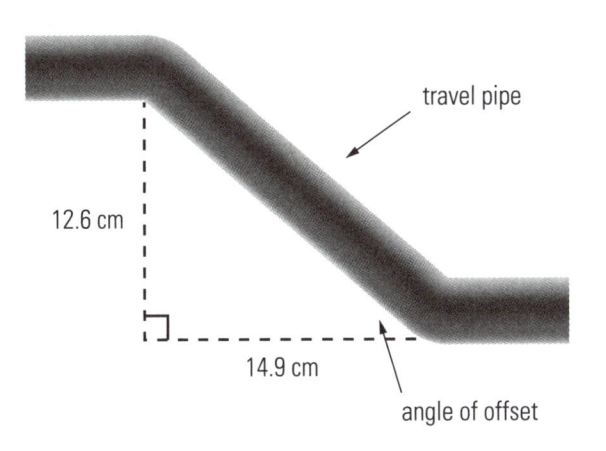

12.6 cm

14.9 cm

travel pipe

angle of offset

The angle of depression is the angle formed between the horizontal and the line of sight looking downward. The angle of elevation is the angle formed by the horizontal and the line of sight while looking upward.

7. A woman is standing on one side of a deep ravine. The angle of depression to the bottom of the far side of the ravine is 52° and the ravine is 120 m across. How deep is the ravine?

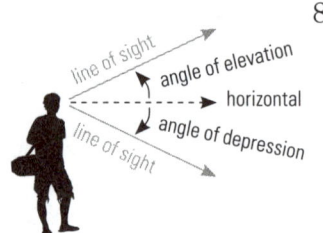

   153.6 m

8. A surveyor must determine the distance, AB, across a river. He stands at point C, downriver 500 m from B, and using his theodolite, measures the angle of vision to A as 28°. How wide is the river? 265.9 m

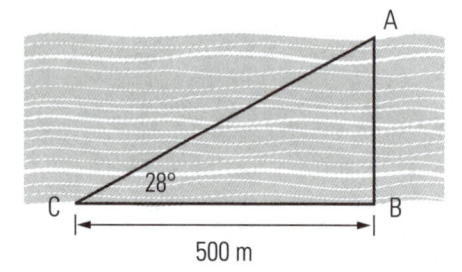

Example 4

Justin wants to line the perimeter of his patio with a paving stone border. What is the perimeter of his patio?

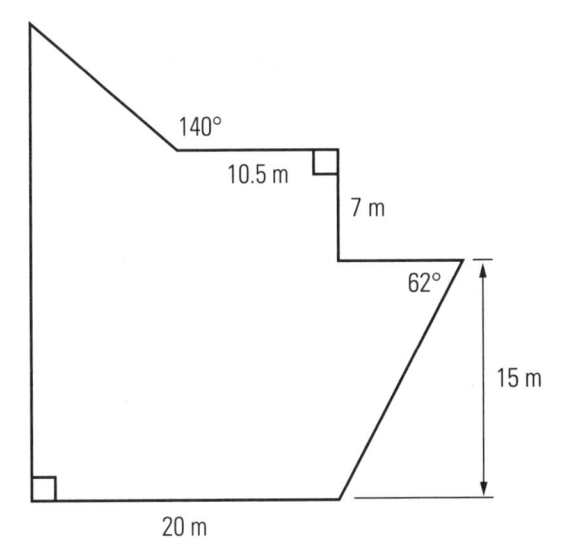

SOLUTION

The patio can be divided into two right triangles and a rectangle.

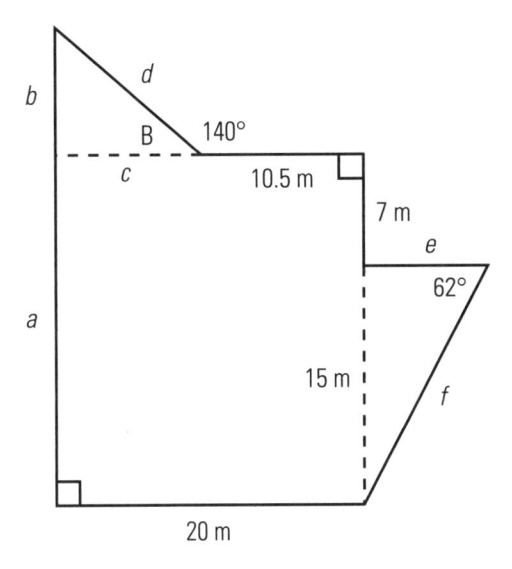

Start by calculating a.

$a = 15$ m $+ 7$ m

$a = 22$ m

Next, $\angle B$ can be calculated by subtraction, because it is supplementary to the 140° angle.

$\angle B = 180° - 140°$

$\angle B = 40°$

Now calculate side length c.

$c = 20$ m $- 10.5$ m

$c = 9.5$ m

Side b can be calculated using the tangent ratio.

$$\tan \theta = \frac{\text{opp}}{\text{adj}}$$

$$\tan B = \frac{b}{c}$$

$$\tan 40° = \frac{b}{9.5}$$

$9.5 \tan 40° = b$

8.0 m $\approx b$

Side d can be calculated using the cosine ratio.

$$\cos \theta = \frac{\text{adj}}{\text{hyp}}$$

$$\cos B = \frac{c}{d}$$

$$\cos 40° = \frac{9.5}{d}$$

$$d = \frac{9.5}{\cos 40°}$$

$d \approx 12.4$ m

Calculate side e.

$$\tan\theta = \frac{\text{opp}}{\text{adj}}$$

$$\tan 62° = \frac{15}{e}$$

$$e = \frac{15}{\tan 62°}$$

$$e \approx 8.0 \text{ m}$$

And for the last side, f, use the sine ratio.

$$\sin\theta = \frac{\text{opp}}{\text{hyp}}$$

$$\sin 62° = \frac{15}{f}$$

$$f = \frac{15}{\sin 62°}$$

$$f \approx 17.0 \text{ m}$$

Finally, calculate the perimeter of the patio.

$$P = 20 + a + b + d + 10.5 + 7 + e + f$$

$$P = 20 + 22 + 8.0 + 12.4 + 10.5 + 7 + 8.0 + 17.0$$

$$P = 104.9 \text{ m}$$

The perimeter of Justin's patio is about 105 m.

BUILD YOUR SKILLS

9. Pauline is building a fence around her vegetable garden, shown below. What length of fence will she need to build?

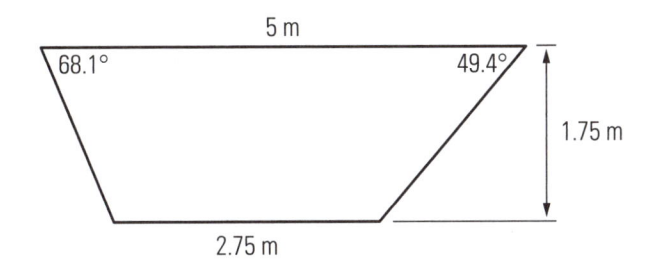

If you grow your own vegetables you can get delicious food and save money in your backyard.

11.94 m

10. Soo-Jin is installing carpet in a den. Using the floorplan below, calculate the area of carpet Soo-Jin will need to buy.

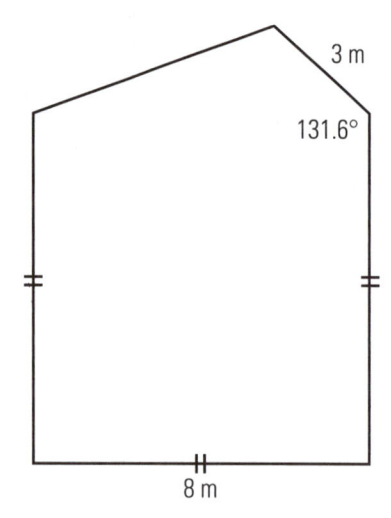

3 m

131.6°

8 m

$72 m^2$

PRACTISE YOUR NEW SKILLS

1. In each triangle, solve for *x*.

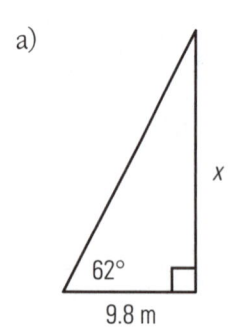

   a)

   $18.4 m$

   62°
   9.8 m
   x

b)

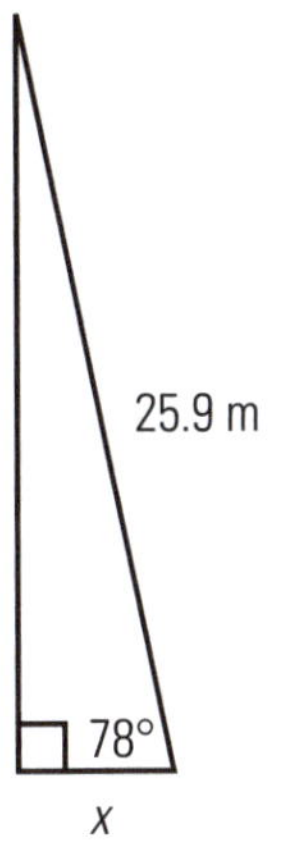
25.9 m
78°
x

5.4m

c)

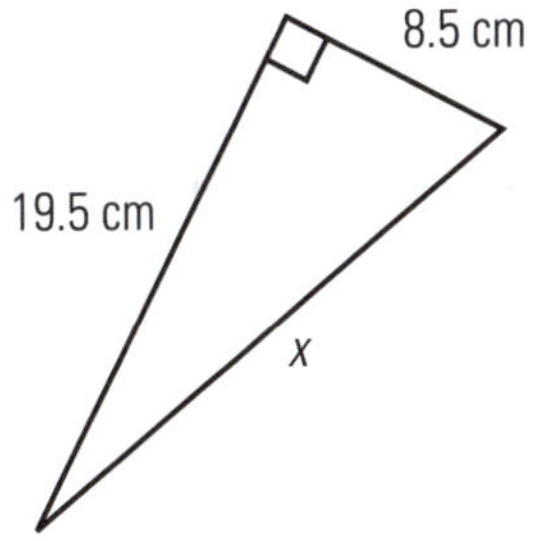
8.5 cm
19.5 cm
x

21.3 cm

d)

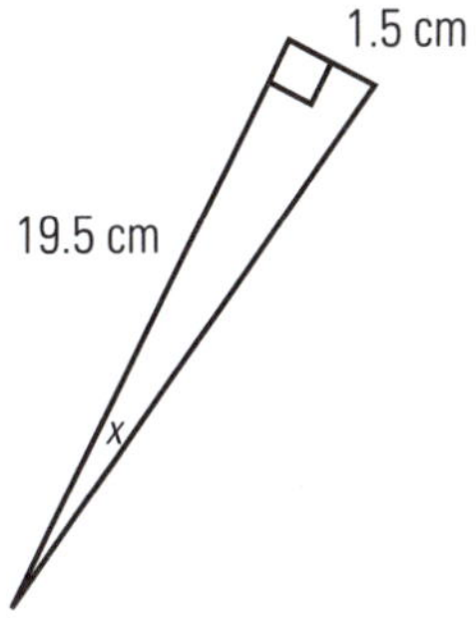
1.5 cm
19.5 cm
x

4.4°

e)

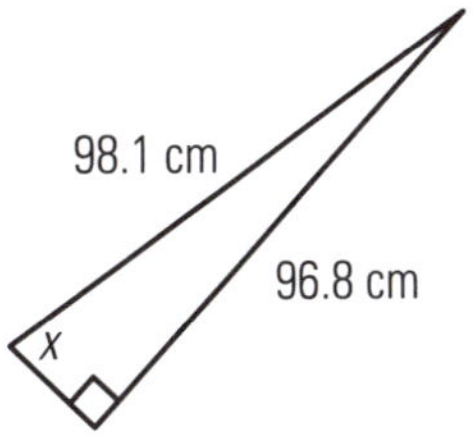
98.1 cm
96.8 cm
x

80.7°

f)

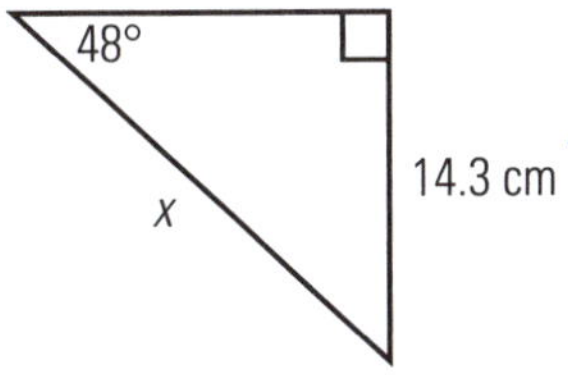
48°
x
14.3 cm

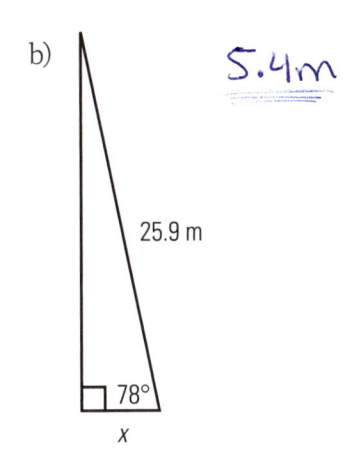

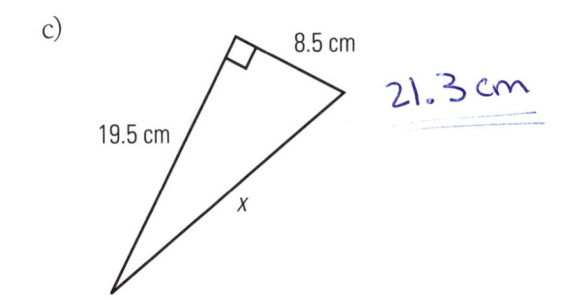

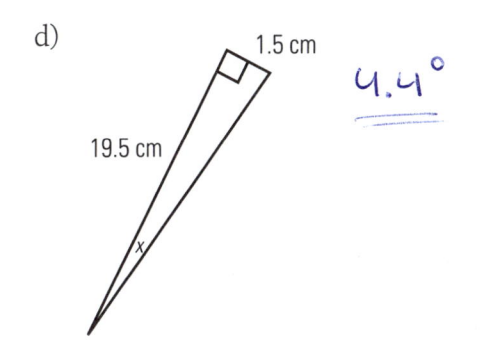

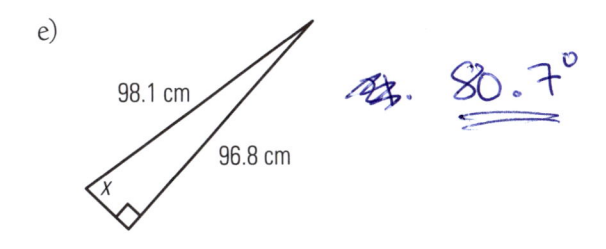

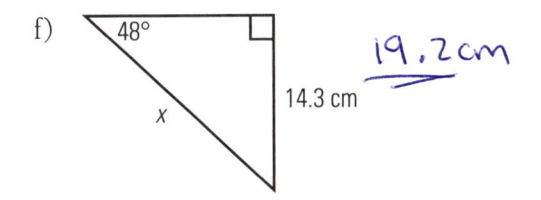

19.2cm

g)

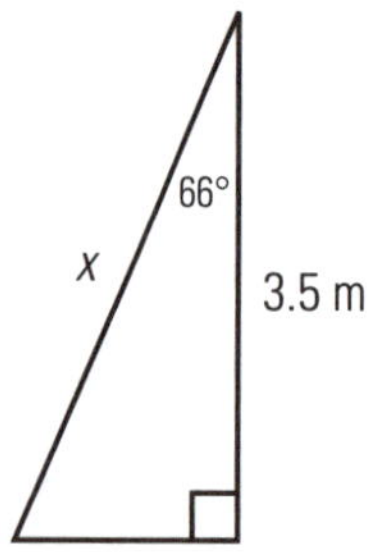

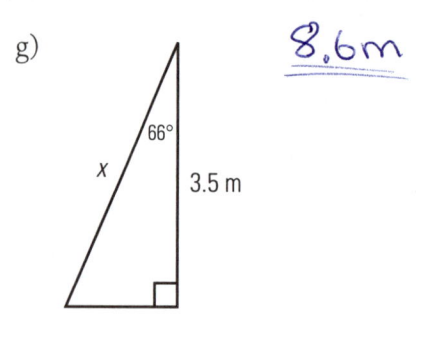

8.6m

h)

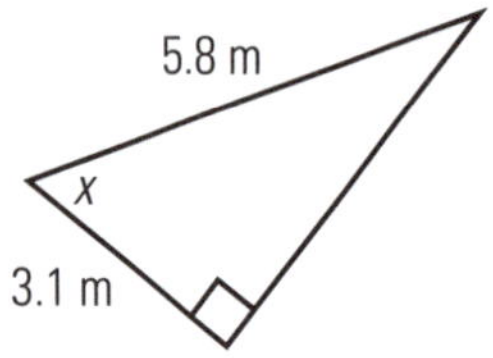

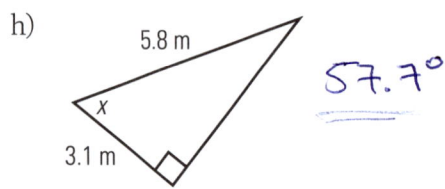

57.7°

2. A ladder placed against a wall forms an angle of 65° with the ground. If the foot of the ladder is 1.8 m from the wall, how long is the ladder?

4.3m

3. A tree casts a shadow that is 12.4 m long and the angle of elevation to the sun is 38°. How tall is the tree? 9.7m

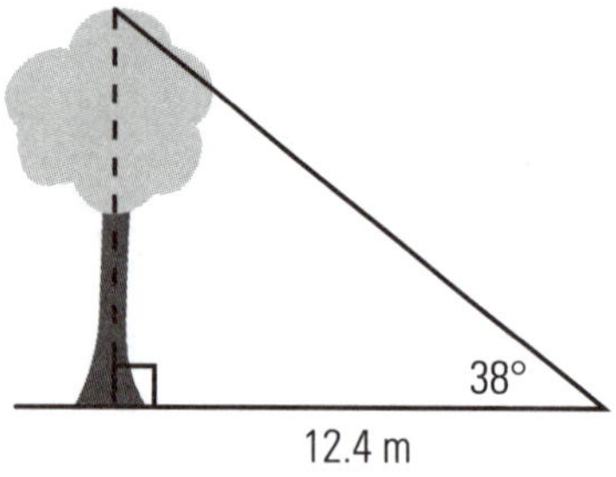

Birch trees need a lot of water to grow. A birch's root system, which gathers water, can spread twice the distance of the tree's height.

4. During a plunge, a submarine travels a distance of 350 m while dropping 200 m. What was its angle of depression, and how far did it travel horizontally?

34.8°, 287.4 m

5. Sasha is building a playhouse for his cousin. He has cut out this piece of plywood for the back of the house. Calculate the indicated dimensions.

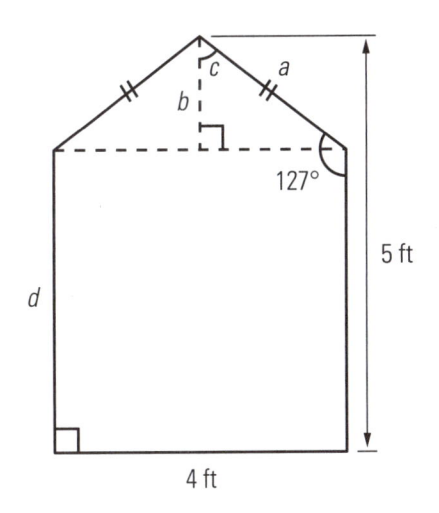

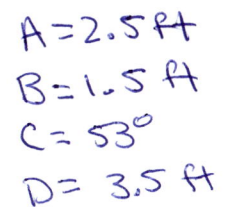

A = 2.5 ft
B = 1.5 ft
C = 53°
D = 3.5 ft

The HMCS *Onondaga* served in the Royal Canadian Navy until it was decommissioned. It is now the only submarine open to the public in Canada and can be found at the maritime museum in Rimouski, Quebec.

4.2 Solving Complex Problems in the Real World

NEW SKILLS: WORKING WITH TWO OR MORE TRIANGLES

Sometimes when working with a problem, you have to break the situation down to two or more triangles and work in steps to solve it. You may need to use values from one triangle to solve another right triangle that shares a common edge.

For more details, see page 185 of *MathWorks 11*.

Example 1

Solve for *x* and *y* in the following diagram.

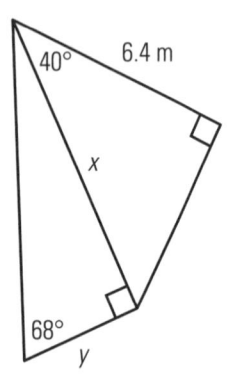

SOLUTION

Use the cosine ratio to find *x*.

$$\cos \theta = \frac{\text{adj}}{\text{hyp}}$$

$$\cos 40° = \frac{6.4}{x}$$

$$x \times \cos 40° = \frac{6.4}{x} \times x$$

$$x \cos 40° = 6.4$$

$$x = \frac{6.4}{\cos 40°}$$

$$x \approx 8.4 \text{ cm}$$

Use the tangent ratio and the value you calculated for *x* to find *y*.

$$\tan \theta = \frac{\text{opp}}{\text{adj}}$$

$$\tan 68° = \frac{8.4}{y}$$

$$y \times \tan 68° = \frac{8.4}{y} \times y$$

$$y \tan 68° = 8.4$$

$$y = \frac{8.4}{\tan 68°}$$

$$y \approx 3.4 \text{ cm}$$

BUILD YOUR SKILLS

1. Calculate x in the following diagram.   5.2 m

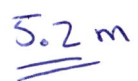

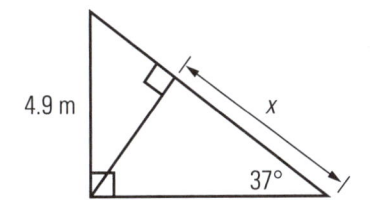

2. Find x and y in the following diagrams. $x = 12.7$ cm, $y = 19.0$ cm

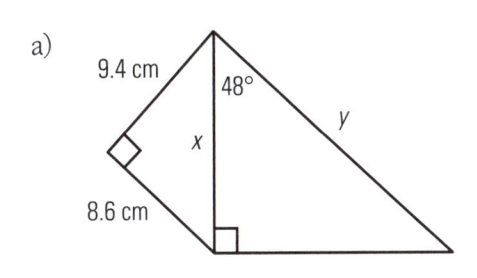

   a)

216 MathWorks 11 Workbook

b)

x = 11.6 m, *y* = 10.0 m

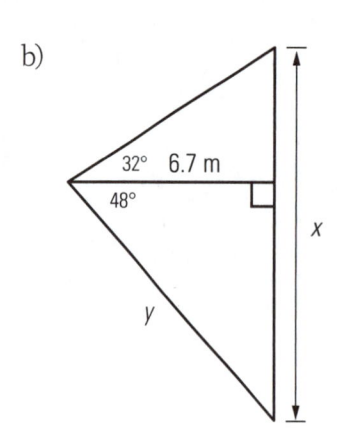

3. Calculate *x*, *y*, and *h* for the following diagram.

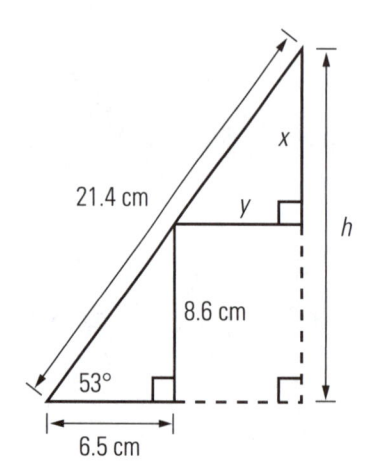

x = 8.5 cm
y = 6.4 cm
h = 17.1 cm

Example 2

A flagpole is supported by two guy wires, each attached to a peg in the ground 4 m from the base of the pole. The guy wires have angles of elevations of 35° and 45°.

a) How much higher up the flagpole is the top guy wire attached?

b) How long is each guy wire?

SOLUTION

Draw a sketch to help you solve this question.

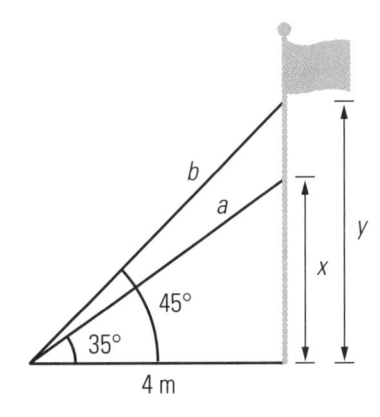

a) Calculate the heights of the guy wires using the tangent ratio.

$$\tan \theta = \frac{\text{opp}}{\text{adj}}$$

$$\tan 35° = \frac{x}{4}$$

$$4 \tan 35° = x$$

$$2.8 \text{ m} \approx x$$

$$\tan \theta = \frac{\text{opp}}{\text{adj}}$$

$$\tan 45° = \frac{y}{4}$$

$$4 \tan 45° = y$$

$$4.0 \text{ m} = y$$

Calculate the difference in heights.

$4.0 - 2.8 = 1.2$ m

The top guy wire is attached 1.2 m higher than the lower wire.

b) To find the lengths of the wires, use the cosine ratio.

Lower wire:

$$\cos \theta = \frac{\text{adj}}{\text{hyp}}$$

$$\cos 35° = \frac{4}{a}$$

$$a \cos 35° = \frac{4}{a} \times a$$

$$a \cos 35° = 4$$

$$a = \frac{4}{\cos 35°}$$

$$a \approx 4.9 \text{ m}$$

Higher wire:

$$\cos \theta = \frac{\text{adj}}{\text{hyp}}$$

$$\cos 45° = \frac{4}{b}$$

$$b \cos 45° = \frac{4}{b} \times b$$

$$b \cos 45° = 4$$

$$b = \frac{4}{\cos 45°}$$

$$b \approx 5.7 \text{ m}$$

The guy wires are approximately 4.9 m and 5.7 m long.

BUILD YOUR SKILLS

4. From the top of a 200 m-tall office building, the angle of elevation to the top of another building is 40°. The angle of depression to the bottom of the second building is 25°. How tall is the second building?   **560 m**

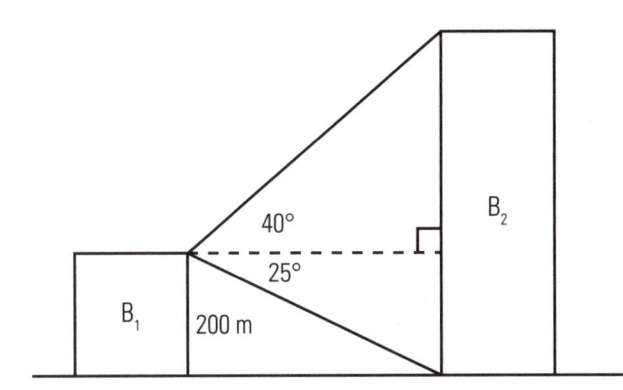

5. An extension ladder must be used at an angle of elevation of 65°. At its shortest length, it is 18 feet long. Fully extended, it has a length of 32 feet.

   a) How much higher up a building will it reach when it is fully extended, compared to its shortest length?

   12.7 ft

   b) How much farther from the house must the base be when it is fully extended, compared to its shortest length?

   5.9 ft

6. Zola can see the top of a 180 m cell phone tower at an angle of elevation of 32°, and Naeem can see it at an angle of elevation of 50°. How far apart are Zola and Naeem if they are on a straight line with the tower? There are two possibilities.

   137 m or 439 m

7. A roller coaster has a track that drops at an angle of depression of 25° from a height of 14.9 m. When it reaches the ground, in travels horizontally for 8 m. It then rises at an angle of elevation of 47° to a height of 26.8 m.

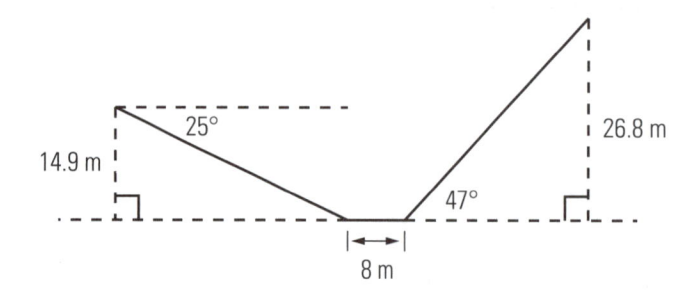

   a) What is the total horizontal distance covered by this portion of track?

   65.0 m

   b) What is the total distance travelled by a car on this portion of the roller coaster track?

   82.6 m

Roller coasters can exert a force on your body comparable to a space shuttle re-entering orbit around Earth.

NEW SKILLS: WORKING WITH TRIANGLES IN THREE DIMENSIONS

In some situations, you may need to work with triangles that are at an angle to each other and share common edges.

For more details, see page 186 of *MathWorks 11*.

Example 3

A box is 10 cm by 12 cm by 15 cm. What is the length of the longest rod that can be carried in it? What angle does it make with the bottom?

SOLUTION

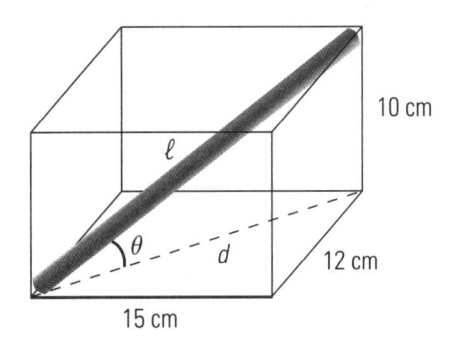

This problem requires two triangles that are at an angle to each other. The first triangle is formed by the diagonal, d, across the bottom of the box and the sides of the box. The diagonal then forms the base of the second triangle, for which the hypotenuse is the rod.

Find the diagonal, d, using the Pythagorean theorem.

$$a^2 + b^2 = d^2$$
$$15^2 + 12^2 = d^2$$
$$\sqrt{15^2 + 12^2} = d$$
$$\sqrt{225 + 144} = d$$
$$d \approx 19.2 \text{ cm}$$

Find the length of the rod, ℓ, again using the Pythagorean theorem.

$$a^2 + b^2 = \ell^2$$
$$19.2^2 + 10^2 = \ell^2$$
$$\sqrt{19.2^2 + 10^2} = \ell$$
$$\sqrt{368.64 + 100} = \ell$$
$$21.6 \text{ cm} \approx \ell$$

The longest rod that can be carried in the box is about 21.6 cm.

To find the angle, θ, you can use any one of the trigonometric ratios but the tangent is the best choice because it uses only one rounded value (d).

$$\tan \theta = \frac{\text{opp}}{\text{adj}}$$

$$\tan \theta = \frac{10}{19.2}$$

$$\theta = \tan^{-1}\left(\frac{10}{19.2}\right)$$

$$\theta \approx 27.5°$$

The rod will make an angle of about 27.5° with the bottom of the box.

BUILD YOUR SKILLS

8. An airplane is flying 100 km north and 185 km west of an airport. It is flying at a height of 7 km.

   a) What is the straight-line distance to the airport?

   210.4 km

   b) What is the angle of elevation of the airplane, from the point of view of the airport?

   1.9°

9. Sylvie and Mathieu are bird-watching. They both spot a nest at the top of a tree. Mathieu is 89 m from the tree. The angle between Sylvie's line of sight and Mathieu is 73°. The angle of elevation from Sylvie to the top of the tree is 35°. What is the height of the nest?

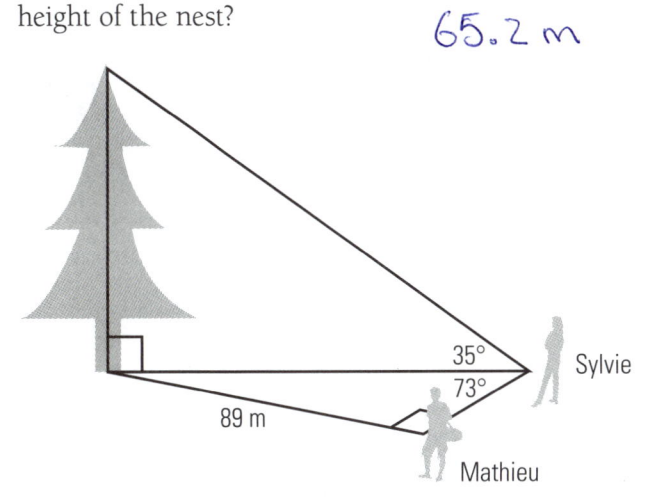

65.2 m

PRACTISE YOUR NEW SKILLS

1. In each diagram, solve for the indicated sides and angles.

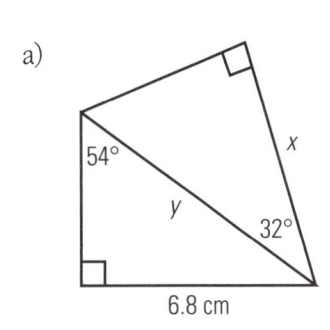

   a) *x = 7.1 cm*
      y = 8.4 cm

b)

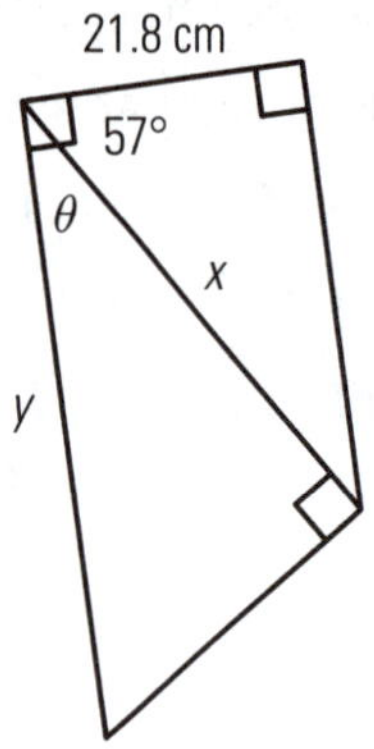
21.8 cm
57°
θ
x
y

θ = 33°
x = 40 cm
y = 47.7 cm

c)

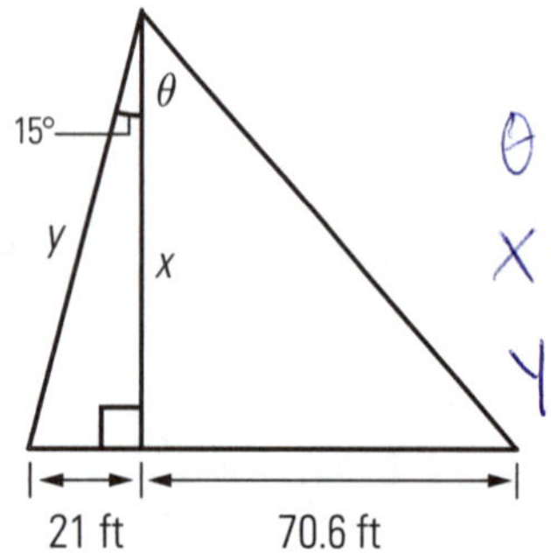
θ
15°
y
x
21 ft
70.6 ft

θ = 42.0°
x = 78.4 ft
y = 81.1 ft

2. An asymmetrical roof has measurements shown in the diagram below. If the vertical supports are each two feet apart, calculate the measure of ∠G and the slant heights (lengths x and y) of the roof.

G = 43.2°
x = 8.5 ft
y = 11.0 ft

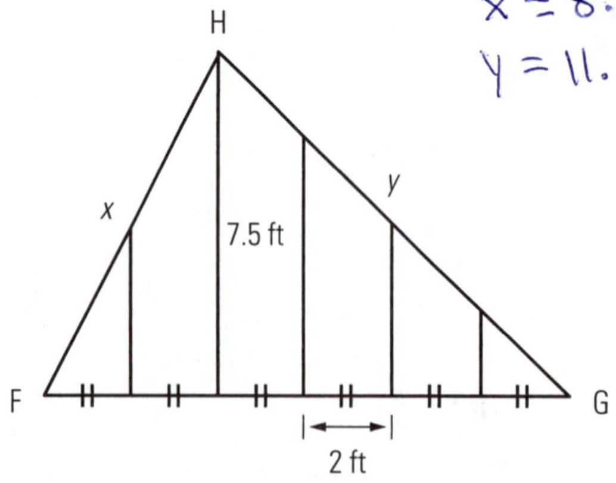
H
x
7.5 ft
y
F
G
2 ft

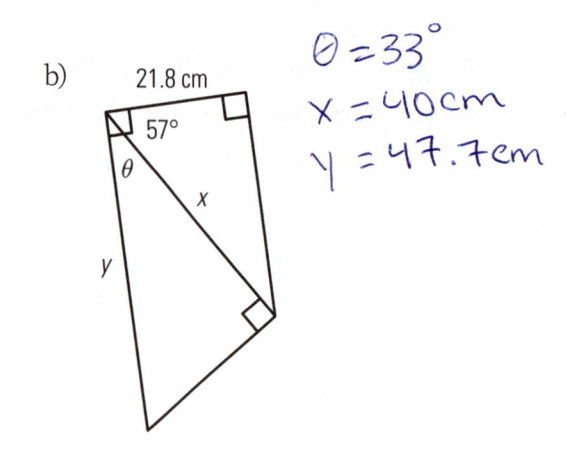

3. Geneviève is standing on the top of a building that is 109 m tall. At an angle of elevation of 41°, she views the top of the neighbouring building, which is 147 m tall.

   a) How far apart are the buildings?

   43.7 m

   b) If Geneviève looks down to the base of the neighbouring building, what is the angle of depression?

   68.2°

4. Malcolm is on a canoe trip, travelling across a lake. He sees a tall tree on the shoreline in the distance, and wants to estimate its height. He estimates that he is about 100 m from the tree, and that the angle of elevation to the top of the tree is about 20°.

   a) What is the height of the tree?

   36.4 m

   Make sure you wear your life jacket if you go on a canoe trip.

   b) If Malcolm paddles closer to the tree and then views the top at an angle of elevation of 36°, how much closer to the tree will he have paddled?

   49.9 m

5. Tamiko wants to calculate the height of a cliff that drops straight down into a river. From one point along the opposite shoreline, the angle of elevation to the top of the cliff is 32°. Tamiko walks 200 m along the shore, and calculates the angle between her original position and the new position to be 38°. What is the height of the cliff?

160 m

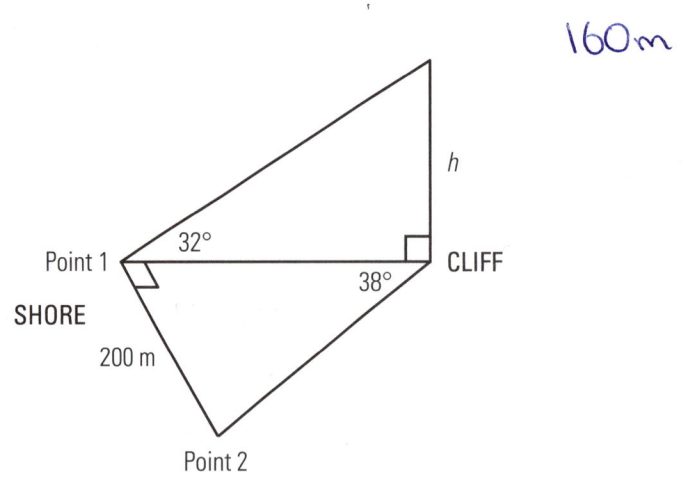

CHAPTER TEST

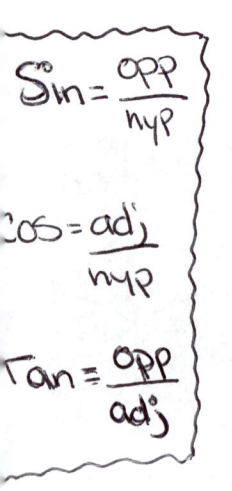

$Sin = \dfrac{opp}{hyp}$

$Cos = \dfrac{adj}{hyp}$

$Tan = \dfrac{opp}{adj}$

1. Find x in each of the following diagrams.

   a) *hyp, 3.8 m, opp: x, 47°, adj*

   2.8 m

   $\sin 47 = \dfrac{x}{3.8}$
   $= 2.77914$

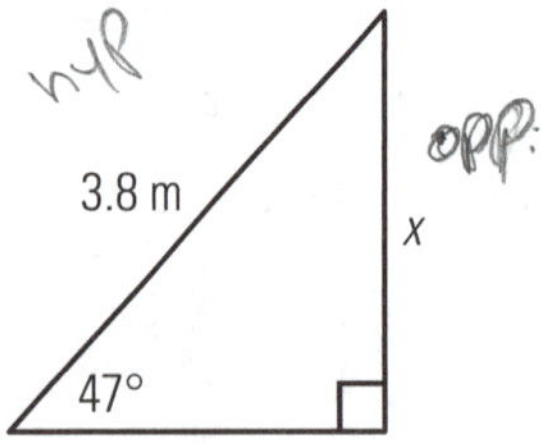

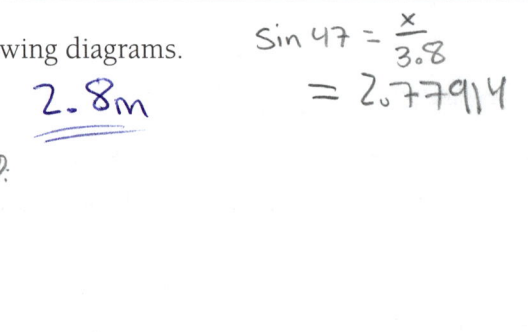

   b) *4.3 cm, 7.5 cm, x*

   35.0°

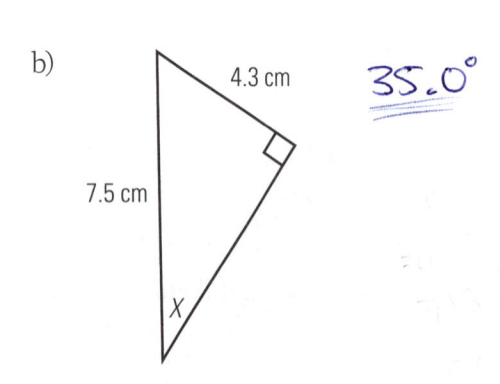

73.9°

c)

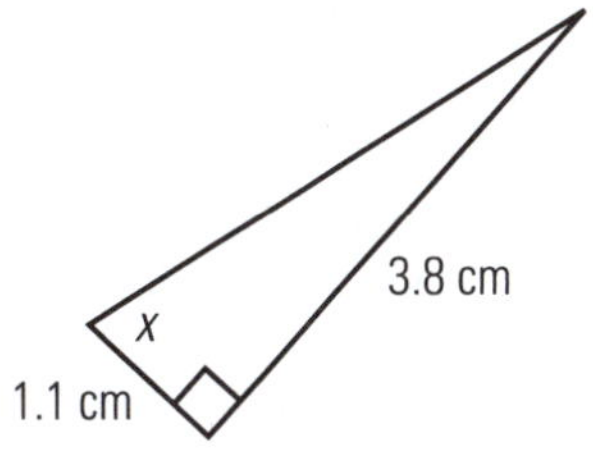
x
3.8 cm
1.1 cm

d)

38 39.8 in

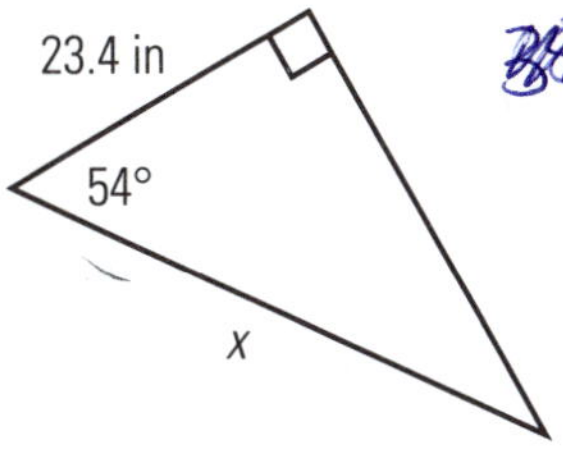
23.4 in
54°
x

2. Solve for the variables shown in the following diagrams.

a)

x = 10.1 cm
y = 47.7°

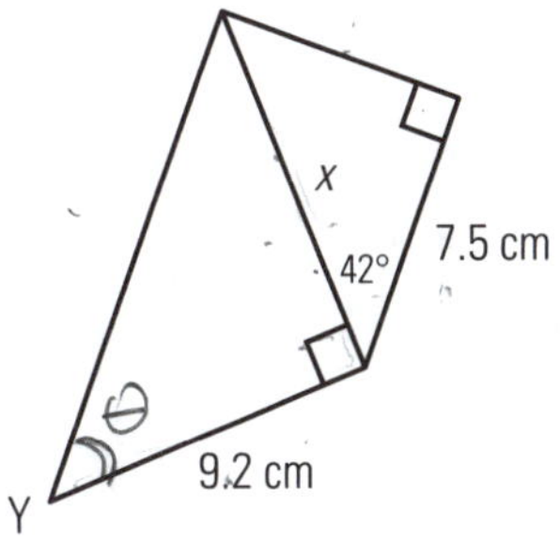
x
42°
7.5 cm
9.2 cm
Y

b)

x = 53.6°
y = 8.4 cm
z = 10.4 cm

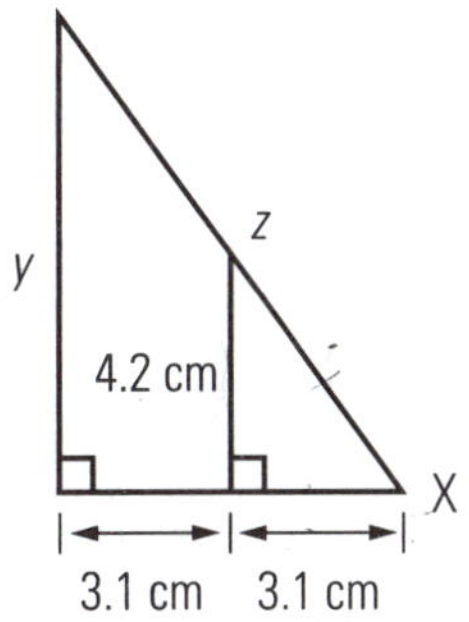
y
z
4.2 cm
X
3.1 cm
3.1 cm

c)

X = 5.9 cm
Y = 48°
Z = 2.9 cm

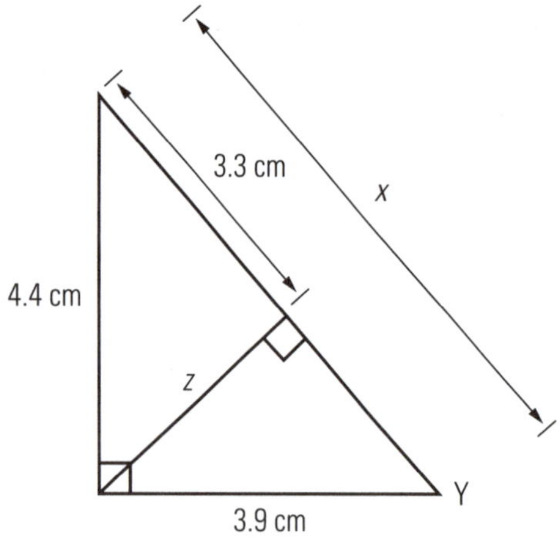

Many patterns can be used to make a patio from paving stones.

3. Paolo is making a patio with paving stones. He needs to know how many square metres of paving stones to buy. Calculate the area of his patio.

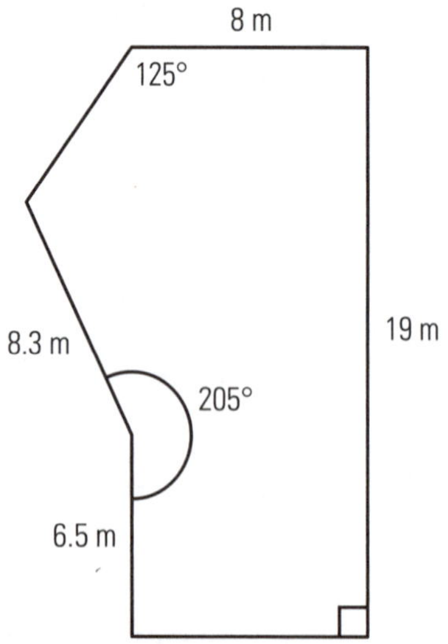

173.9 m²

4. A kite has the dimensions indicated. What is the length of the kite?

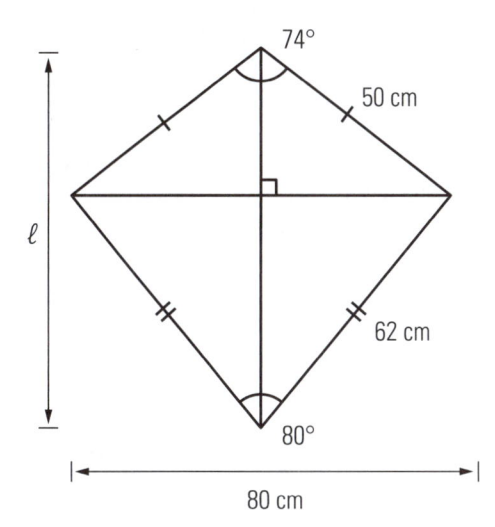

87.4 cm

5. Chung-ho is standing on the top of a building that is 135 m tall. The angle of depression to the top of the building next door is 71°. The angle of depression to the base of the building is 77°. The buildings are 31 m apart. How tall is the other building?

45 m

6. Bernhardt and Julia are observing an eagle's nest in a tree. Julia is 75 m from the tree, and sees it at an angle of elevation of 42°.

   a) How high up the tree is the nest?

   67.5 m

   b) Bernhardt is standing 30 m behind Julia. At what angle of elevation does he see the nest?

   32.7°

7. An airplane is flying 75 km south and 35 km west of an airport. It is flying at a height of 6 km.

   a) What is the straight-line distance to the airport?

   83.0 km

   b) What is the angle of elevation of the airplane, from the point of view of the airport?

   4.1°

Chapter 5
Scale Representations

Blueprints are an example of scale representation. Carpenters and contractors need to know how to read scale statements and scale diagrams to accurately construct buildings.

Scale Drawings and Models 5.1

REVIEW: PROPORTIONAL REASONING

In this chapter, you will use proportional reasoning to calculate the sizes of different objects.

A proportion is a statement of equality between two rates or two ratios. A ratio is a comparison between two numbers with the same units. A rate is a comparison between two numbers with different units.

Example 1

The ratio of the length to the width of a rectangle is 5:3. If the rectangle is 24 cm wide, how long is it?

SOLUTION

A ratio of 5:3 can be written as a fraction, in the form $\frac{5}{3}$. Let ℓ be the length of the rectangle. Set up a proportion to solve for ℓ.

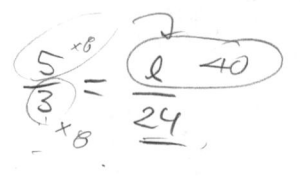

$$\frac{5}{3} = \frac{\ell}{24}$$

$$24 \times \frac{5}{3} = \frac{\ell}{24} \times 24 \qquad \text{Multiply both sides by the same number.}$$

$$8 \times \frac{5}{1} = \ell \qquad \text{Simplify.}$$

$$40 = \ell$$

The length is 40 cm.

ALTERNATIVE SOLUTION

In the above example, both sides of the equation were multiplied by the lowest common denominator, 24. You can also multiply by the product of the denominators—in this case, 3 × 24. You will get the same answer, but it will just take more steps.

$$\frac{5}{3} = \frac{\ell}{24}$$

$$3 \times 24 \times \frac{5}{3} = \frac{\ell}{24} \times 24 \times 3$$

$$\cancel{3} \times 24 \times \frac{5}{\cancel{3}} = \frac{\ell}{\cancel{24}} \times \cancel{24} \times 3 \qquad \text{Multiply both sides by the product of the denominators.}$$

$$24 \times 5 = 3\ell \qquad \text{Simplify.}$$

$$120 = 3\ell$$

$$\frac{120}{3} = \frac{3\ell}{3}$$

$$40 = \ell \qquad \text{Divide both sides by 3 to isolate } \ell.$$

The length is 40 cm.

Chapter 5 Scale Representations 233

BUILD YOUR SKILLS

1. Solve for x.

a) $\dfrac{3}{8} = \dfrac{x}{168}$

b) $\dfrac{x}{13} = \dfrac{7}{91}$

c) $\dfrac{x}{7} = \dfrac{30}{105}$

d) $\dfrac{408}{x} = \dfrac{4}{9}$

e) $\dfrac{90}{198} = \dfrac{5}{x}$

f) $\dfrac{34}{289} = \dfrac{2}{x}$

2. Solve the following proportions to one decimal place.

a) $\frac{5}{6} = \frac{12}{x}$

14.4

b) $\frac{7}{15} = \frac{9}{k}$

19.3

$\frac{15}{7} = \frac{k}{9}$ ×9

$\frac{15 \times 9}{7} = 19.3$

c) $\frac{1.2}{4.9} = \frac{m}{7.3}$

1.8

d) $\frac{p}{85} = \frac{76}{39}$

165.6

$\frac{76 \times 85}{39} =$

3. The ratio of Tom's age to Mary's is 3:4. If Tom is 15, how old is Mary?

20 years

Tom : Mary
3 : 4
15 : x

$\frac{3}{15} = \frac{4}{x}$

$\frac{15}{3} = \frac{x}{4}$ ×4

$\frac{15 \times 4}{3} = 20$

4. If Georgina travels 355 km in 7 hours, how far will she travel in 8.5 hours at the same rate? *speed*

431 km

$\frac{355 \text{ km}}{7 \text{ h}} = \frac{x}{8.5 \text{ h}}$ ×8.5

$\frac{355 \times 8.5}{7} = 431.0 \text{ km}$

speed = $\frac{distance}{time}$

scale statement: a ratio that shows the relationship between the sizes of two objects

scale factor: a number by which all the dimensions of an original figure are multiplied to produce an enlargement or a reduction

NEW SKILLS: WORKING WITH SCALE STATEMENTS

A **scale statement** is a ratio that compares the size of a model to the size of the original object. For example, a model might be given a scale statement of 3:5; this means that 3 units on the model represent 5 units on the original object.

A **scale factor** is the number by which the measurements of one object must be multiplied to give the measurements of the other object. It is the ratio of corresponding lengths of two similar geometric figures.

For more details, see page 210 of *Mathworks 11*.

Chapter 5 Scale Representations 235

Example 2

Write a scale statement for the reduced or enlarged object, and calculate the scale factor used to create the reduced or enlarged object.

a) original: (triangle, 6 cm base)   model: (triangle, 3 cm base)

$3\boxed{:}6 = \dfrac{\boxed{3}}{6} = \dfrac{1}{2}$

$\dfrac{5 \div 5}{20 \div 5} = \boxed{\dfrac{1}{4}}$

$\dfrac{9 \div 3}{27 \div 3} = \dfrac{3 \div 3}{9 \div 3} = \boxed{\dfrac{1}{3}}$

$\dfrac{9 \div 3}{12 \div 3} = \dfrac{3}{4}$

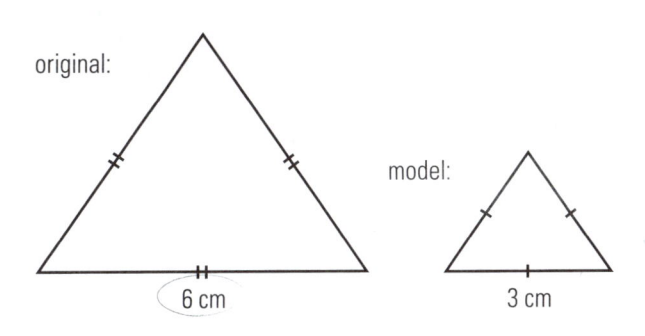

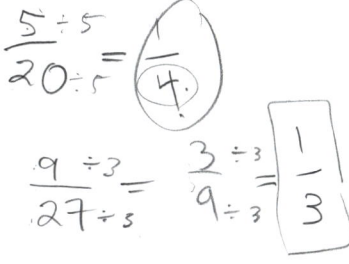

b) original: (box 1 cm × 2 cm × 3 cm)   model: (box 5 cm × 10 cm × 15 cm)

① Try dividing the denominator by the numerator... If it gives you a whole #, then yay!!

② Find a # that is divisible by the two #'s.

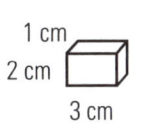

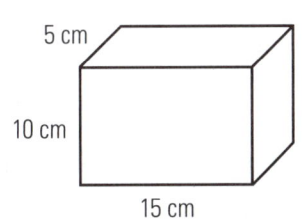

c) A man in a photograph is 2 cm tall. His actual height is 1.8 m.

SOLUTION

a) The side length of the original is 6 cm and of the model is 3 cm. The scale statement for the model is written as follows.

scale statement = model:original

scale statement = 3:6

scale statement = 1:2

The model is smaller than the original. Calculate the scale factor.

scale factor = $\dfrac{\text{model}}{\text{original}}$

scale factor = $\dfrac{3}{6}$

scale factor = $\dfrac{1}{2}$

Each dimension of the original must be multiplied by $\dfrac{1}{2}$ to get the dimensions of the model.

b) The length of the original box is 3 cm and of the model is 15 cm. The scale statement for the model is written as follows.

scale statement = model:original

scale statement = 15:3

scale statement = 5:1

The original is smaller than the model. Calculate the scale factor.

scale factor = $\dfrac{\text{model}}{\text{original}}$

scale factor = $\dfrac{15}{3}$

scale factor = $\dfrac{5}{1}$

scale factor = 5

Each dimension of the original must be multiplied by 5 to get the dimensions of the model.

c) Both measures must be expressed in the same units, so convert the man's actual height to centimetres. The man is 180 cm tall.

scale statement = photograph:original

scale statement = 2:180

scale statement = 1:90

scale factor = $\dfrac{\text{photograph}}{\text{original}}$

scale factor = $\dfrac{2}{180}$

scale factor = $\dfrac{1}{90}$

The actual height of the man must be multiplied by $\dfrac{1}{90}$ to calculate his height in the photograph.

mm → cm → m → km

Chapter 5 Scale Representations 237

BUILD YOUR SKILLS

5. The distance between Vancouver and Winnipeg is approximately 1850 km in a straight line. The distance on a map is 3.7 cm. Write a scale statement for the map. What scale factor was used to make the map?

   1:50 000 000   Fraction

   SS: 3.7 cm : 185,000,000 cm

   SF: $\dfrac{3.7 \div 3.7}{185,000,000 \div 3.7} = \dfrac{1 \text{ cm}}{50\,000\,000 \text{ cm}}$

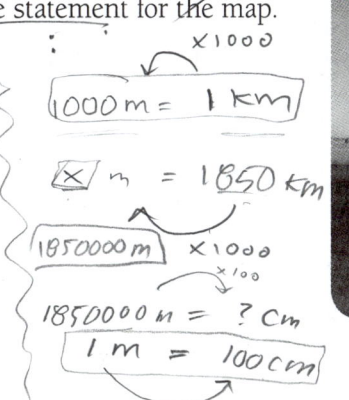

   Side work:
   1000 m = 1 km
   ☒ m = 1850 km
   1 850 000 m   ×1000
   1 850 000 m = ? cm   ×100
   1 m = 100 cm
   1850 km ×100 = 185 000 000 cm

   The road from Winnipeg to Vancouver passes by hundreds of hectares of agricultural land.

6. A photograph of a strand of human hair shows the hair magnified by a factor of 200.

   a) Write a scale statement for the photograph.
      200 : 1

      $\dfrac{\text{model}}{\text{original}} = \text{factor} = \dfrac{200}{1}$
      200 : 1

   b) If the photograph shows the hair as 2 cm wide, what is the actual width of the hair?   0.01 cm

      $\dfrac{\text{model}}{\text{original}} = 200$
      $\dfrac{2 \text{ cm}}{x} = \dfrac{200}{1}$ 0.01

7. Trevor Linden, a former player for the Vancouver Canucks, is 1.93 m tall. On a hockey card, he is 5.4 cm tall. What scale was used to print the hockey card?

   1 : 35.7

   $\dfrac{M}{O} = \dfrac{5.4 \text{ cm}}{1.93 \text{ m}}$

   $= \dfrac{5.4 \text{ cm}}{193 \text{ cm}} = \dfrac{1}{35.7}$

   1.93 = 100
   1 m = 100 cm
   1.93 = 193 cm

   1 × 1 = 1
   1 × 2 = 2

Example 3

On a blueprint, $\frac{1}{4}$ inch is equal to 1 foot.

a) Write this as a scale statement, in the form 1:x.

b) What is the actual length of a room that measures $3\frac{3}{4}$ inches on the blueprint?

SOLUTION

a) To write a scale statement, both measurements need to be in the same units. Convert 1 foot to inches.

scale statement = blueprint:original

scale statement = $\frac{1}{4}$:12

The statement needs to be written in the form 1:x. Multiply both sides by 4 to eliminate the fraction.

scale statement = $(4 \times \frac{1}{4})$:(12×4)

scale statement = 1:48

The scale is therefore 1:48.

b) Let x represent the actual length of the room. Set up a proportion to solve for x.

$$\frac{1}{48} = \frac{3.75}{x}$$

$$x \times 48 \times \frac{1}{48} = \frac{3.75}{x} \times 48 \times x$$

$$x = 3.75 \times 48$$

$$x = 180$$

The room is 180 inches long. Convert this to feet.

180 in ÷ 12 in/ft = 15 ft

The actual room is 15 feet long.

ALTERNATIVE SOLUTION

You could calculate the length of the room using the scale 0.25 in:1 ft. It becomes a rate question; you just have to remember that the units are not the same for the denominator and the numerator.

$$\frac{0.25 \text{ in}}{1 \text{ ft}} = \frac{3.75 \text{ in}}{x \text{ ft}}$$

$$\frac{0.25}{1} = \frac{3.75}{x}$$

$$x \times 0.25 = \frac{3.75}{x} \times x$$

$$0.25x = 3.75$$

$$\frac{0.25x}{0.25} = \frac{3.75}{0.25}$$

$$x = 15$$

The actual room is 15 feet long.

In this case, the answer is given in feet because the unit of the denominator was feet.

BUILD YOUR SKILLS

8. In a picture, a man measures 2.3 cm. His actual height is 1.78 m. He is standing beside a flagpole that measures 7.6 cm in the picture. What is the actual height of the flagpole, to the nearest tenth of a metre?

   5.9 m

9. A beluga whale that is actually 4.2 m long is represented in a children's picture book with the following picture.

   a) Measure the drawing and write a scale statement for the picture.

   Scale: 1:84 picture is 5 cm long

   b) An alligator is drawn at the same scale. In the drawing, it is 5.9 cm long. How long is the actual alligator?

   5.0 m

   c) How tall will an ostrich be in the picture if it is actually 1.9 m tall?

   2.3 cm

10. The scale used in a drawing is 12.5:1.

    a) What is the actual size of a mite that is drawn as 3.8 cm long?

    0.30 cm or 3 mm

    b) A cat is about 30 cm tall. How tall would it be drawn using this scale?

    375 cm or 3.75 m

    c) Do you think it is useful to use the same scale to draw both the mite and the cat? Why or why not?

    It's unlikely that the same scale would be used because the sizes are very different. For a cat, you would probably use a scale of 1:6. You would represent it smaller than it actually is.

PRACTISE YOUR NEW SKILLS

1. A 7.8-m object is represented in a picture as being 1.5 cm. What is the scale factor?

    $\dfrac{1}{520}$

2. The shoreline of Great Bear Lake is approximately 2719 km (not counting islands). If a map is drawn with a scale of 3 cm:100 km, how long would the shoreline be on the map?

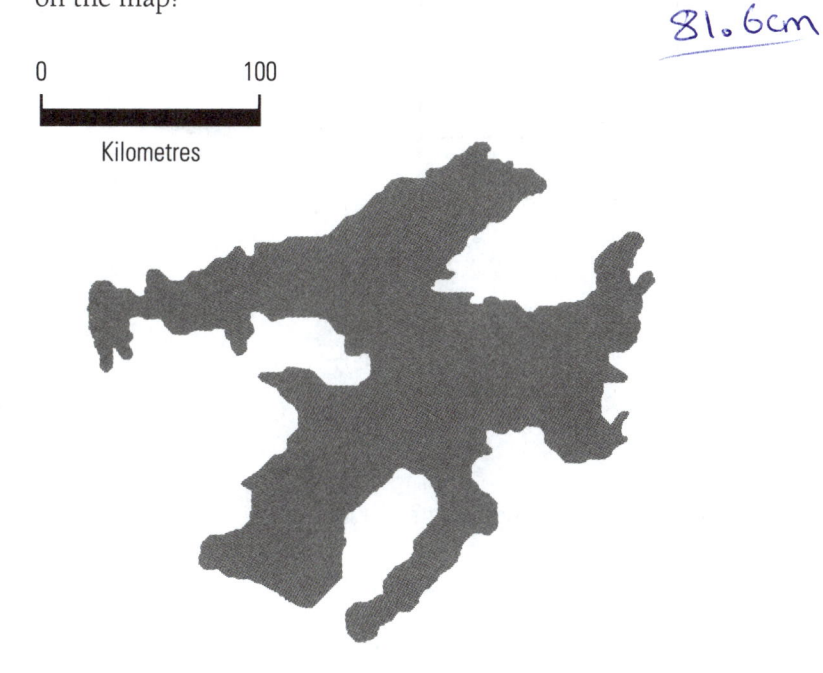

    81.6 cm

    0   100
    Kilometres

3. The diagram below shows a house floor plan. The indicated wall (ℓ) in the actual master bedroom is 12.5 feet long.

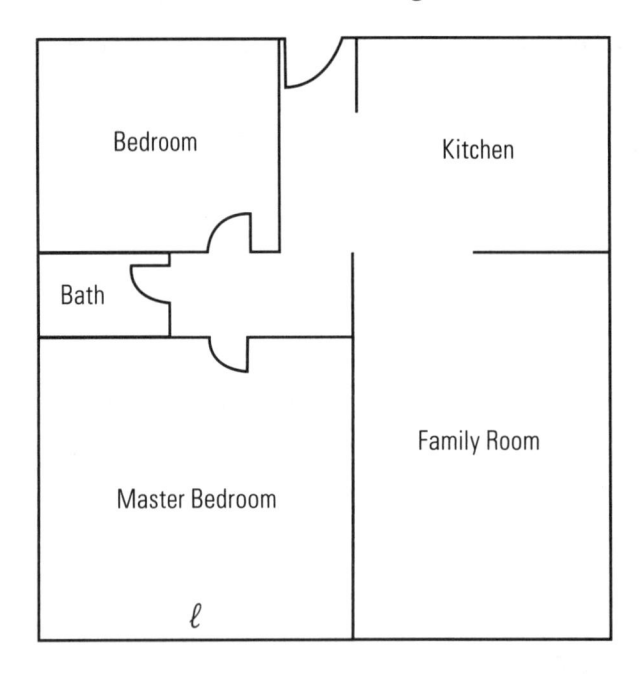

a) What scale was used to draw the floor plan?

b) What are the dimensions of the family room?

c) What are the dimensions of the smaller bedroom?

4. The tallest building in Canada is First Canadian Place in Toronto. The tower is 298 m tall, and the antenna reaches to 355 m. A model of the building, without the antenna, is 11.9 cm tall.

   a) What scale was used to build the model?

   b) How long will the antenna on the model be?

Toronto's First Canadian Place is Canada's tallest office/residential building. The tallest structure in Canada is Toronto's CN Tower, at 553 m.

5. A diagram of a bookcase in an instruction booklet uses a scale of 1:30. If the diagram is 7.8 cm tall, 5.4 cm wide, and 1 cm deep, what are the actual dimensions of the bookcase?

6. A scale model has been built of downtown Calgary. The TD Canada Trust Building is 16.6 cm tall and the Nexen Building is 15.0 cm tall. If the scale used is 1 cm:10 m, what is the actual difference in the heights of the two buildings?

The Calgary Tower is one of the most recognizable features of the Calgary skyline. The tower, with a circular observation deck at the top, is 191 m tall.

Two-Dimensional Representations

5.2

NEW SKILLS: WORKING WITH VIEWS AND COMPONENT PARTS DIAGRAMS

A **view** or an **elevation** is a flat representation of each side or face of a figure. While a view shows what the sides of an object look like, you must remember that sometimes there are parts that are not visible from the sides, such as the seam allowance needed in sewing or a screw in the underside of table. A **component parts diagram** shows all the parts needed to assemble an object.

For more details, see page 219 of *Mathworks 11*.

view: a scale drawing that shows one plane of an object

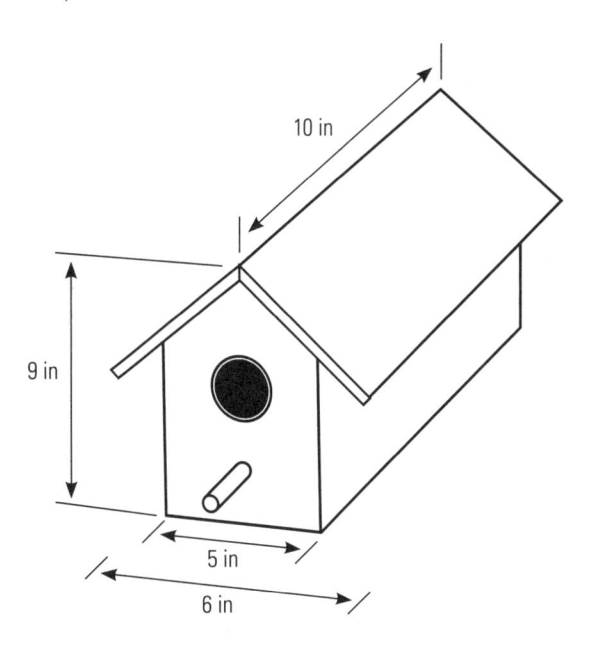

elevation: another term for view

component parts diagram: a 2-D scale drawing that shows each part of an object

Example 1

A simple birdhouse is rectangular in shape with a slanted roof. Draw the view of each face, labelled with the dimensions.

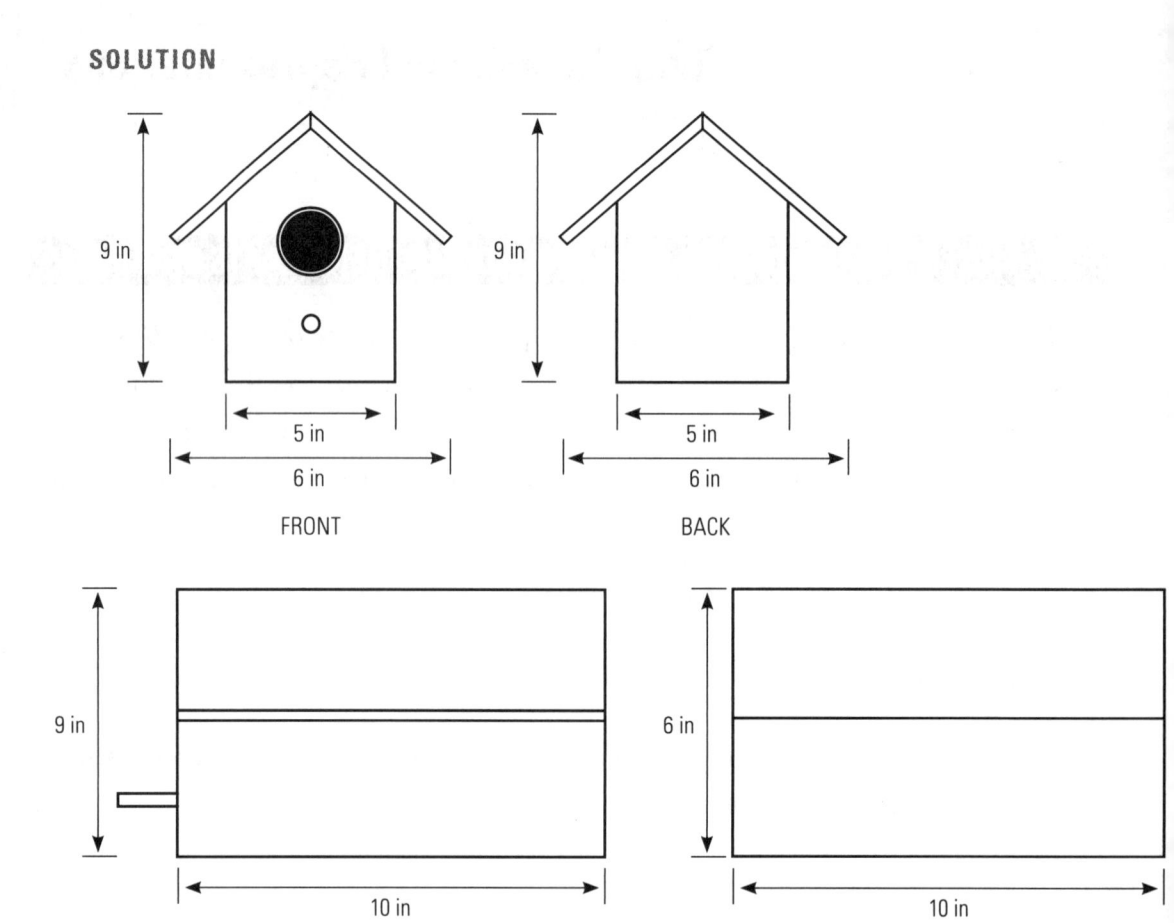

SOLUTION

9 in

5 in
6 in
FRONT

9 in

5 in
6 in
BACK

9 in

10 in
SIDE

6 in

10 in
TOP

BUILD YOUR SKILLS

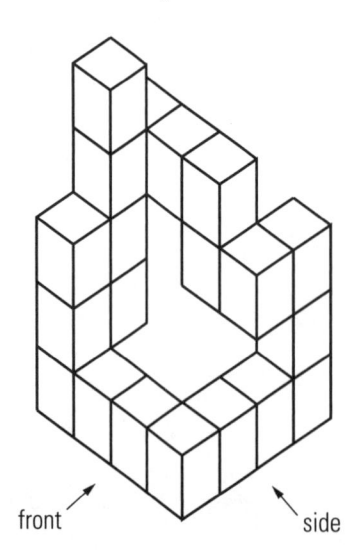

1. Sketch the top, front, and side views of this set of blocks.

front   side

2. a) Draw the front view of this set of blocks.

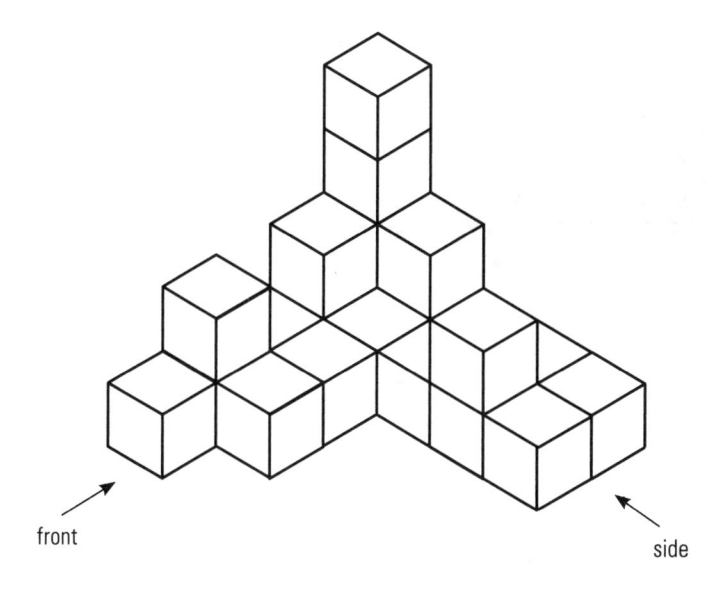

   b) Do you have enough information to draw the top and side views?
      Why or why not?

3. Sketch the top, front, and side views of this toolbox. Label the dimensions.

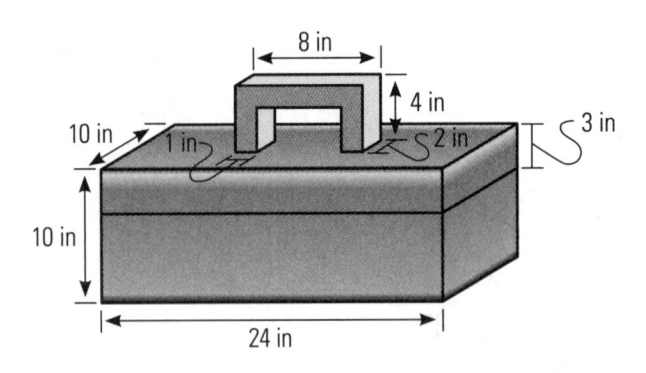

4. Sketch the front and side views of this doghouse. Label the dimensions.

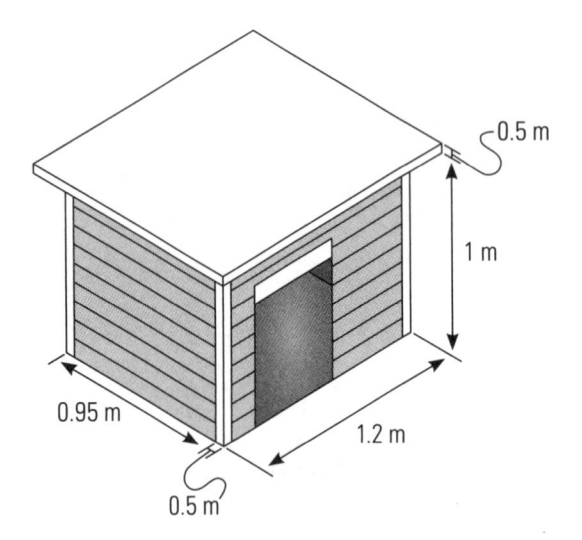

Example 2

Edison is building a toy box for his son in the shape of a rectangular prism. The box is to be 120 cm long, 60 cm deep, and 60 cm high.

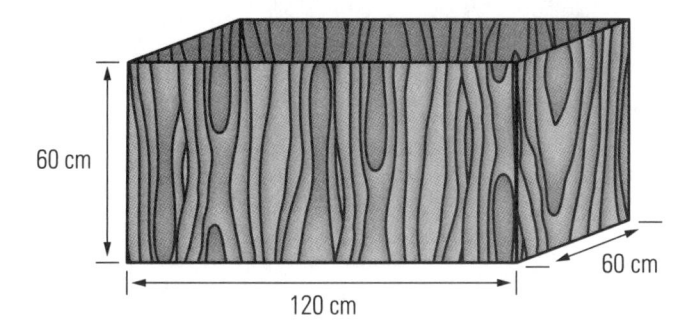

Draw the component parts using a scale of 1:15.

SOLUTION

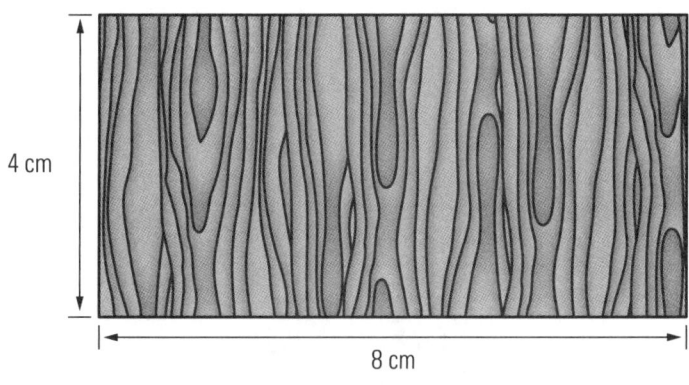

8 cm

4 cm

FRONT, BACK, AND BOTTOM

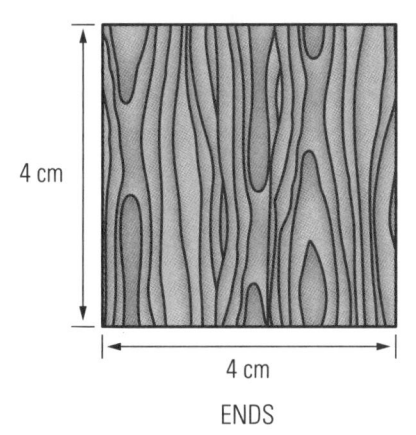

4 cm

4 cm

ENDS

BUILD YOUR SKILLS

5. Draw the component parts of this bookcase. Label the dimensions.

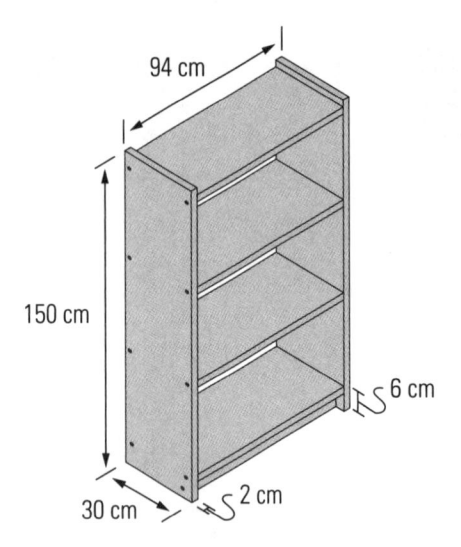

94 cm
150 cm
30 cm
6 cm
2 cm

6. Rebecca is making a patchwork quilt. She has chosen a simple design called the basic four-patch block. Each finished four-patch block is to be 1 foot by 1 foot.

   Quilt makers are able to make intricate and beautiful designs using geometry.

   a) What scale has been used to draw the diagram?

   b) Rebecca cut out squares that are 6 inches by 6 inches. Will her pieces form the quilt she planned? Why or why not?

   c) If the seam allowance is to be $\frac{3}{8}$ inch, what size must she cut each block?

7. Draw the component parts of this kitchen table, at an appropriate scale. Label the dimensions.

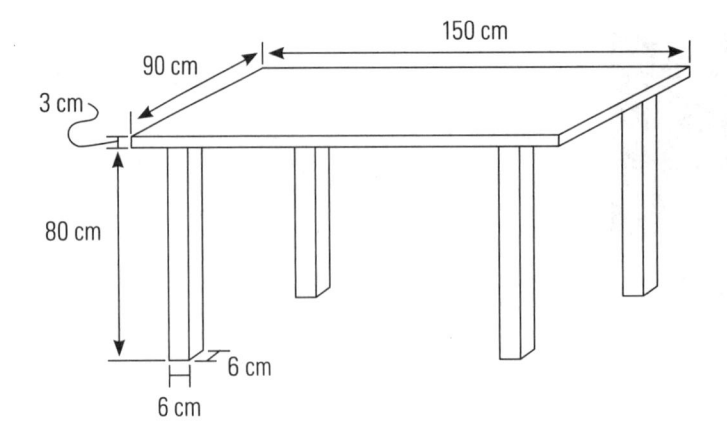

PRACTISE YOUR NEW SKILLS

1. Sketch the top, front, and side views of this set of blocks.

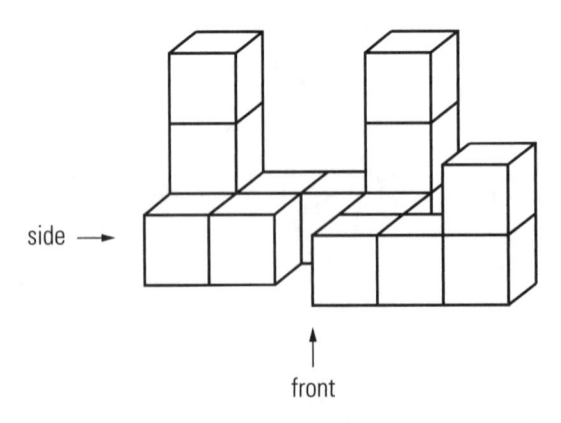

2. a) Draw the front, top, and side views of this set of blocks.

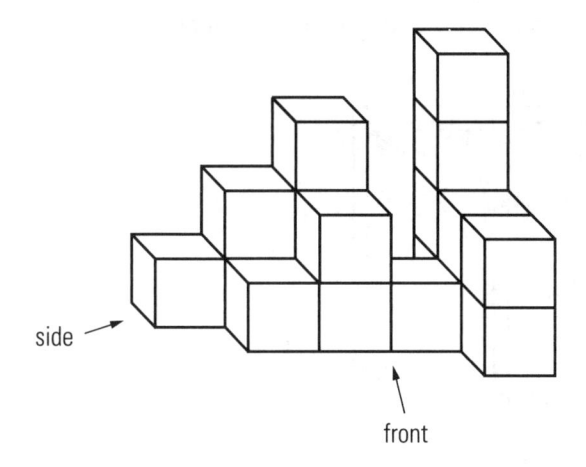

   b) Do you have enough information to draw the back view? If so, draw it. If not, explain why not.

3. The following diagram shows the design of a desk organizer. Draw the front and top views of the organizer, using the measurements given and a scale of 1:6.

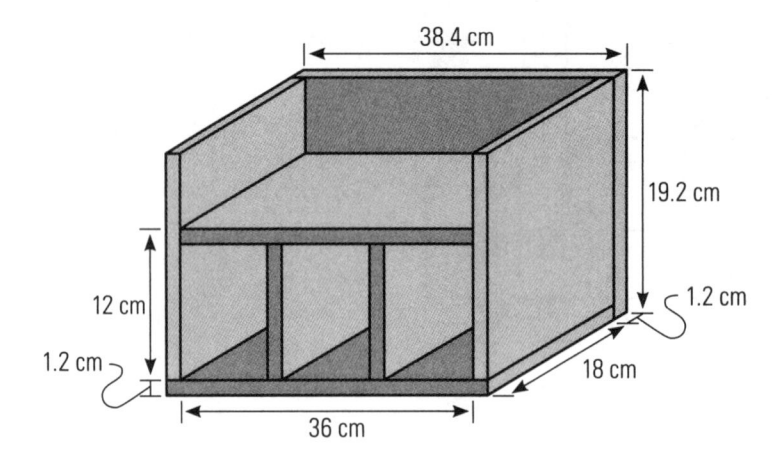

4. Richard is making a model village to go with his model train set. He wants to build a set of three row houses like those shown in this scale drawing.

Building model train sets is a popular hobby.

a) Measure the width and height of the houses with a ruler. If each house is actually 14 metres tall and 7 metres wide, what scale was used to draw the diagram?

b) The scale of Richard's train set is 1:100. What will the front dimensions of his model houses be?

c) Can you draw top and side views of the houses? Why or why not?

5. Jamila built a bird feeder with eight holes (two on each side). She wants to prepare instructions and diagrams so that others can make the same bird feeder.

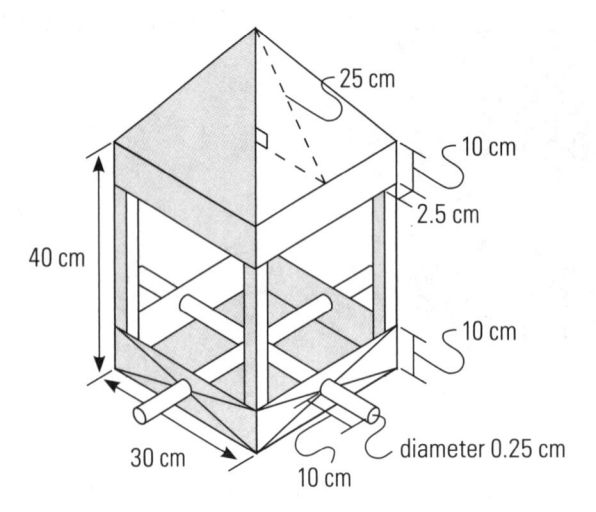

a) What views and measurements will she need to provide?

b) Draw to scale the view(s) needed to build the bird feeder. Write a scale statement for your diagrams.

6. Feed bins for horses need to be carefully designed so that it is easy to remove the feed and replenish it when the bin is empty. Jasper is building a new feed bin for his stables. He has found the following diagram of a bin that will hold about 200 kg of oats. He wants to estimate the amount of material needed. Draw the component parts of the bin, and label them with their dimensions. You can ignore the thickness of the wood.

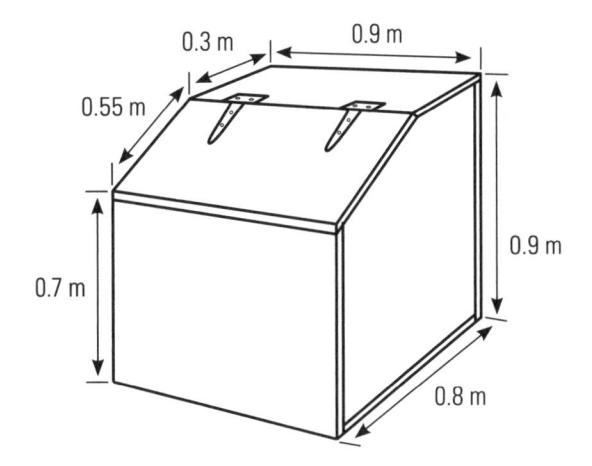

Horses can eat about 2–2.5% of their body weight in dry feed each day. They eat hay and grass as well as grains.

7. Draw the component parts of this boot rack, and label them with their dimensions. Note that the dowels sink 1 cm into the bottom rail.

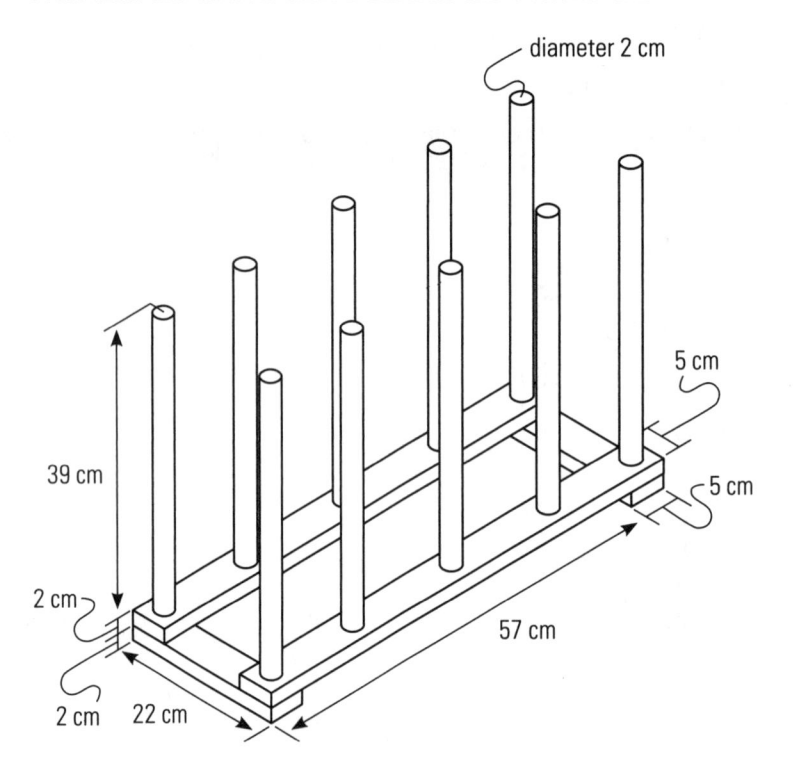

Three-Dimensional Representations 5.3

NEW SKILLS: WORKING WITH ISOMETRIC DRAWINGS

An **isometric drawing** is a way of representing a three-dimensional figure on a two-dimensional plane. Isometric drawings are drawn to scale. Lines that are parallel in real life are parallel in the drawing. Lines measured 30° from the horizontal are used to show width and height. When doing isometric drawings, it is easiest to use isometric dot paper.

For more details, see page 232 of *MathWorks 11*.

isometric drawing: a representation of a 3-D object where the same scale is used to draw the object height, width, and depth

Example 1

Use isometric dot paper to draw a cube with sides that are each 3 units long.

SOLUTION

Start with the bottom corner closest to you (point A). Make sure you draw it at a point on the isometric dot paper that will allow space for your diagram. In each case, make the segment 3 units long. Follow these steps:

- Draw line segment AB vertically.
- Draw AC and BD at an angle 30° counterclockwise from the horizontal.
- Join C and D.
- Draw AE and BF at 30° in the opposite direction from AC.
- Join E and F.
- Draw FG and DG to meet above A and B.

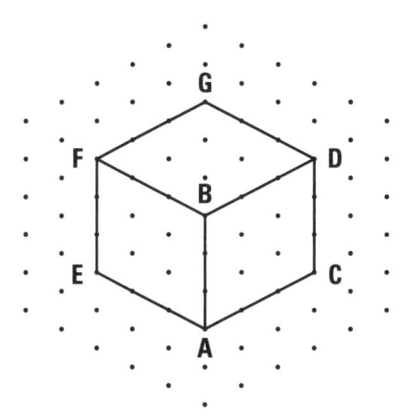

BUILD YOUR SKILLS

1. In the following isometric drawing of a room, the front wall is 18 feet long. Find the lengths of walls x, y, and z and the height (h) of the room.

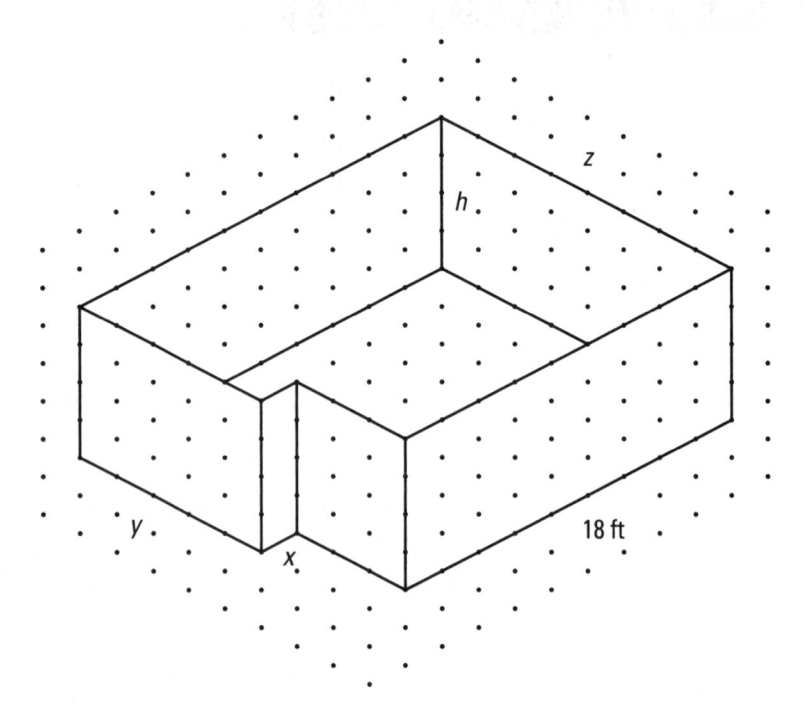

2. Draw the shape below as an isometric drawing, at a scale of 1:20. Use the indicated edge as your starting line.

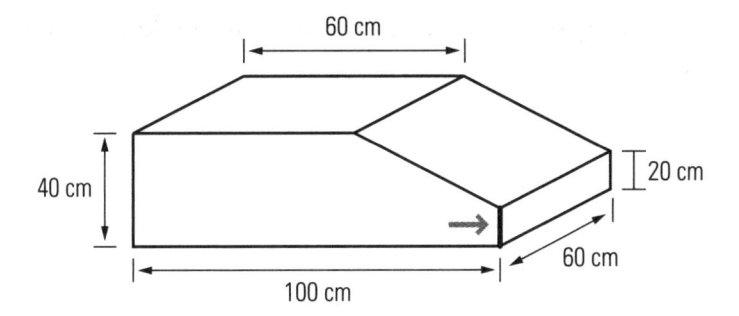

3. Using an appropriate scale, draw an isometric image of the storage unit using the indicated edge as your starting line.

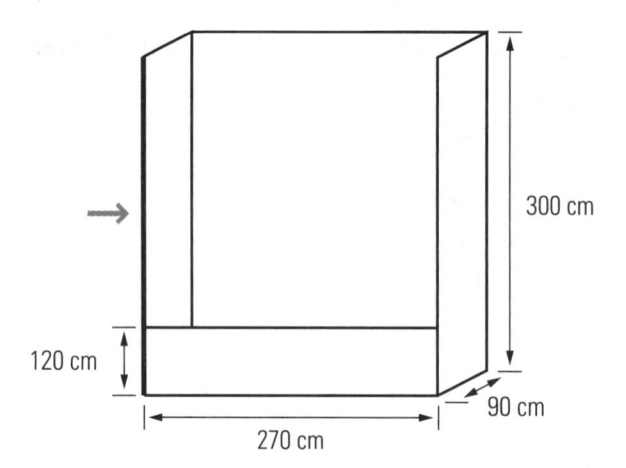

300 cm

120 cm

270 cm

90 cm

NEW SKILLS: WORKING WITH PERSPECTIVE DRAWINGS

A **perspective drawing** is a drawing that tries to represent objects as we actually see them. It uses the idea that parallel lines appear to intersect at a point on the **horizon line**. This point is called the **vanishing point**. In perspective drawing, objects that are farther away appear smaller.

perspective drawing: a representation of a 3-D object in 2-D; objects appear smaller in the distance, and the vanishing point is used to create a sense of depth and space

horizon line: a horizontal line (not always visible) that is at the eye level of the viewer in a perspective drawing

vanishing point: the point on the horizon line at which parallel lines appear to converge in a perspective drawing

Example 2

Use perspective drawing to create an image of a rectangular prism.

SOLUTION

Draw a horizon line and a vanishing point (H). Draw a rectangle below and to one side of the vanishing point.

Draw lines from the corners of the rectangle to the vanishing point.

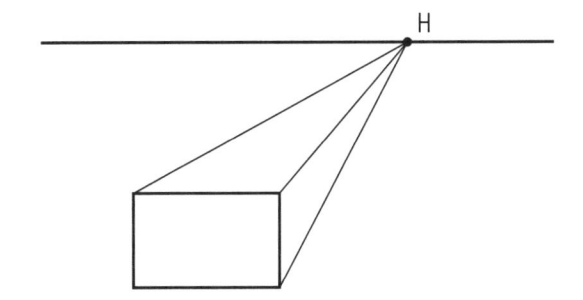

Choose a point, X, on the line joining the upper left corner to the vanishing point and draw a line parallel to the top of your rectangle from X to Y, a point on the line that goes from from the upper right corner to the vanishing point.

This photograph of a road disappearing into the distance is an example of a perspective image.

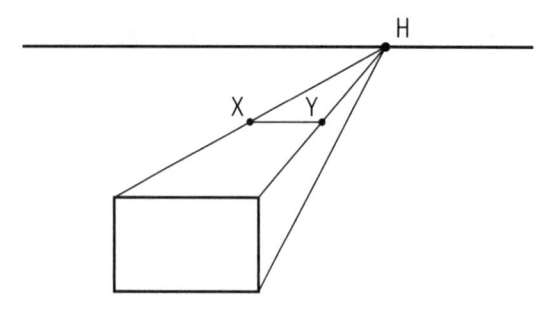

Draw a vertical line from point Y to the line joining the bottom right of the rectangle to the vanishing point, at point Z.

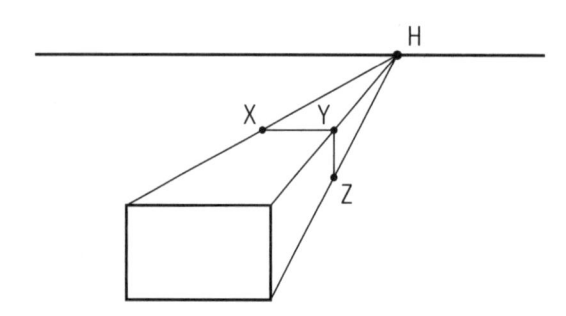

Once you have completed the prism, you can erase the horizon line and the lines connecting the prism to the vanishing point.

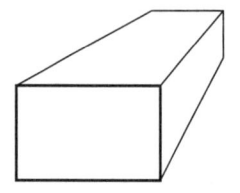

BUILD YOUR SKILLS

4. Draw two perspective drawings of this rectangular prism, using the two vanishing points given. Do your two perspective drawings look the same? Why or why not?

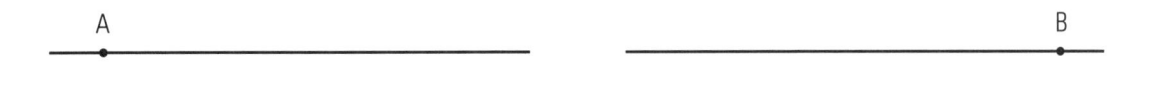

A   B

5. Draw a perspective drawing of a prism with the front face given below.

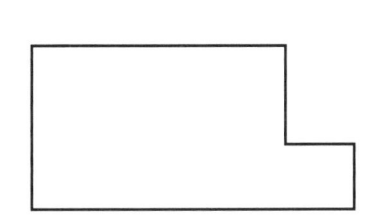

V

6. Create a perspective drawing of a four-legged coffee table for which the front view is given below.

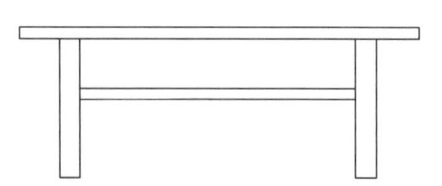

NEW SKILLS: WORKING WITH EXPLODED DIAGRAMS

exploded diagram: a 3-D representation of an object that shows how the components connect together; components are shown separated but in their relative positions, and dotted lines show where the pieces fit together

An **exploded diagram** shows the relationship of the component parts of an object. It is a diagram that shows you how to construct the object; you might see such a diagram in the instructions for furniture that you assemble from a kit, or with a model or toy that needs assembling. An exploded diagram can be drawn using either isometric or perspective drawing techniques.

Example 3

Sketch an exploded diagram of the shelving unit below.

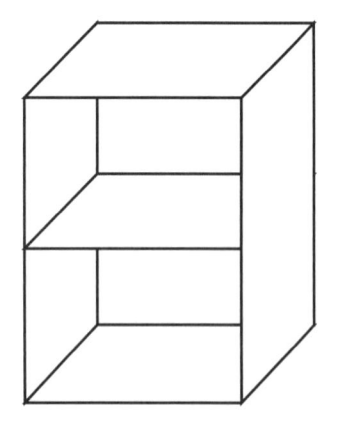

SOLUTION

The component parts are the back, sides, top, bottom, and shelf.

Begin by drawing the back, then each of the other parts separately in a way that shows how they fit together.

Draw dashed lines to show how the parts connect.

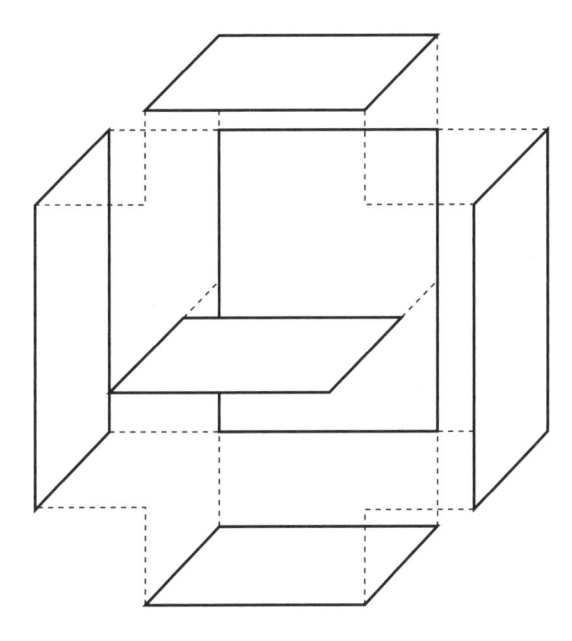

BUILD YOUR SKILLS

7. Sketch an exploded view of this flower planter.

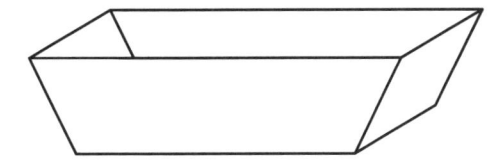

8. Sketch an exploded view of this box.

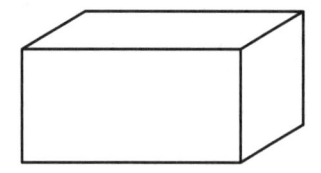

9. Given the exploded view below, sketch what the bookcase would look like.

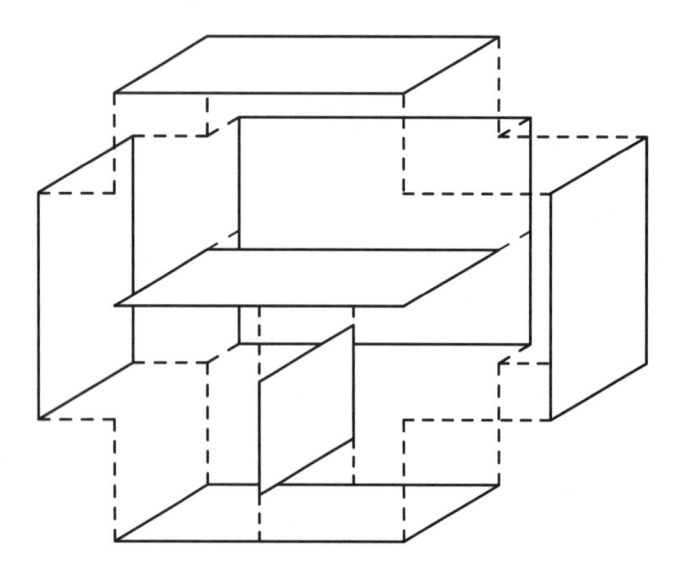

PRACTISE YOUR NEW SKILLS

1. Draw isometric representations of the following objects, using the given shape as the front face. Extend the drawings to create prisms of the length indicated.

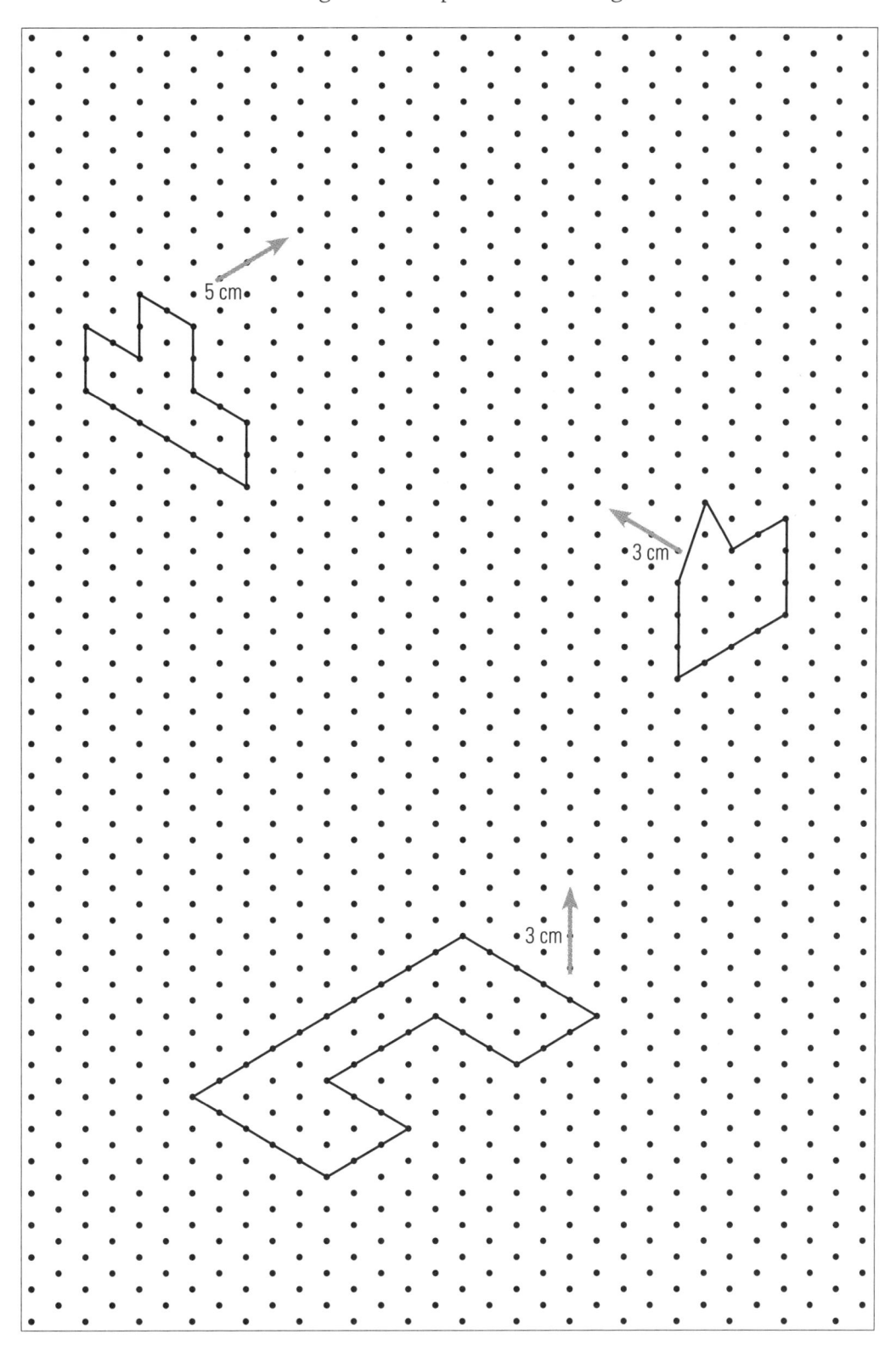

2. Use isometric dot paper to draw a set of 3 stairs. Make each stair 3 units wide, 3 units deep, and 1 unit high.

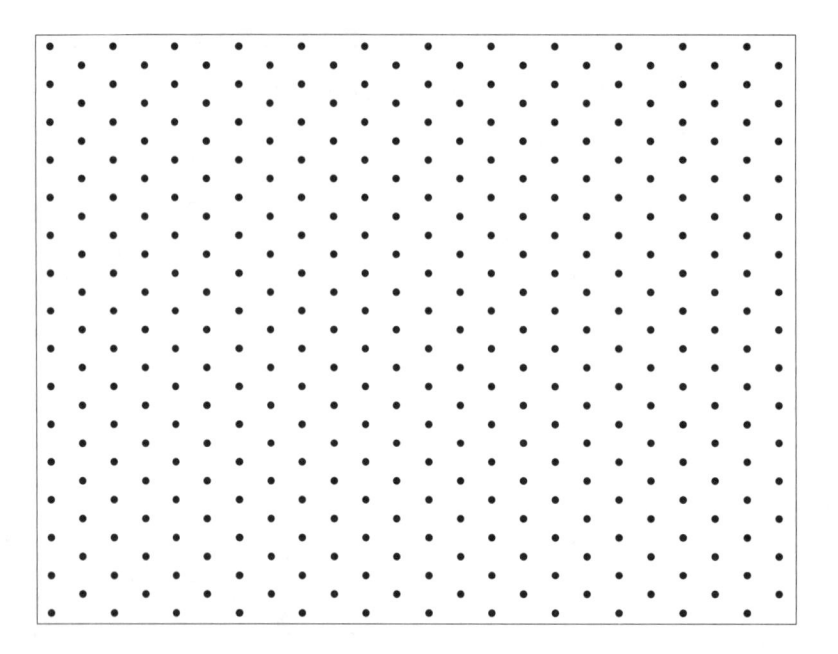

3. Draw two perspective drawings of this staircase, using the two vanishing points given.

a)

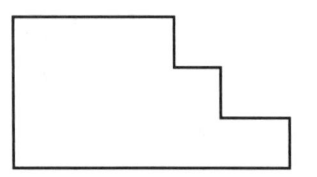

b) ———•————————

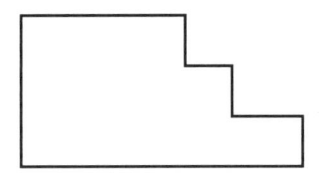

c) Why do they look different?

4. Draw the component parts of this magazine rack, and label them with their dimensions.

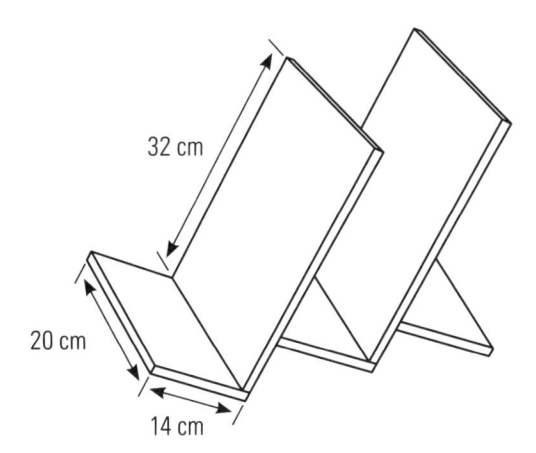

5. Alexandra is building bookends for her younger brother. She has found the following drawing.

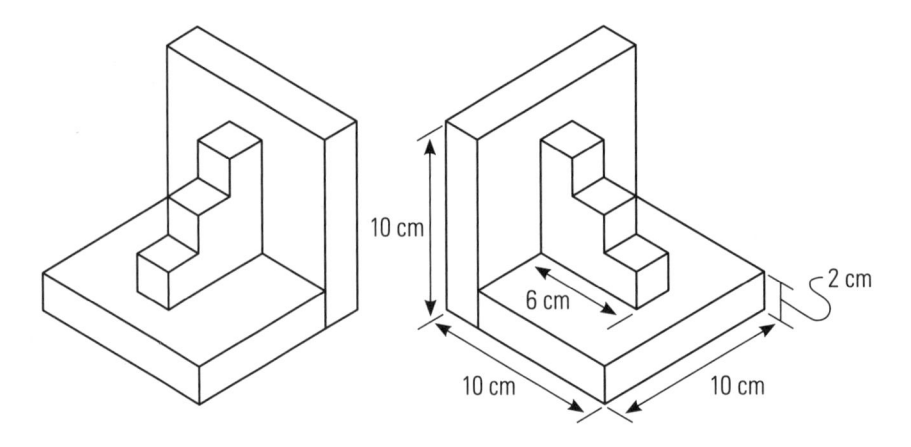

a) To help Alexandra build the bookends, draw the component parts and label them with their dimensions.

b) Draw an exploded diagram of the bookends that could be used as assembly instructions.

CHAPTER TEST

1. A model airplane is made on a scale of 1:128.

   a) What is the scale factor of the model?

   b) If the airplane model has a wingspan of 30 cm, what is the wingspan of the actual airplane?

   Model airplanes can be built as static models not intended to fly, or as flying models. Many people collect scale models of commercial and military airplanes.

2. The distance between two cities on a map is 7 cm. The actual distance between the two cities is 350 km. What is the scale used on this map? Write your answer in the most simplified form.

3. In a photograph, a man is 1.3 cm tall and a flagpole is 4.8 cm tall. If the man is 190 cm in real life, how tall is the flagpole, to the nearest centimetre?

4. Charlotte is building a dollhouse that is a scale replica of her own house. One of the windows on the front of the house is 105 cm wide and 126 cm high. On the dollhouse, the window is 7 cm wide.

a) Write a scale statement for the dollhouse.

b) What scale factor is Charlotte using to build the dollhouse?

c) What is the height of the window on the dollhouse?

5. Draw front, top, and side views of these stacked cubes.

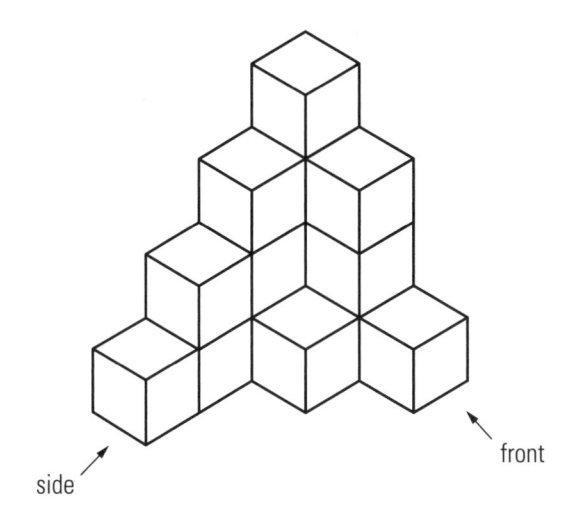

6. Draw a perspective drawing of a prism that has the front face shown. Use the horizon line and vanishing point given.

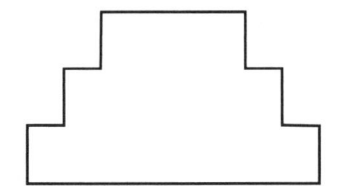

7. An industrial designer has created a chair made out of concrete for an outdoor recreation area. Using the isometric dot grid below, draw an isometric drawing of the chair from the corner indicated.

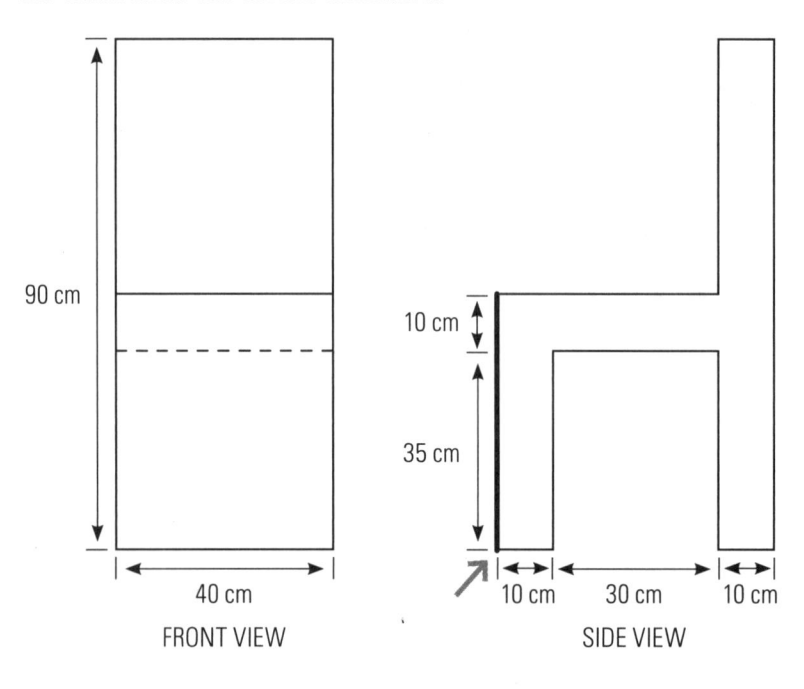

90 cm

40 cm

FRONT VIEW

10 cm

35 cm

10 cm 30 cm 10 cm

SIDE VIEW

8. Kenji is a woodworking teacher. He has built the wooden stool shown below, and he would like to make instructions for his students to build copies of the stool.

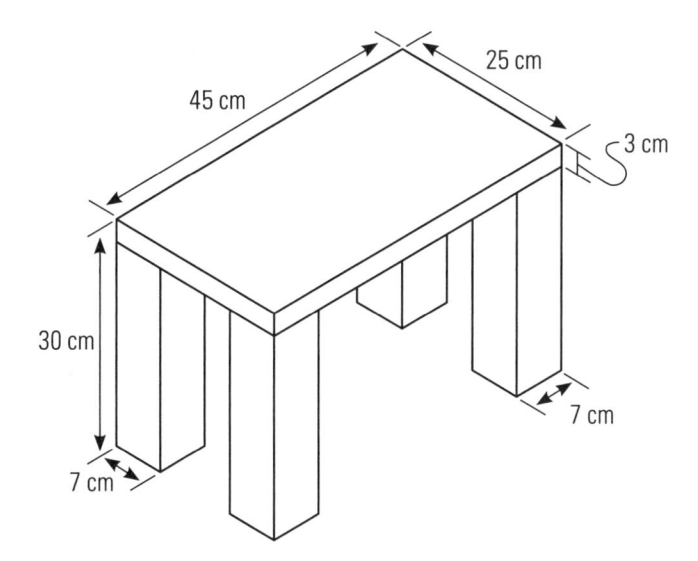

25 cm
45 cm
3 cm
30 cm
7 cm
7 cm

a) Draw the component parts of the stool to an appropriate scale. Label the parts with their dimensions and write a scale statement for your diagram.

b) Draw an exploded diagram of the stool that shows how to assemble it.

Chapter 6
Financial Services

Keeping track of your own finances is very important. It lets you save money for important things like vacations, cars, paying your taxes, and buying your first home.

Choosing an Account 6.1

NEW SKILLS: REVIEWING YOUR BANKING OPTIONS

In this chapter you will look at different banking options and services in Canada. This may be useful for you even if you already have a bank account and are familiar with banking services.

There are many different types of accounts offered by banks. Each bank has its own particular names for the accounts, but most are some form of chequing account or savings account.

Different fees and interest are attached to each type of account, and each allows for different types of transactions. In order to earn interest, some accounts require a minimum balance.

Banks also offer different services such as self-service via Automatic Teller Machines (ATMs) and computer (online payments and transfers), and full-service at the bank with the help of a teller. To use an ATM, you need a bank card and a Personal Identification Number (PIN).

For more details, see page 254 of *MathWorks 11*.

Use the following chart to answer the questions in this section.

NORTHWEST BANK OF CANADA SERVICE PACKAGES				
	Value Account	Self-service Account	Full-service Account	Bonus Savings Account
Monthly fee	$3.90	$10.90 Students and Youth (under 18) save 50% on the monthly fee	$24.50	No fee
Fee waived on minimum monthly balance	$1000.00	$1500.00	$2000.00	
Transactions covered by monthly fee: • cheques • withdrawals • bill payments • debit purchases • transfers to other Northwest Bank of Canada accounts	10 self-service	25 self-service	40 self-service or teller-assisted No annual fee for a credit card	2 debit transactions
Charge for additional transactions not covered by monthly fee	Self-service $0.50 each Teller-assisted $1.00 each	Self-service $0.50 each Teller-assisted $1.00 each	Self-service $0.25 each	Self-service or teller-assisted $1.25 each
Non-Northwest Bank of Canda ATM withdrawals	$1.50 each	$1.50 each		
Interest				Daily interest that grows with your balance
TRANSACTION TYPES				

Self-service: Any transaction that does not require a bank teller. This includes withdrawals, deposits, cheques, money transfers, direct payment purchases, and transactions made at an ATM, by telephone, or online.

Teller-assisted: Includes all transactions that require a teller, such as in-branch withdrawals, transfers, bill payments, and traveller's cheque and foreign currency purchases.

Example 1

In one month, Mary makes 2 deposits and 5 cash withdrawals at Northwest Bank ATMs. She pays 4 bills online. She maintains a balance of over $1000.00. Calculate her fees for each of the accounts. Which account would you advise her to use?

SOLUTION

Calculate how many self-service transactions Mary makes.

2 + 5 + 4 = 11

Value Account:
The $3.90 fee is waived, because Mary maintains a balance over $1000.00.
The account covers 10 self-service transactions for free. Mary will be charged for the 11th transaction at a rate of $0.50.

Her fees for the Value Account are $0.50.

Self-service Account:
She pays a fee of $10.90. It is not waived, because she does not maintain the minimum monthly balance of $1500.00.
This account offers 25 free self-service transactions, so all of Mary's transactions are covered.

Her fees for the Self-Service Account are $10.90.

Full-service Account:
She pays a fee of $24.50. It is not waived, because she does not maintain the minimum monthly balance of $2000.00.
This account offers 40 free self-service or teller-assisted transactions, so all of Mary's transactions are covered.

Her fees for the Self-Service Account are $24.50.

Bonus Savings Account:
There is no monthly fee on this account, but only 2 debit transactions are free. Mary will have to pay $1.25 per transaction for the 9 other transactions.

9 × $1.25 = $11.25

Her fees for the Bonus Savings Account are $11.25.

Mary should use the Value Account because the fees are the lowest.

Be careful when you withdraw money from an ATM. Pay attention not just to fees that the owners of the machine warn you about, but also fees charged by your bank.

BUILD YOUR SKILLS

Use the Northwest Bank of Canada Service Packages table on p. 280 to answer these questions.

1. Frédéric makes 2 direct deposits per month and pays 4 bills online. Last month, he also made 5 cash withdrawals and 10 debit purchases with his bank card. He maintains a minimum monthly balance of $1500.00. Calculate his service charges for the month if he had a: *Self-service transaction: 2+4+5+10 = 21*

   a) Value Account.

   monthly fee: 0

   10 out of 21 are free

   $0.50 for other 11,

   $0 + 0.50 \times 11 = \$5.50$

   b) Self-service Account.

   $0

2. Thom made 29 self-service transactions on his bank account last month. He kept a minimum balance of $900.00. What would his service charges be if he had a:

   a) Bonus Savings Account?

   b) Full-service Account?

3. In one month, Li Ping made 4 self-service deposits and 4 self-service withdrawals on her account. She visits a teller on two occasions, once to make a foreign currency purchase and once to pay a bill. Her minimum monthly balance was $965.95. She has a Value Account. What are her fees?

Example 2

The following is Onani's accounting of his transactions for the past month. He has a Value Account.

Transaction	Description	Withdrawal	Deposit	Balance
				$4398.40
ATM	Cash	$100.00		
ATM (non-Northwest Bank)	Cash (other ATM)	$40.00		
Bank card	Lunch	$12.95		
Bank card	Groceries	$174.32		
ATM	Birthday gift		$50.00	
Teller	Phone bill	$62.31		
Auto-withdrawal	Car payment	$275.48		
ATM	Cash	$100.00		
Direct deposit	Paycheque		$586.21	
Auto-withdrawal	Rent	$790.00		
Bank card	Groceries	$58.21		
Bank card	Lunch	$8.59		
Direct deposit	Paycheque		$586.21	
Teller	Gas bill	$107.45		

a) How much will Onani pay in extra transaction fees?

b) What will his balance be at the end of the month?

SOLUTION

a) Onani made 12 self-service transactions, one of which was at a non-Northwest Bank ATM. His account offers 10 free self-service transactions. He will pay $0.50 for 1 extra transaction, and $1.50 for the non-Northwest Bank ATM transaction.

He made 2 teller-assisted transactions, which will each cost $1.00.

Calculate his total service charges.

$0.50 + $1.50 + $1.00 + $1.00 = $4.00

Onani will pay $4.00 in extra transaction fees.

b) Calculate Onani's final balance by subtracting each withdrawal from his opening balance, and adding each deposit. Remember to include transaction fees.

To determine if Onani maintained the minimum monthly balance, calculate his account balance after each transaction. Remember to include the service charges.

Transaction	Description	Withdrawal	Deposit	Balance
				$4398.40
ATM	Cash	$100.00		$4398.40 – $100.00 = $4298.40
ATM (non-Northwest Bank)	Cash (other ATM)	$40.00+ *$1.50 service charge*		$4298.40 – $40.00 – $1.50 = $4256.90
Bank card	Lunch	$12.95		$4256.90 – $12.95 = $4243.95
Bank card	Groceries	$174.32		$4243.95 – $174.32 = $4069.63
ATM	Birthday gift		$50.00	$4069.63 + $50.00 = $4119.63
Teller	Phone bill	$62.31 + *$1.00 service charge*		$4119.63 – $62.31 – $1.00 = $4056.32
Auto-withdrawal	Car payment	$275.48		$4056.32 – $275.48 = $3780.84
ATM	Cash	$100.00		$3780.84 – $100.00 = $3680.84
Direct deposit	Paycheque		$586.21	$3680.84 + $586.21 = $4267.05
Auto-withdrawal	Rent	$790.00		$4267.05 – $790.00 = $3477.05
Bank card	Groceries	$58.21		$3477.05 – $58.21 = $3418.84
Bank card	Lunch	$8.59		$3418.84 – $8.59 = $3410.25
Direct deposit	Paycheque	+ *$0.50 service charge*	$586.21	$3410.25 + $586.21 – $0.50 = $3995.96
Teller	Gas bill	$107.45 + *$1.00 service charge*		$3995.96 – $107.45 – $1.00 = $3887.51

His account never had less than $3410.25 in it at one time. This means that he did maintain the minimum monthly balance of $1000.00. He will not have to pay the monthly account fee of $3.90.

His account balance at the end of the month is $3887.51.

BUILD YOUR SKILLS

Use the Northwest Bank of Canada Service Packages table on p. 280 to answer these questions.

4. Fill in the Balance column and calculate Mitra's balance at the end of the month if she has a Full-service Account.

Transaction	Description	Withdrawal	Deposit	Balance
				$1798.53
Direct deposit	Paycheque		$1432.51	
ATM	Cash	$200.00		
Bank card	Groceries	$63.95		
Bank card	Clothes	$75.32		
Bank card	Movie	$24.50		
Teller	Hydro bill	$89.56		
Direct deposit	Paycheque		$1432.50	
ATM	Cash	$100.00		
Auto-withdrawal	Loan payment	$375.86		
Bank card	Groceries	$154.32		
Bank card	Gas	$56.23		
Bank card	Dinner	$25.38		
Auto-withdrawal	Rent	$575.00		
Bank card	Books	$123.45		

5. Marek has a Value Account and makes the following transactions. What is his balance at the end of the month?

Transaction	Description	Withdrawal	Deposit	Balance
				$532.89
ATM	Cash	$50.00		
Bank card	Movie/snack	$18.54		
Auto-deposit	Paycheque		$238.21	
Auto-payment	Loan	$385.21		
Bank card	Groceries	$115.87		
ATM	Cash	$100.00		

6. Calculate Noah's balance at the end of the month if he has a Bonus Savings Account.

Transaction	Description	Withdrawal	Deposit	Balance
				$785.53
ATM	Cash	$40.00		
ATM	Cash	$100.00		
Bank card	Groceries	$45.98		
Bank card	Movie	$12.95		
ATM	Babysitting		$30.00	
Bank card	Snacks	$9.59		
Direct deposit	Paycheque		$187.37	
Auto-withdrawal	Telephone	$58.82		
ATM	Cash	$100.00		

PRACTISE YOUR NEW SKILLS

Use the Northwest Bank of Canada Service Packages table on p. 280 to answer these questions.

1. Georgina has an account that has no monthly fees. However, she must pay $0.50 for every self-service transaction and $2.00 for any full-service transaction. She made 8 self-service and 3 full-service transactions last month. What were her service charges?

2. Rolfe has $2675.32 in his Self-service Account. If he makes 4 deposits and 6 withdrawals of $100.00 each during the month, what will his fees be?

3. Patrice is trying to determine what account he should open.

    - He has about $3500.00 that he can deposit.
    - He estimates that he can save $500.00 per month to add to that.
    - He regularly makes 3 online payments per month.
    - He withdraws money from an ATM almost every week (an average of 4 times per month).
    - He uses his bank card about 8 times a month to make purchases.

    Which would be the best for him and why? Show necessary calculations.

4. Jeanette has a Value Account and makes the following transactions in one month.

   a) Fill in the table and calculate her balance at the end of the month.

Transaction	Description	Withdrawal	Deposit	Balance
				$4986.54
ATM	Cash	$250.00		$4736.54
Bank card	Dinner	$25.32		$4711.22
Bank card	Groceries	$145.93		$4565.29
Direct deposit	Paycheque		$524.66	$5089.95
Bank card	Movie	$12.98		$5076.97
ATM	Cash	$100.00		$4976.97
Bank card	Gas	$48.96		$4928.01
Teller	Utilities	$123.23		$4804.78
Auto-withdrawal	Rent	$550.00		$4254.78
Direct deposit	Paycheque		$524.65	$4779.43
Bank card	Groceries	$165.24		$4614.19
ATM	Cash	$100.00		$4514.19
Teller	Phone	$47.25		$4466.94
Bank card	Misc.	$12.32		$4454.62
Bank card	Dinner	$15.88		$4438.74
ATM	Cash	$200.00		$4238.74
Bank card	Prescription	$32.54		$4206.20

   b) Do you think this is the best type of account for her? Why or why not?

5. Determine the balance in her Value Account if Mariya made the following transactions during the month:

   - opening balance of $432.98;

   - 3 ATM withdrawals of $200.00 each;

   - full-service payment of phone bill of $68.21;

   - bank card payments of $103.56 for groceries, $12.87 for a movie, $15.89 and $22.48 for meals;

   - direct deposit of paycheque $658.42; and

   - online payment of her credit card bill of $243.56.

Do you shop for your own groceries? How much will you spend when you do?

6.2 Simple and Compound Interest

NEW SKILLS: WORKING WITH SIMPLE INTEREST

Interest is an amount of money paid or charged for when you deposit or borrow money.

simple interest: interest calculated as a percentage of the principal

Simple interest is interest paid only on the initial amount deposited or the amount borrowed, called the **principal**. The **term** is the length of time in years over which the money is deposited or borrowed. The interest rate is often expressed "per annum," which means per year.

principal: the original amount of money invested or borrowed

The amount of simple interest accumulated on an investment or loan is calculated using the following formula:

$$I = Prt$$

term: the length of time over which money is invested or borrowed

I is the amount of interest earned or due.

P is the principal.

r is the annual interest rate, expressed as a decimal.

t is the term of the investment or loan.

For an investment, you can calculate the total value at the end of the term using this formula.

$$A = P + I$$

A is the final value of the investment.

For more details, see page 264 of *MathWorks 11*.

Example 1

You would like to invest $5000.00 in an account that offers simple interest. Calculate how much the investment would be worth at each of the following rates and terms:

a) 3.00% per annum over a 2-year term;

b) 3.75% per annum over a 4-year term; and

c) 1.75% per annum over a 15-month term.

SOLUTION

a) First, change the interest rate to a decimal: 3% is equal to 0.03. The principal is $5000.00, and the term is 2 years.

   Use the formula for simple interest.

   $I = Prt$

   $I = (\$5000.00)(0.03)(2)$

   $I = \$300.00$

   You will earn $300.00 on the investment.

   Calculate the final value.

   $A = P + I$

   $A = \$5000.00 + \$300.00$

   $A = \$5300.00$

   The investment would be worth $5300.00 at the end of the investment term.

b) Convert the rate to a decimal.

   $3.75 \div 100 = 0.0375$

   Use the formula for simple interest.

   $I = Prt$

   $I = (\$5000.00)(0.0375)(4)$

   $I = \$750.00$

   Calculate the final value.

   $A = P + I$

   $A = \$5000.00 + \$750.00$

   $A = \$5750.00$

   The investment would be worth $5750.00 at the end of the investment term.

c) Convert the rate to a decimal.

1.75 ÷ 100 = 0.0175

You need to change 15 months to years. Divide by 12.

15 months ÷ 12 months/year = 1.25 years

$I = Prt$

$I = (\$5000.00)(0.0175)(1.25)$

$I \approx \$109.38$

$A = P + I$

$A = \$5000.00 + \$109.38$

$A = \$5109.38$

The investment would be worth $5109.38 at the end of the investment term.

BUILD YOUR SKILLS

1. Calculate the amount of simple interest earned on each of the following principal amounts at the rate and term given.

   a) Principal: $1000.00   Rate: 2.50% per annum   Term: 1 year

   b) Principal: $1000.00   Rate: 5.00% per annum   Term: 1 year

   c) Principal: $1000.00   Rate: 2.50% per annum   Term: 2 years

   d) Principal: $2000.00   Rate: 2.50% per annum   Term: 1 year

e) What happens to the amount of interest earned when the principal and the term stay the same but the rate doubles?

f) What happens to the amount of interest earned if the principal and the rate stay the same but the term doubles?

2. Calculate the value of an investment of $600.00 after 5 years, invested at a simple interest rate of 3.75% per annum.

3. How much money would you have after 10 years if you deposited $1000.00 at a rate of 4.50% simple interest per annum?

NEW SKILLS: WORKING WITH COMPOUND INTEREST

Compound interest is a type of interest that is calculated on the principal, plus any interest previously earned. For example, if you invest money for two years but earn interest annually, the second year of interest will be calculated on the value of the investment after one year; that is, on the principal plus one year of interest. You will earn more interest than would be earned at simple interest.

As with simple interest, compound interest is stated as a rate per annum. If the interest is compounded annually, this means that the interest is applied to the account once a year. The **compounding period** of the investment is one year. Investments can have different compounding periods:

- interest calculated semi-annually has 2 compounding periods per year;
- interest calculated quarterly has 4 compounding periods per year;

compound interest: interest calculated on the principal plus interest earned in prior compounding periods

compounding period: the time between calculations of interest

- interest calculated monthly has 12 compounding periods per year; and
- interest calculated daily has 365 compounding periods per year.

Compound interest is calculated using the following formula.

$$A = P\left(1 + \frac{r}{n}\right)^{nt}$$

A is the final value of the investment (principal plus interest).

P is the principal.

r is the annual interest rate expressed as a decimal.

n is the number of compounding periods in a year.

t is the term of the investment or loan in years.

For more details, see page 266 of *MathWorks 11*.

Example 2

a) Calculate the interest you would earn on $1000.00 deposited in an account that pays 4.00% interest per annum, compounded annually if you left it for 2 years.

b) Compare this to what you would get with simple interest.

SOLUTION

a) The rate of 4.00% expressed as a decimal is 0.0400. There is one compounding period per year.

Use the formula for compound interest.

$$A = P\left(1 + \frac{r}{n}\right)^{nt}$$

$$A = (\$1000.00)\left(1 + \frac{0.0400}{1}\right)^{(1 \times 2)}$$

$$A = (\$1000.00)(1.04)^2$$

$$A = \$1081.60$$

If you earned compound interest, your investment would be worth $1081.60 after 2 years.

ALTERNATIVE SOLUTION

You could calculate the value of the investment using the simple interest formula. First calculate the value after 1 year.

$I = Prt$

$I = (\$1000.00)(0.0400)(1)$

$I = \$40.00$

$A = P + I$

$A = \$1000.00 + \$40.00$

$A = \$1040.00$

After the first year, the investment would be worth $1040.00. This amount would then serve as the principal for the second year of investment.

$I = Prt$

$I = (\$1040.00)(0.0400)(1)$

$I = \$41.60$

$A = P + I$

$A = \$1040.00 + \$41.60$

$A = \$1081.60$

Your investment would be worth $1081.60 after 2 years.

b) Calculate how much interest you would earn at simple interest.

$I = Prt$

$I = (\$1000.00)(0.0400)(2)$

$I = \$80.00$

Calculate the total value of the investment.

$A = P + I$

$A = \$1000.00 + \$80.00$

$A = \$1080.00$

If you earned simple interest, your investment would be worth $1080.00 after 2 years.

$1081.60 − $1080.00 = $1.60

Your investment would be worth $1.60 more if invested in an account that offered compound interest.

BUILD YOUR SKILLS

4. Calculate the final value of a deposit of $5000.00 invested at 3.00% per annum, compounded annually, for 2 years.

5. Calculate the difference between the final values of the following two investments after 3 years:

    - $4000.00 invested at 3.50% per annum, compounded annually; and
    - $4000.00 invested at 3.50% simple interest.

6. Calculate how much interest you would earn on a deposit of $8000.00 invested at 2.50%, compounded annually, for a term of 5 years.

Example 3

Calculate the final value of a deposit of $1000.00 invested at a rate of 2.80% per annum for 4 years, with the following compounding periods:

a) semi-annual;

b) quarterly; and

c) monthly.

SOLUTION

a) The rate of 2.80% expressed as a decimal is 0.0280. A semi-annual compound period means that interest is earned twice a year. Use the compound interest formula to calculate the final value.

$$A = P\left(1 + \frac{r}{n}\right)^{nt}$$

$$A = (\$1000.00)\left(1 + \frac{0.0280}{2}\right)^{(2\times 4)}$$

$$A = (\$1000.00)(1 + 0.014)^8$$

$$A = (\$1000.00)(1.014)^8$$

$$A \approx \$1117.64$$

b) A quarterly compound period means that interest is earned 4 times a year. Use the compound interest formula to calculate the final value.

$$A = P\left(1 + \frac{r}{n}\right)^{nt}$$

$$A = (\$1000.00)\left(1 + \frac{0.0280}{4}\right)^{(4\times 4)}$$

$$A = (\$1000.00)(1 + 0.007)^{16}$$

$$A = (\$1000.00)(1.007)^{16}$$

$$A \approx \$1118.08$$

When investing your money it's good to consult with loved ones. Your investments could affect them, too.

c) A monthly compound period means that interest is earned 12 times a year. Use the compound interest formula to calculate the final value.

$$A = P\left(1 + \frac{r}{n}\right)^{nt}$$

$$A = (\$1000.00)\left(1 + \frac{0.0280}{12}\right)^{(12 \times 4)}$$

$$A = (\$1000.00)(1 + 0.0023)^{16}$$

$$A = (\$1000.00)(1.007)^{16}$$

$$A \approx \$1137.99$$

BUILD YOUR SKILLS

7. Calculate the final value of an investment of $4000.00 that earns interest at a rate of 4.00% per annum for 8 years, with the following compounding periods:

   a) annual;

   b) semi-annual;

   c) quarterly; and

   d) monthly.

8. What is the difference in the amount of interest you will get on $10 000.00 deposited at 3.75% per annum for one year if it is compounded annually compared to daily (assume a 365-day year)?

Example 4

Calculate the value of an investment of $5000.00 that earns interest at a rate of 2.95% per annum, compounded semi-annually, for 3 years. Use a table to show the value of the investment at the end of each compounding period.

SOLUTION

Use the simple interest formula ($I = Prt$) to calculate the interest earned each period.

The interest rate of 2.95% is 0.0295 expressed as a decimal.

Interest is compounded semi-annually, so there are 2 interest periods per year, for a total of 6 interest periods over 3 years. Each interest period is 0.5 years.

INTEREST TABLE

Interest period	Investment value at beginning of period	Interest earned ($I = Prt$)	Investment value at end of period
1	$5000.00	$5000.00 × 0.0295 × 0.5 = $73.75	$5000.00 + $73.75 = $5073.75
2	$5073.75	$5073.75 × 0.0295 × 0.5 ≈ $74.84	$5073.75 + $74.84 = $5148.59
3	$5148.59	$5148.59 × 0.0295 × 0.5 ≈ $75.94	$5148.59 + $75.94 = $5224.53
4	$5224.53	$5224.53 × 0.0295 × 0.5 ≈ $77.06	$5224.53 + $77.06 = $5301.59
5	$5301.59	$5301.59 × 0.0295 × 0.5 ≈ $78.20	$5301.59 + $78.20 = $5379.79
6	$5379.79	$5379.97 × 0.0295 × 0.5 ≈ $79.35	$5379.79 + $79.35 = $5459.14

The investment will be worth $5459.14 at the end of the term.

You can use the compound interest formula to check your calculations.

$$A = P\left(1 + \frac{r}{n}\right)^{nt}$$

$$A = (\$5000.00)\left(1 + \frac{0.0295}{2}\right)^{(2 \times 3)}$$

$$A = (\$5000.00)(1.01475)^6$$

$$A \approx \$5459.14$$

BUILD YOUR SKILLS

9. Use a table to show how much a deposit of $3000.00, invested at 3.25% per annum, compounded quarterly for 2 years, would be worth at the end of each compounding period.

INTEREST TABLE

Interest period	Investment value at beginning of period	Interest earned (I = Prt)	Investment value at end of period

NEW SKILLS: USING THE RULE OF 72

Rule of 72: a way to estimate the time it takes for an investment to double in value

If you are investing your money, you may try to estimate how much interest you will earn over the term. There is an easy way to estimate how long it will take you to double your investment if it is compounded annually. It is called the **Rule of 72**. The approximate time in years is calculated by dividing 72 by the interest rate expressed as a percent.

Years to double investment = 72 ÷ (interest rate as a percent)

For more details, see page 270 of *MathWorks 11*.

Example 5

Approximately how long will it take an investment of $5000.00, invested at a rate of 3.75% per annum, compounded annually, to double in value?

SOLUTION

Use the Rule of 72.

Years to double investment = 72 ÷ (interest rate as a percent)

Years to double investment = 72 ÷ 3.75

Years to double investment = 19.2

It would take just over 19 years for an investment earning a rate of 3.75% to double in value.

BUILD YOUR SKILLS

10. Use the Rule of 72 to estimate how long it would take the following investments to double in value:

    a) $6000.00 invested at 4.00% per annum, compounded annually;

    b) $1000.00 invested at 2.45% per annum, compounded annually; and

    c) $1000.00 invested at 1.95% per annum, compounded annually.

11. If you wanted to double your money in 15 years, at what rate of interest would you need to invest your money?

PRACTISE YOUR NEW SKILLS

1. Calculate the amount of simple interest earned and the final value for each of the following investments.

    a) Principal: $400.00   Rate: 1.25% per annum   Term: 8 years

b) Principal: $750.00   Rate: 2.75% per annum   Term: 5 years

c) Principal: $1000.00   Rate: 4.50% per annum   Term: 10 years

d) Principal: $1200.00   Rate: 3.95% per annum   Term: 9 years

2. Use the investment information given in Question #1. How much would each investment be worth if interest were compounded monthly?

3. Use a table to show how much a deposit of $1000.00, invested at 3.85% per annum, compounded semi-annually for 2 years, would be worth at the end of each compounding period.

INTEREST TABLE

Interest period	Investment value at beginning of period	Interest earned (I = Prt)	Investment value at end of period

4. Tameka deposits $4000.00 into an investment account that offers 3.00% interest per annum, compounded daily.

   a) How much will her investment be worth after 3 years?

   b) How much will it be worth after 10 years?

5. An investment offers a rate of 2.80% per annum, compounded annually.

   a) Use the Rule of 72 to determine about how long it will take for the value to double. Round your answer to the nearest whole year.

   b) Use the compound interest formula and an investment of $1000.00 to check your answer to a). What is the value after that number of years?

6. Réjean has a $1000.00 investment that offers an interest rate of 2.50% per annum, compounded monthly.

   a) If he invests it for 5 years, how much will the investment be worth at the end of the term?

   b) Approximately how long will it take for his investment to double in value?

7. Which is the better investment over 5 years:

    - an investment that offers a rate of 1.90% per annum, compounded annually; or

    - an investment that offers at rate of 1.75% per annum, compounded monthly?

8. Calculate the final value of an investment of $5000.00 over a term of 10 years and a rate of 2.60% at the following compounding periods:

    a) annual;

    b) quarterly;

    c) monthly; and

    d) daily.

Credit Cards and Store Promotions 6.3

NEW SKILLS: WORKING WITH CREDIT CARDS

In the last section, you calculated how much interest you would earn on different investments. The rates of interest for most secure investments are fairly low. However, if you borrow money or use a credit card and do not pay it off each month, the **finance charges**, or rates of interest, are much higher on what you owe. While you may get as little as 1.50% on an investment, you may have to pay 19.50% or more on a loan or unpaid credit card balance!

finance charge: the total amount of interest paid to borrow a sum of money

For more details, see page 276 of *MathWorks 11*.

Example 1

Sheng Li has a $4384.76 unpaid balance on his credit card that charges an interest rate of 19.50% per annum. The payment was due on March 23.

a) His minimum payment is $50.00 or 10% of the outstanding balance, whichever is more. What is the minimum he must pay?

b) What will his balance be on April 15?

SOLUTION

a) Calculate 10% of his unpaid balance.

$4384.76 × 0.10 ≈ $43.85

This is less than $50.00, so Sheng Li's minimum payment is $50.00.

b) Convert the rate, 19.50% to a decimal, 0.1950.

Calculate the number of days, including March 23 and April 15. There are 31 days in March, so Sheng Li will be charged interest for 9 days that month and 15 days in April.

9 + 15 = 24 days

Sheng Li will be charged simple interest for the term. Since the interest is per year, the number of days needs to be divided by 365 (days per year).

$I = Prt$

$I = (\$4384.76)(0.1950)(24 \div 365)$

$I \approx \$56.22$

Calculate the total amount due.

$A = P + I$

$A = \$4384.76 + \$56.22$

$A = \$4440.98$

As of April 15, Sheng Li would owe $4440.98.

BUILD YOUR SKILLS

1. Calculate the interest due on the following credit card balances:

    a) an unpaid balance of $2076.54 at a rate of 19.50% for 15 days;

    b) an unpaid balance of $1007.48 at a rate of 21.50% for 38 days; and

    c) an unpaid balance of $2019.64 at a rate of 18.50% for 18 months.

2. Marcia's credit card company charges 24.00% per annum, counting each day that an amount is owed. Her only purchase was an item for $568.93. She did not pay on the due date, March 10. How much will she owe on the next statement date, April 2, if she doesn't make any other purchases?

Credit card interest rates can be expensive if you don't pay your balance off every month.

3. Harley used her credit card to make the following purchases during the month. She does not have to pay interest on purchases during the month, only on outstanding balances. Her credit card company charges 18.50% per annum.

Date	Item	Amount
November 2	Groceries	$124.32
November 7	Dress	$187.54
November 12	Dinner	$32.42
November 16	Groceries	$154.21
November 21	Gas	$54.24
November 23	Plane ticket	$654.32

a) What is her balance due on the statement date, November 28?

b) If the minimum payment is 5% or $10.00, whichever is greater, what is Harley's minimum payment?

c) If she pays only the minimum and doesn't use the card between then and the next statement date, how much will she owe on her December 28 statement?

Example 2

Daphne is charged 18.95% per annum on her credit card balances. She used her card, which had no previous balance, to make a purchase of $2198.95. She did not use the card again before her statement dated April 29.

On May 2, Daphne paid the minimum payment of 5%.

On May 6, Daphne took a **cash advance** of $95.10 on her credit card.

If she makes no other transactions, how much will Daphne owe on her May 29 statement?

cash advance: a withdrawal of cash from an ATM or bank teller charged to a credit card; interest is usually calculated from the day of the withdrawal

SOLUTION

Calculate Daphne's minimum payment.

$2198.95 × 0.05 ≈ $109.95

Calculate Daphne's unpaid balance as of May 2.

$2198.95 − $109.95 = $2089.00

Daphne is charged daily interest on the unpaid balance as of April 29. Calculate how many days of interest she will be charged.

2 days (April 29–30) + 29 days (May 1–29) = 31 days

$I = Prt$

$I = (\$2089.00)(0.1895)(31 ÷ 365)$

$I = \$33.62$

Daphne will be charged daily interest on the cash advance beginning immediately. Calculate how much interest she will be charged on the new purchase over 24 days (May 6–29, including May 6).

$I = Prt$

$I = (\$95.10)(0.1895)(24 ÷ 365)$

$I = \$1.18$

Add the interest amounts, the unpaid balance, and the amount of the cash advance.

$2089.00 + $33.62 + $1.18 + $95.10 = $2218.90

On her next statement, Daphne will owe $2218.90.

BUILD YOUR SKILLS

4. Javier's credit card charges 24.90% interest per annum. He used his credit card, which had no previous balance, to take out a cash advance of $550.00 on December 10. Interest is calculated starting on the day of the withdrawal.

   a) Javier's next statement is dated December 21. For how many days is interest calculated for the balance on this statement?

   b) How much will he owe on his December 21 statement?

   c) What is the actual cost of the cash withdrawal, if he pays his bill in full on January 10?

5. Marie-Josée is charged 21.95% per annum on her credit card balances. She used her card, which had no previous balance, to make the following purchases:

   - $28.95 for dinner;

   - $45.39 for gas; and

   - $106.15 for groceries

   These items appeared on her statement dated October 29.

   By the due date, Marie-Josée paid the minimum payment (5% or $10.00, whichever is greater).

   On November 12, Marie-Josée made another purchase of $119.65 on her credit card.

   If she makes no other purchases or payments, how much will Marie-Josée owe on her next statement dated November 29?

NEW SKILLS: WORKING WITH STORE PROMOTIONS

down payment: a partial payment sometimes required at the time of purchase

Stores often offer promotions where you can purchase an item with little or no **down payment**. These offers allow you to purchase an item without having to pay for it in full until months or years later. However, these offers usually come with high interest rates.

Be sure you understand the details of a store promotion before signing an agreement.

For more details, see page 283 of *MathWorks 11*.

Example 3

Zaynab is buying a new stove, listed at $989.95. The store has an offer of "Nothing down, and 4 easy monthly payments of $265.00."

a) What is the total cost of the stove on the payment plan?

b) Use the simple interest formula to calculate what rate of interest is being charged.

SOLUTION

a) Calculate the total cost of the payment plan.

   4 × $265.00 = $1060.00

b) Calculate the difference between the cost in a) and the list price.

   $1060.00 − $989.95 = $70.05

   The payment plan charges $70.05 in interest.

   The payments must be made within 4 months; divide this by the number of months per year to calculate the term.

$$I = Prt$$

$$\$70.05 = (\$989.95)(r)\left(\frac{4}{12}\right)$$

$$\$70.05 = (\$989.95)\left(\frac{1}{3}\right)r$$

$$\$70.05 = \frac{\$989.95r}{3}$$

$$3 \times \$70.05 = \$989.95r$$

$$\frac{3 \times \$70.05}{\$989.95} = r$$

$$0.212 \approx r$$

Convert the decimal to a percent.

0.212 × 100 = 21.2

The rate of interest is approximately 21.2% per annum.

The first meal ever cooked with an electric stove was made by Canadian inventor Thomas Ahearn in 1892. The "Electric Dinner" featured consommé royal soup, Saginaw trout, sugar-cured ham, stuffed loin of veal, lamb cutlets, apple pie, and chocolate cake.

BUILD YOUR SKILLS

6. Sol is buying a new TV. The cash price is $1675.89, or he can take the store promotion: "24 easy monthly payments of $75!" If Sol chooses the store promotion, what annual rate of interest will he pay for the TV?

7. A store offers a bike for $689.98. You want to purchase it, but cannot pay cash. Your payment options are:

   Option 1: 10% down payment then 6 monthly payments of $115.00.

   Option 2: No down payment and 24 monthly payments of $35.00.

   Option 3: Pay using a cash advance on your credit card. You would be charged interest at an annual rate of 20.95%, and you expect that it will take you 20 days to pay the credit card balance.

   Which payment plan offers the better deal?

8. Jacquie bought a new car. The cash price was $24 789.00, but she is paying in monthly installments of $450.00 for 60 months. What interest rate is she paying?

PRACTISE YOUR NEW SKILLS

1. Calculate the interest due on the following credit card balances:

   a) an unpaid balance of $2987.69 at a rate of 21.50% for 45 days; and

   b) an unpaid balance of $1539.99 at a rate of 20.95% for 6 months.

2. Simona's credit card company charges interest at a rate of 19.50% per annum. On her statement dated June 18, she owed $1630.45. She paid only the minimum (5% or $10.00, whichever is greater). How much will she owe on her next statement (July 18) if she does not use her credit card again before the statement date?

3. Vlad's credit card charges 18.50% per annum interest. On his June 12 statement, he had a balance of $398.51. By the due date, he made the minimum payment (5% or $10.00, whichever is greater). On June 14, he made a purchase of $575.54.

   a) If he makes no other purchases or payments, what will his balance be on his next statement, dated July 12?

b) On his July 12 statement, what will his minimum payment be?

4. George wants to buy a new living room set. His payment options are:

   Option 1: Pay $2543.90 cash.

   Option 2: Store payment plan of 6 monthly payments of $435.00.

   Option 3: Pay using a cash advance on his credit card. He would be charged interest at an annual rate of 22.75%, and he expects that it would take him 30 days to pay the credit card balance.

   a) If he chooses Option 2, how much will he pay in interest?

   b) If he chooses Option 3, how much will he pay for the living room set?

5. Considering interest rate only, which is the better option on a $859.40 purchase?

   Option 1: 4 monthly payments of $220.00

   Option 2: 6 monthly payments of $150.00

6.4 Personal Loans, Lines of Credit, and Overdrafts

At times you may want or have to borrow money from a lending institution such as a bank or credit union to make a large purchase such as a house or a car. There are different ways to borrow money.

- A loan is a fixed amount of money that you borrow all at once. Interest is calculated from the date you receive the money until the final date of the loan. When you take out the loan, you usually sign an agreement of how much you will pay for a certain length of time. This time is referred to as the **amortization period**.

- A bank **line of credit** allows you to borrow money as needed up to a pre-approved amount. You will be charged interest only on the amount of money used.

- Your bank may also offer **overdraft protection**, which allows you to withdraw more money than you have in the bank. There is often a fee and interest attached to this.

- You will hear of some places that offer you emergency loans, often called **payday loans**. These are usually not a good idea as they charge very high rates of interest.

If you do not make your loan payments as agreed, you are said to **default**, and legal action can be taken against you.

For more details, see page 288 of *MathWorks 11*.

amortization period: the time required to pay back a loan

line of credit: an approved loan amount that you can draw on as needed, with interest charged on the money used

overdraft protection: an agreement with a bank that allows you to withdraw more money from an account than you have in it, up to a specified amount

payday loan: a small, short-term loan with a high interest rate

default: failure to repay a loan

Example 1

Richard's car insurance of $1400.00 was due in two days and he did not have the cash available. He went to a payday loan store for a loan. He had to repay the store $1635.20 within 14 days.

a) What was the daily interest rate for the loan?

b) What was the annual interest rate for the loan?

SOLUTION

a) Calculate how much interest Richard paid.

$1635.20 − $1400.00 = $235.20

Use the simple interest formula, with t given in days.

$$I = Prt$$
$$\$235.20 = (\$1400.00)(r)(14)$$
$$\$235.20 = \$19\,600.00r$$
$$\frac{\$235.20}{\$19\,600.00} = r$$
$$0.012 = r$$

Convert the interest rate to a percent.

0.012 × 100 = 1.20%

The daily interest rate is 1.20%.

b) Multiply by the number of days per year to find the annual interest rate.

1.20 × 365 = 438%

The annual interest rate is 438%.

ALTERNATIVE SOLUTION

Calculate the annual interest rate using the formula for simple interest.

$$I = Prt$$
$$\$235.20 = (\$1400.00)(r)(14 \div 365)$$
$$\$235.20 = \$53.9686r$$
$$\frac{\$235.20}{\$53.9686} = r$$
$$4.36 \approx r$$

Convert the interest rate to a percent.

4.36 × 100 = 436%

The annual interest rate is 436%. (Note that this is slightly different from the first solution due to rounding.)

BUILD YOUR SKILLS

1. Barou borrowed $250.00 from a payday loan company and had to repay $275.00 in 15 days. Calculate the annual interest rate.

   Payday loans give you quick access to cash, but are very costly.

2. Hayden borrowed $400.00 and paid back $415.00 in 10 days.

    a) What was the annual interest rate?

    b) What was the daily interest rate?

3. Chantal borrowed $200.00 from a payday loan store. She paid back the loan plus interest 7 days later. The interest rate was 395% per annum. How much interest did she pay?

Example 2

Safia borrowed $500.00 from a payday loan store and agreed to repay it in 30 days at a rate of 1.15% per day. How much will Safia have to repay?

SOLUTION

She must pay 1.15% per day for 30 days. Use the simple interest formula with the daily rate and a term of 30 days.

$I = Prt$

$I = (\$500.00)(0.0115)(30)$

$I = \$172.50$

Add to calculate how much Safia will pay.

$A = P + I$

$A = \$500.00 + \$172.50$

$A = \$672.50$

Safia will have to pay the loan store $672.50.

BUILD YOUR SKILLS

4. Arleta borrowed $500.00 for 25 days at 1.12% per day. How much did she have to repay?

5. Helen agreed to pay $781.50 to a company that lent her $750.00 at 1.05% per day. How many days did she have the money?

6. Hans borrowed $1000.00 for 60 days at a rate of 0.50% per day.

   a) How much will he have to repay?

   b) What is the annual interest rate?

Example 3

Stanley borrowed $4500.00 from his credit union to do some home renovations. The loan has an annual interest rate of 5.75% and an amortization period of 3 years.

You will need the Personal Loan Payment Calculator table on p. 320 to answer the following questions.

a) What is Stanley's monthly payment?

b) Calculate the total amount he will pay over 3 years.

c) Calculate the finance charge on the loan.

Some types of renovations are best to get professionals to do. What renovations can you do yourself?

SOLUTION

a) Using the Personal Loan Payment Calculator table, look up the interest rate of 5.75% in the left-hand column. In that row, look at the entry under the 3-year term: it is $30.31 for a loan of $1000.00.

To calculate the monthly payment, divide the amount of the loan by $1000.00 and multiply by $30.31.

($4500.00 ÷ $1000.00) × $30.31 ≈ $136.40

Stanley's monthly payment will be $136.40.

b) Stanley will pay the monthly amount for 3 years.

3 years × 12 months/year × $136.40/month = $4910.40

He will pay a total of $4910.40 for the loan.

c) Calculate the difference between the principal and the amount Stanley repaid.

$4910.40 − $4500.00 = $410.40

The finance charge on Stanley's loan was $410.40.

PERSONAL LOAN PAYMENT CALCULATOR:
MONTHLY PAYMENT PER $1000.00 BORROWED (INTEREST COMPOUNDED MONTHLY)

Interest rate (%)	Term in years				
	1	2	3	4	5
3.00	84.69	42.98	29.08	22.13	17.97
3.25	84.81	43.09	29.19	22.24	18.08
3.50	84.92	43.20	29.30	22.36	18.19
3.75	85.04	43.31	29.41	22.47	18.30
4.00	85.15	43.42	29.52	22.58	18.42
4.25	85.26	43.54	29.64	22.69	18.53
4.50	85.38	43.65	29.75	22.80	18.64
4.75	85.49	43.76	29.86	22.92	18.76
5.00	85.61	43.87	29.97	23.03	18.87
5.25	85.72	43.98	30.08	23.14	18.99
5.50	85.84	44.10	30.20	23.26	19.10
5.75	85.95	44.21	30.31	23.37	19.22
6.00	86.07	44.32	30.42	23.49	19.33
6.25	86.18	44.43	30.54	23.60	19.45
6.50	86.30	44.55	30.65	23.71	19.57
6.75	86.41	44.66	30.76	23.83	19.68
7.00	86.53	44.77	30.88	23.95	19.80
7.25	86.64	44.89	30.99	24.06	19.92
7.50	86.76	45.00	31.11	24.18	20.04
7.75	86.87	45.11	31.22	24.29	20.16
8.00	86.99	45.23	31.34	24.41	20.28
8.25	87.10	45.34	31.45	24.53	20.40
8.50	87.22	45.46	31.57	24.65	20.52
8.75	87.34	45.57	31.68	24.77	20.64
9.00	87.45	45.68	31.80	24.89	20.76
9.25	87.57	45.80	31.92	25.00	20.88
9.50	87.68	45.91	32.03	25.12	21.00
9.75	87.80	46.03	32.15	25.24	21.12
10.00	87.92	46.14	32.27	25.36	21.25

BUILD YOUR SKILLS

For these questions, you will need the Personal Loan Payment Calculator table on p. 320.

7. Calculate the monthly payment, the total amount paid, and the finance charge for the following loans:

   a) $3000.00 at 9.00% per annum for 2 years;

   b) $2125.00 at 7.25% per annum for 3 years; and

   c) $11 500.00 at 4.75% per annum for 4 years.

8. Adele wants to buy a used car that costs $2900.00. She has $1100.00 saved up for a down payment.

   a) How much will Adele have to borrow to buy the car?

b) She can get a loan at 6.50% per annum with an amortization period of 2 years. What will be her monthly payment?

c) What will be the total she pays for the loan?

d) How much will the car cost?

PRACTISE YOUR NEW SKILLS

For some of these questions, you will need to use the Personal Loan Payment Calculator table on p. 320.

1. Shey needed $850.00 cash to pay an emergency vet bill. He went to a payday loan store and agreed to pay $950.00 on payday, which is 12 days away.

   a) What is the daily interest rate for the loan?

   b) What is the annual interest rate?

Dogs and cats can get ear mites in their ear canals. Make sure you take your pets to the vet if they are sick.

2. Carmen borrowed $250.00 from a payday loan store and agreed to repay it in 18 days, at a rate of 1.17% per day. How much did she have to repay?

3. Calculate the monthly payment, the total amount paid, and the finance charge for the following loans:

    a) $2500.00 at 8.00% per annum for 3 years;

    b) $10 000.00 at 6.25% per annum for 5 years; and

    c) $1500.00 at 3.75% per annum for 2 years.

4. Jackson borrowed $5000.00 from the bank to buy a car. The loan has an annual interest rate of 7.00% and an amortization period of 2 years.

    a) What is Jackson's monthly payment?

    b) Calculate the total amount he will pay over 2 years.

    c) Calculate the finance charge on the loan.

According to Statistics Canada the average Canadian watches 15 hours of TV a week.

5. Manon is buying a new TV. The TV costs $3499.99 in the store. She has only $1000.00 saved up to use as a down payment. She has the following payment options:

   Option 1: Get a loan from the bank at 6.50% per annum over 2 years, and pay cash.

   Option 2: Take the store payment plan of a $50.00 down payment and 12 monthly payments of $325.00.

   Option 3: Take out a payday loan. She would be required to pay 1.12% daily interest, and would have to repay the loan within 30 days.

   a) With Option 1, how much would Manon pay per month?

   b) Calculate the total cost of each of Manon's payment options. Which option should she choose?

CHAPTER TEST

For some of these questions, you will need to use the Personal Loan Payment Calculator table on p. 320.

1. For a fee of $6.00 per month, Salma is allowed an unlimited number of deposits and 10 self-service withdrawal transactions on her bank account. Each additional self-service transaction costs $0.50. Each full-service transaction costs $1.50. If she keeps a minimum balance of $2000.00 her monthly fee is waived.

   Calculate Salma's balance after each transaction.

Transaction	Description	Withdrawal	Deposit	Balance
				$2879.54
ATM	Cash	$200.00		
Direct deposit	Paycheque		$457.21	
Bank card	Groceries	$172.12		
Bank card	Gas	$42.54		
ATM	Cheque—reimbursement		$175.64	
Bank card	Dinner	$32.42		
ATM	Cash	$100.00		
Auto-withdrawal	Hydro	$112.21		
Direct deposit	Paycheque		$457.21	
Auto-withdrawal	Rent	$645.00		
Bank card	Car repairs	$276.97		
Bank card	Movie	$28.12		
ATM	Cash	$200.00		

2. Jamal has invested $5000.00 in an account that earns 2.50% simple interest per annum for a term of 10 years.

   a) How much interest will he earn?

   b) How much will his investment be worth at the end of the term?

3. An investment earning simple interest at a rate of 1.10% per annum for a term of 5 years earned $82.50 in interest. What was the principal?

4. Calculate the final value after 10 years if you invest $5000.00 at 2.5% per annum, compounded annually.

5. Calculate the amount of interest earned in 10 years on $1000.00 invested at 3.00% per annum, compounded monthly.

6. Calculate the interest due on the following credit card balances:

   a) An unpaid balance of $1629.53 at a rate of 19.50% for 21 days; and

   b) An unpaid balance of $2639.99 at a rate of 22.95% for 30 days.

7. Monique's credit card charges interest of 20.85% per annum on unpaid balances. On her March 12 statement, she had a balance of $739.65. By the due date, she made the minimum payment (5% or $10.00, whichever is greater). On March 16, she made a purchase of $179.39.

   a) If she makes no other purchases or payments, what will her balance be on her next statement, dated April 12?

   b) On her April 12 statement, what will her minimum payment be?

8. Harpreet took out a payday loan of $500.00. He had to repay $540.00 within 7 days.

   a) What was the daily interest on the loan?

   b) What was the annual interest?

9. Nathaniel wants to buy a new bicycle. His payment options are:

   Option 1: Pay $2055.99 cash. He only has $400.00 saved up, so he can take out a loan for the rest from his bank at a rate of 7.25% per annum over 2 years.

   Option 2: Take the store payment plan of 12 monthly payments of $180.00.

   a) If he chooses Option 1, what will his monthly payments be?

   b) If he chooses Option 2, what annual rate of interest will he pay?

   c) Calculate the total cost of each option. Which option should he choose, and why?

Chapter 7
Personal Budgets

Making a budget can help you to reach a financial goal, such as a large purchase.

Preparing to Make a Budget — 7.1

NEW SKILLS: WORKING WITH INCOME AND EXPENSES

In this chapter, you will consider what income you might make and what it might cost you to live. Will you have enough money to pay all your expenses? You need to make a **budget**, an estimated plan of income and expenses. To do this, you have to consider:

- Your income: Is it regular or does it vary? Variable income is income where the amount changes over time and/or is not received on a regular basis (for example, commissions, tips, or piecework).

budget: a balanced statement of projected income and expenses

recurring expenses:
expenses that occur on a regular basis

- Your expenses: Which ones are **recurring** and regular (for example, car payments or rent), and which ones vary (for example, buying new clothes)? What are your possible unexpected expenses (for example, an emergency vet bill for a sick pet)?
- Your savings: What do you want to save for?

For more details, see page 302 of *MathWorks 11*.

Example 1

Janice had the following income and expenses during the past month. Identify the income and expenses. Classify the income as regular or variable, and the expenses as recurring, variable, or unexpected.

Paycheque	$500.00
Gas	$34.86
Cell phone bill	$42.89
New boots	$189.54
Paycheque	$500.00
Birthday gift from grandparents	$100.00
Car loan payment	$275.00
New hard hat for work, to replace lost hat	$29.95
Eating out	$25.78

A hard hat is an essential piece of safety equipment in many jobs.

SOLUTION

Separate the entries into two columns, income and expenses.

JANICE'S MONTHLY INCOME AND EXPENSES	
Income	Expenses
Paycheque: $500.00	Gas: $34.86
Paycheque: $500.00	Cell phone bill: $42.89
Birthday gift from grandparents: $100.00	New boots: $189.54
	Car loan payment: $275.00
	New hard hat for work, to replace lost hat: $29.95
	Eating out: $25.78

Examine each item under income. The two paycheques look like they are regular income, since they are both for the same amount. The birthday gift is variable income, because it is not received regularly.

Recurring expenses would probably be the car loan payment and the cell phone bill. Gas, new boots, and eating out are probably variable expenses. Buying the new hard hat is an unexpected expense.

Sometimes it is not easy to classify items as regular or variable because it may depend on usage.

BUILD YOUR SKILLS

1. Classify the following types of income as regular or variable, and explain your reasoning.

Item	Classification	Reason
Semi-monthly paycheque		
Birthday gift		
Tips		
Interest from investment		
Tax refund		

2. Classify the following expenses as recurring, variable, or unexpected. Explain your reasoning.

Item	Classification	Reason
Rent		
New shoes		
Loan payment		
Car repairs		
Groceries		
Meal at restaurant		
Replacing broken cell phone		
Car insurance		

3. Classify the following as income or expenses. Identify the income as regular or variable and the expenses as recurring, variable, or unexpected.

Item	Income	Expense
Paycheque: $250.98		
John's birthday: $54.25		
Commission: $75.00		
Babysitting: $40.00		
Paycheque: $123.42		
Loan payment: $125.00		
Donation to earthquake relief fund: $25.00		
Car insurance: $115.32		
Savings: $50.00		
Rent: $450.00		
Cell phone bill: $45.00		
Meal at restaurant: $56.76		

Example 2

Carlos has made a list of his income and expenses for one month.

Income		Expenses	
Semi-monthly paycheque	$539.92	Rent	$445.00
Semi-monthly paycheque	$539.92	Food	$195.00
		Entertainment	$79.85
		Utilities	$45.15
		Transportation	$75.00
		Clothing	$72.95
		Cell phone bill	$47.95
		Miscellaneous	$25.00

a) He plans to put any extra income into a savings account. How much money does he have to put into savings?

b) How much money can Carlos save over the course of one year?

c) What percentage of his income do Carlos's savings represent?

d) Carlos hopes to buy a new computer in one year. He expects it will cost $1500.00. How much more would he need to save per month to be able to afford it? Suggest one way he could do this.

SOLUTION

a) Calculate Carlos's total income.

$539.92 + $539.92 = $1079.84

Calculate his total expenses.

$445.00 + $195.00 + $79.85 + $45.15 + $75.00 + $72.95 + $47.95 + $25.00 = $985.90

Subtract expenses from income to calculate how much he could put into savings.

$1079.84 − $985.90 = $93.94

Carlos can put $93.94 into a savings account.

b) Calculate his savings for one year.

$93.94 × 12 = $1127.28

After one year, Carlos will have $1127.28 saved.

c) In one month, Carlos earns $1079.84 and saves $93.94. Calculate what percentage his savings are of his income.

$$\frac{\$93.94}{\$1079.84} \times 100 \approx 8.7\%$$

Carlos saves about 9% of his income.

Computers get faster and more efficient every year. How often do you think you'll need to buy one?

d) The computer will cost $1500.00. Divide by 12 to find how much Carlos would have to save per month.

$1500.00 ÷ 12 = $125.00

Calculate how much more this is than what Carlos is currently saving.

$125.00 − $93.94 = $31.06

To be able to afford the computer, Carlos will have to put $31.06 more into savings each month.

Suggestions for how Carlos could save extra money:

- Food and entertainment are variable expenses. He could spend less on them per month and put more money into savings.

- Clothing is a variable expense, so Carlos will probably not spend the same amount each month. He can save some of this money for the computer.

BUILD YOUR SKILLS

4. Tonia has made a list of her income and expenses for one month. She will put any extra income into savings. If she has an unexpected car repair that costs $243.25, how much will she save this month?

Income		Expenses	
Paycheque (week 1)	$450.00	Rent	$775.00
Paycheque (week 2)	$450.00	Groceries	$225.39
Paycheque (week 3)	$450.00	Renter's insurance	$74.00
Paycheque (week 4)	$450.00	Clothing	$66.79
		Entertainment	$47.59
		Utilities	$84.00
		Transportation	$250.00

5. Franklin earns $2456.85 each month. He expects the following expenses this month:

Expenses	
Mortgage payment	$1250.46
Groceries	$250.00
Insurance	$135.76
Entertainment	$50.00
Utilities/phone	$245.00
Transportation	$250.00
Miscellaneous	$100.00

   If he saves the rest, how much can he save in a year? What percentage of his income does this represent?

6. Marion has the following monthly income and expenses. She puts any extra income into savings.

Income		Expenses	
Semi-monthly pay	$1037.72	Rent	$825.00
Semi-monthly pay	$1037.72	Utilities (phone, gas, hydro)	$110.00
		Entertainment	$100.00
		Loan payment	$150.00
		Renter's insurance	$25.00
		Transportation	$225.00
		Groceries	$275.00
		Clothing	$100.00
		Charity	$25.00
		Miscellaneous	$50.00

   After three months, Marion wants to buy a new TV that costs $1399.99. Will she have enough saved to pay cash?

Example 3

Rachelle's budgeted income and expenses are shown below. She wants to replace her car in one year. She expects that she will be able to sell her old car for $1500.00. Assuming she saves any extra income, how much money will she have for a new car?

A car is a big purchase; plan wisely for it.

Income		Expenses	
Regular pay	$1100.00	Rent	$500.00
Tutoring	$300.00	Utilities	$150.00
Babysitting	$250.00	Car Insurance	$125.00
		Gas	$80.00
		Clothing	$100.00
		Groceries	$175.00
		Entertainment	$50.00
		Miscellaneous	$25.00

SOLUTION

Add to find her monthly expenses.

$500.00 + $150.00 + $125.00 + $80.00 + $100.00 + $175.00 + $50.00 + $25.00
= $1205.00

Add to find her monthly income.

$1100.00 + $300.00 + $250.00 = $1650.00

Subtract her expenses from her income.

$1650.00 − $1205.00 = $445.00

She should be able to save $445.00 per month.

Calculate her total savings after one year.

$445.00 × 12 = $5340.00

Add the amount she expects to earn from the sale of her car.

$5340.00 + $1500.00 = $6840.00

Rachelle will have $6840.00 saved for her new car.

BUILD YOUR SKILLS

7. Aidan earns $1588.25 per month and has about $1275.00 in expenses per month. If he saves the rest, how many months will it take him to save for a new computer if the one he wants costs $1798.98? (Ignore taxes.)

8. Karen's monthly income is $2379.00 and her monthly expenses are as follows.

Expenses	
Rent	$775.00
Utilities	$175.00
Car payment	$342.00
Car insurance	$123.00
Renter's insurance	$42.00
Groceries	$225.00
Gas	$90.00
Entertainment	$75.00
Miscellaneous	$50.00

In January, Karen starts saving for a trip in July that will cost her $3000.00. Will she have enough saved by the beginning of July? How much more/less will she have in savings?

PRACTISE YOUR NEW SKILLS

1. Wong has recorded his income and expenses below. Identify the income and expenses. Classify the income as regular or variable, and the expenses as recurring or variable.

Item	Income	Expense
Paycheque		
Rent		
Car insurance		
Gas		
Clothing		
Cell phone bill		
Mother's Day gift for mom		
Groceries		
Present for Joan		
Entertainment		
Mowing lawns		
Utilities		

2. Hannah has made a list of her incomes and expenses for one month.

Income		Expenses	
Semi-monthly paycheque	$400.00	Rent	$395.00
Tips	$140.00	Loan payment	$85.00
Yard and house work	$150.00	Car (gas and insurance)	$185.00
Tutoring	$150.00	Clothing	$75.00
Semi-monthly paycheque	$400.00	Food	$170.00
		Entertainment	$50.00
		Miscellaneous	$25.00
		Cell phone	$40.00

Doing a bit of yard work can supplement your income.

a) How much will Hannah be able to save each month?

b) What percentage of her income do her savings represent?

c) After 6 months, Hannah wants to buy a new bicycle that costs $1199.99. Will she have enough money saved?

3. Perseus has regularly saved $125.00 per month since be began working 8 months ago. He has planned a trip in 6 months, which will cost him $1900.00. How much more does he have to save each month to have enough for the trip?

4. Shonda has listed her income and expenses for one month. She has regular income from a part-time job, and also earns money from tutoring and babysitting.

Babysitting	$40.00
Babysitting	$40.00
Cell phone	$40.00
Entertainment	$105.00
Food	$195.00
Loan payment	$65.00
Paycheque	$375.00
Paycheque	$375.00
Rent	$425.00
Renter's insurance	$25.00
Transportation	$80.00
Tutoring	$50.00
Tutoring	$100.00
Tutoring	$50.00

a) Sort the items listed into income and expenses.

Income		Expenses	

b) Calculate her total income and expenses.

c) How much can Shonda save in one year? Include any assumptions you made.

d) What percentage of her income do her savings represent?

7.2 The Budgeting Process

NEW SKILLS: CREATING A BUDGET

In order to create an accurate budget, you need to have a good idea of your total income and expenses. To make a personal budget, you could keep track of your income and expenses for a few months, and use these financial transactions to estimate what you will spend and earn in the future.

A budget is a plan for the future, so it is an estimate, because you cannot know exactly how much you will have to spend on every item in the future. To create a conservative budget, you should underestimate your income and overestimate your expenses.

surplus: the amount by which income exceeds expenses

If your income is higher than your expenses, you have a **surplus**. If you have a surplus in your budget, that money should be allocated to an item such as "savings" or "unexpected expenses" to balance your budget.

deficit: the amount by which expenses exceed income

If your expenses are higher than your expenses, you have a **deficit**. You will need to adjust your spending, reducing your expenses in some areas to balance your budget.

To make your budget, you will need to group your expenses into categories such as housing, food, transportation, and entertainment. Each category can include several transactions. For example, the food category can include four purchases at the grocery store and three meals eaten at restaurants.

For more details, see page 313 of *MathWorks 11*.

Example 1

Kate works on salary and earns $2259.09 per month. She kept track of her monthly expenses for a period of 6 months.

Item	April	May	June	July	August	September
Rent	$450.00	$450.00	$450.00	$450.00	$450.00	$450.00
Utilities, phone, cable, internet	$150.00	$125.00	$125.00	$155.00	$150.00	$200.00
Groceries	$260.00	$300.00	$100.00	$275.00	$150.00	$125.00
Car payment	$175.00	$175.00	$175.00	$175.00	$175.00	$175.00
Gas	$90.00	$125.00	$100.00	$200.00	$50.00	$100.00
Restaurant meals	$120.00	$90.00	$150.00	$120.00	$100.00	$120.00
Entertainment	$75.00	$85.00	$50.00	$325.00	$350.00	$200.00
Car insurance	$115.00	$115.00	$115.00	$115.00	$115.00	$115.00
Clothing	----	$75.00	$350.00	$45.00	$90.00	----
Miscellaneous	$75.00	$50.00	$50.00	$100.00	$50.00	$75.00

a) Use this information to calculate her average monthly expenses in each category for the 6-month period.

b) Create a possible conservative budget for Kate. If she has a surplus, allocate the extra money to savings.

SOLUTION

a) Calculate the average of each category.

Rent:

This is a fixed amount of $450.00 per month.

Utilities, phone, cable, internet:

($150.00 + $125.00 + $125.00 + $155.00 + $150.00 + $200.00) ÷ 6 ≈ $150.83

Groceries:

($260.00 + $300.00 + $100.00 + $275.00 + $150.00 + $125.00) ÷ 6 ≈ $201.67

Car payment:

This is a fixed amount of $175.00 per month.

Gas:

($90.00 + $125.00 + $100.00 + $200.00 + $50.00 + $100.00) ÷ 6 ≈ $110.83

Restaurant meals:

($120.00 + $90.00 + $150.00 + $120.00 + $100.00 + $120.00) ÷ 6 ≈ $116.67

Entertainment:

($75.00 + $85.00 + $50.00 + $325.00 + $350.00 + $200.00) ÷ 6 ≈ $180.83

Car insurance:

This is a fixed amount of $115.00 per month..

Clothing:

($0 + $75.00 + $350.00 + $50.00 + $90.00 + $0) ÷ 6 ≈ $94.17

Miscellaneous:

($75.00 + $50.00 + $50.00 + $100.00 + $50.00 + $75.00) ÷ 6 ≈ $66.67

> Even though there are two months in which Kate did not spend money on clothes, those months still need to be considered in the average.

b) To create a conservative budget, underestimate Kate's income and overestimate her expenses in each category, except for fixed expenses.

KATE'S MONTHLY BUDGET			
Income		*Expenses*	
Regular	$2200.00	Rent	$450.00
		Utilities, phone, cable, internet	$200.00
		Groceries	$250.00
		Car payment	$175.00
		Gas	$150.00
		Restaurant meals	$125.00
		Entertainment	$200.00
		Car insurance	$115.00
		Clothing	$100.00
		Miscellaneous	$100.00
Total income	$2200.00	*Total expenses*	$1865.00

There is a surplus in the budget.

$2200.00 − $1865.00 = $335.00

Kate can put this money into savings.

Also, she can group some of the expenses into broader categories.

- Groceries and restaurant meals can be combined in the category food.

- Car payment, gas, and car insurance can be combined in the category transportation.

Redo the budget with these groupings, and with the surplus allocated to savings.

KATE'S MONTHLY BUDGET			
Income		Expenses	
Regular	$2200.00	Rent	$450.00
		Utilities, phone, cable, internet	$200.00
		Food	$375.00
		Transportation	$440.00
		Entertainment	$200.00
		Clothing	$100.00
		Miscellaneous	$100.00
		Savings	$335.00
Total income	$2200.00	Total expenses	$2200.00

BUILD YOUR SKILLS

1. Craig and Stéfanie live in Vancouver, BC. They are creating a budget to help them control their spending. Craig earns semi-monthly pay of $1400.00. Stéfanie's semi-monthly pay is $1385.00. They have kept track of their other expenses for 4 months.

CRAIG AND STÉFANIE'S MONTHLY EXPENSES				
Item	November	December	January	February
Mortgage payment	$1850.00	$1850.00	$1850.00	$1850.00
Utilities	$175.00	$175.00	$175.00	$175.00
Cat care	$75.00	----	----	$100
Clothing	----	$250.00	$175.00	$90.00
Food	$375.00	$420.00	$500.00	$250.00
Gas	$150.00	$120.00	$200.00	$125.00
Car insurance	$112.00	$112.00	$112.00	$112.00
Gifts	$275.00	$200.00	----	$25.00
Entertainment	$100.00	$150.00	$75.00	$125.00
Loan payment	$150.00	$150.00	$150.00	$150.00
Home insurance	$122.00	$122.00	$122.00	$122.00
Trip fund	$250.00	$250.00	$250.00	$250.00
Cell phones	$135.00	$135.00	$135.00	$135.00
Miscellaneous	$125.00	$175.00	$75.00	$100.00

Not all vacations have to be expensive. Camping can be a cost-effective way to get out of town.

a) Use their financial records to create a conservative monthly budget for Craig and Stéfanie.

b) If they follow this budget, how much money will they be able to save in one year?

2. Minh has kept track of his finances over the last 4 months. Averages for his income and spending are listed below.

MINH'S INCOME AND EXPENSES			
Income		*Expenses*	
Regular	$1665.00	Rent	$640.00
Tips	$300.00	Utilities, phone, cable, and internet	$115.00
		Food	$275.00
		Transportation	$100.00
		Entertainment	$200.00
		Other	$475.00

a) Create a conservative monthly budget for Minh. Allocate any surplus to savings.

b) Minh wants to buy a new pair of skis at the beginning of the next ski season, which is 6 months away. The skis he wants cost $1059.99. Will he be able to afford the skis?

3. Georgina earns approximately $3050.00 per month. She has made the following list of her expenses.

Income	Amount
Mortgage	$1025.00/month
Car insurance	$122.00/month
House repairs	$800.00/year
House taxes	$4200.00/year
Gifts	$500.00/year
Charity	$300.00/year
Gas	$120.00/month
Loan payment	$220.00/month
Miscellaneous	$150.00/month
Entertainment	$150.00/month
Home insurance	$1500.00/year
Clothing	$125.00/month
Car maintenance	$500.00/year
Food	$350.00/month
Skiing season's pass	$650.00/year

A season's pass can be expensive, but if you enjoy skiing enough it can be worth it.

a) Create a conservative monthly budget for her.

b) How much money can she save per year?

c) What percentage of her income goes into savings?

d) If Georgina wanted to begin saving more money, what are two changes she could make to her spending?

Example 2

Manny has two part-time jobs. At one, he works 20 hours per week and earns $12.75 per hour. At the second, he works 15 hours per week at $18.20 per hour.

He has created a budget and expects to save 10% of his salary. How many weeks will it take him to save $900.00?

SOLUTION

Calculate Manny's weekly income at each job.

Job 1: 20 × $12.75 = $255.00

Job 2: 15 × $18.20 = $273.00

Add to find his total income.

$255.00 + $273.00 = $528.00 per week

Calculate 10% of his income.

$528.00 × 0.10 = $52.80

Manny saves $52.80 per week.

Divide $900.00 by $52.80.

$900.00 ÷ $52.80 ≈ 17

It will take Manny about 17 weeks to save $900.00.

BUILD YOUR SKILLS

4. Janae works as a server and earns an hourly wage plus tips. She works about 40 hours per week, at a rate of $10.75 per hour. She takes home about $500.00 in tips each month. Her fixed and variable expenses account for about 80% of her income.

   a) How much money does Janae put into savings each month? (Assume there are 4 weeks in a month.)

   b) Janae spends about $75.00 a week on food. What percentage of her income does this represent?

5. Justin works on contract as a landscaper. He earns about $2700.00 a month. He is creating a budget and wants to put 12% of his income into savings.

   a) If he follows his budget, how much will he save each month?

   b) How long will it take him to save $1500.00?

6. Veejay is saving for his college tuition. Since his parents do not charge him room and board, he plans on saving 55% of his income. If he earn $1725.00 month, how long will it take him to save the $6000.00 he needs for tuition and $550.00 for books?

Setting aside money for college is a good way to avoid student loans.

PRACTISE YOUR NEW SKILLS

1. Pierre has kept a record of his spending over the past 4 months. He earns semi-monthly pay of $1475.59.

Item	August	September	October	November
Mortgage payment	$1450.00	$1450.00	$1450.00	$1450.00
Utilities/phone	$139.00	$142.00	$142.00	$159.00
Groceries	$276.00	$312.00	$248.00	$363.00
Loan repayment	$250.00	$250.00	$250.00	$250.00
Charity	$100.00	$25.00	----	$30.00
Entertainment	$95.00	$128.00	$212.00	$145.00
Transportation	$245.00	$189.00	$196.00	$212.00
Miscellaneous	$84.00	$98.00	$75.00	$54.00

a) Create a conservative budget for Pierre.

b) Approximately how much will he save in a month? A year?

2. Chantal has kept track of her income and expenses over the last 6 months. Averages for her income and spending are shown.

CHANTAL'S MONTHLY INCOME AND EXPENSES

Income		Expenses	
Semi-monthly	$1110.00	Rent	$675.00
Semi-monthly	$1110.00	Utilities, phone, cable, and internet	$150.00
Tips	$135.00	Food	$395.00
		Transportation	$285.00
		Entertainment	$125.00
		Other	$350.00

a) Create a conservative monthly budget for Chantal. Allocate any surplus to savings.

b) What percentage of her income is Chantal putting into savings?

c) How long will it take Chantal to save up for a new computer, which she estimates will cost about $1000.00?

3. Marcel is looking for a new apartment. He works for 40 hours a week at a job that pays $14.50 an hour. He usually works 6 hours of overtime, paid at time and a half, each month. He estimates his monthly expenses as follows.

Expenses	
Rent	?
Utilities, phone, cable, and internet	$125.00
Food	$250.00
Transportation	$165.00
Savings for a trip to Ecuador	$300.00
Loan payment	$350.00
Other	$400.00

a) What is the maximum rent Marcel can pay, and still be able to afford his other expenses?

b) Marcel's trip to Ecuador will cost about $2700.00. How many months will it take him to save up for the trip?

7.3 Analyzing a Budget

NEW SKILLS: ADJUSTING A BUDGET

People often find that once they create a budget, either they cannot stay on it, or their situation changes and they need to make adjustments.

One useful tool for analyzing budgets is a circle graph, because it shows which categories make up the biggest expenses.

For more details, see page 327 of *MathWorks 11*.

Example 1

Patrice has budgeted to put $35.00 a week into savings. This accounts for 12% of her income.

a) What is Patrice's weekly income?

b) If she follows her budget, how much will she have saved in one year?

c) If her salary increases by 3% and she continues to put 12% of her income into savings, how much will she save in a year?

SOLUTION

a) Set up a proportion to calculate Patrice's income. Let x represent Jessica's income; put this over 100% (her whole income). On the other side of the equation, put her savings, which are equal to 12% of her income.

$$\frac{x}{100} = \frac{\$35.00}{12}$$
$$x = \frac{\$35.00}{12} \times 100$$
$$x \approx \$291.67$$

Patrice earns $291.67 per week.

b) Multiply this by 52 weeks.

$35.00 × 52 = $1820.00

In one year, she will save $1820.00.

c) Calculate 3% of her weekly income.

$291.67 × 0.03 = $8.75

Add to her original salary.

$291.67 + $8.75 = $300.42

Her new salary is $300.42 per week. Calculate 12% of this.

$300.42 × 0.12 = $36.05

Multiply this by 52 weeks.

$36.05 × 52 = $1874.60

With the increase in salary, Patrice's savings will be $1874.60 per year.

BUILD YOUR SKILLS

1. Sukh works full-time but is saving up for a part-time college course. He estimates that he will need $6000.00 in savings to cover extra expenses while he studies.

   a) He budgets to save 15% of his salary each month. If he earns $2865.00 a month, how many months will he have to work in order save enough money?

   b) The course starts 12 months from now. What percentage of his salary will Sukh have to save per month in order to be able to afford the course?

2. Juliet's monthly entertainment expenses are $275.00 and account for 12% of her income. She would like to reduce her entertainment spending to 8% of her income.

   a) Calculate her new monthly entertainment budget.

   b) Calculate Juliet's total monthly income.

Example 2

Salima works as a lifeguard and swimming instructor, and she earns about $2400.00 per month. Her average monthly expenses are as follows.

Expenses	
Rent	$760.00
Utilities	$140.00
Food	$400.00
Transportation	$175.00
Entertainment	$200.00
Clothing	$200.00
Savings	$180.00
Other	$345.00

Swimming instructors aren't always in the water. Sometimes they teach aerobics from outside the pool.

Salima has researched spending guidelines. These guidelines give a recommendation of how much of your income you should spend on each category.

Spending Guidelines	
Housing	25–35%
Utilities	5–10%
Food	5–15%
Transportation	5–15%
Entertainment	5–10%
Clothing	2–5%
Savings	5–15%
Other	5–10%

a) What changes need to be made so that Salima's spending falls within the guidelines?

b) What is the maximum that Salima should be spending on food per month?

c) Show Salima's spending on a circle graph.

SOLUTION

a) Calculate what percentage each category represents of Salima's income.

　　Rent:　　　　　　$760.00 ÷ $2400.00 ≈ 0.32

　　　　　　　　　　0.32 × 100 = 32%

　　Utilities:　　　　$140.00 ÷ $2400.00 ≈ 0.06

　　　　　　　　　　0.06 × 100 = 6%

　　Food:　　　　　$400.00 ÷ $2400.00 ≈ 0.17

　　　　　　　　　　0.17 × 100 = 17%

　　Transportation:　$175.00 ÷ $2400.00 ≈ 0.07

　　　　　　　　　　0.07 × 100 = 7%

　　Entertainment:　$200.00 ÷ $2400.00 ≈ 0.08

　　　　　　　　　　0.08 × 100 = 8%

　　Clothing:　　　　$200.00 ÷ $2400.00 ≈ 0.08

　　　　　　　　　　0.08 × 100 = 8%

　　Savings:　　　　$180.00 ÷ $2400.00 ≈ 0.08

　　　　　　　　　　0.08 × 100 = 8%

　　Other:　　　　　$345.00 ÷ $2400.00 ≈ 0.14

　　　　　　　　　　0.14 × 100 = 14%

Compare these percentages to the spending guidelines. Salima is spending more than the recommended amount on food, clothing, and other. She needs to decrease her spending on these items to fall within the guidelines.

b) According to the guidelines, Salima should not spend more than 15% of her income on food. Calculate 15% of $2400.00.

$2400.00 × 0.15 = $360.00

Salima should spend no more than $360.00 on food per month.

c) To construct a circle graph, first calculate how many degrees each percentage of expenses equals.

Rent: $0.32 \times 360° \approx 115°$

Utilities: $0.06 \times 360° \approx 22°$

Food: $0.17 \times 360° \approx 61°$

Transportation: $0.07 \times 360° \approx 25°$

Entertainment: $0.08 \times 360° \approx 29°$

Clothing: $0.08 \times 360° \approx 29°$

Savings: $0.08 \times 360° \approx 29°$

Other: $0.14 \times 360° \approx 50°$

Draw a circle and use a protractor to measure the degrees for each category of expense.

> For a review of how to construct a circle graph, see page 109 of this workbook.

Salima's Monthly Expenses

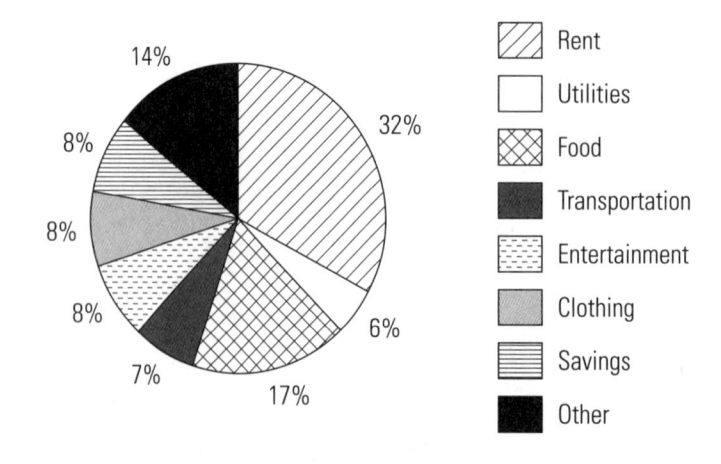

Rent 32%, Food 17%, Transportation 7%, Entertainment 8%, Clothing 8%, Savings 8%, Other 14%, Utilities 6%

BUILD YOUR SKILLS

3. Petra has created the following monthly budget.

PETRA'S MONTHLY BUDGET			
Income		*Expenses*	
Regular	$1400.00	Rent	$550.00
		Utilities, phone, cable, internet	$175.00
		Food	$325.00
		Transportation	$75.00
		Entertainment	$50.00
		Clothing	$100.00
		Miscellaneous	$100.00
		Charitable donations	$25.00
		Savings	$100.00
Total income	$1400.00	Total expenses	$1500.00

a) Petra's budget has a deficit. Suggest how she can adjust her spending to create a balanced budget. Explain your reasoning.

b) Construct a circle graph that shows Petra's new budget.

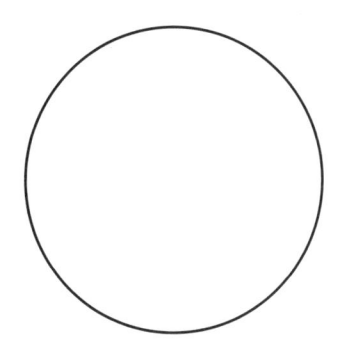

4. Sammy earns about $1500.00 per month and has the following expenses.

Expenses	
Housing	$400.00
Food	$225.00
Transportation	$350.00
Entertainment	$250.00
Charitable donations	$25.00
Savings	$50.00
Other	$200.00

Housing costs can be the biggest part of your monthly budget. Think carefully when you choose a place to live.

a) He has found the following spending guidelines for people living in his area.

Spending Guidelines	
Housing	25–35%
Food	10–20%
Transportation	10–15%
Entertainment	5–10%
Charitable donations	2–10%
Savings	5–10%
Other	5–10%

How does his spending compare to the guidelines? In what categories does he need to adjust his spending?

b) If Sammy does not make any changes to his spending, how much money will he save in one year?

c) Make a new budget for Sammy that falls within the spending guidelines. Construct a circle graph that shows his new budget.

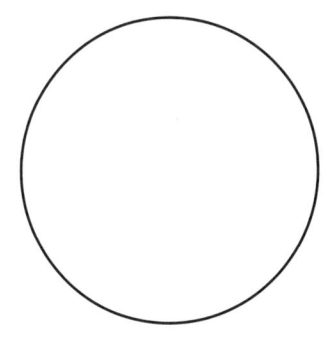

5. Willa earns $3532.00 a month and has been given the following budget guidelines.

Spending Guidelines	
Housing	30–35%
Utilities	5–10%
Transportation	8–12%
Debt repayment	0–12%
Savings	at least 10%
Food	12–18%
Recreation	6–12%
Heath and personal care	8–15%

Willa's housing costs are $1250.00 per month, and her utilities cost $235.00 per month. Willa wants to save 15% of her money and pay off her loans as fast as possible.

a) Construct a conservative budget for Willa.

b) Make a circle graph to show her spending.

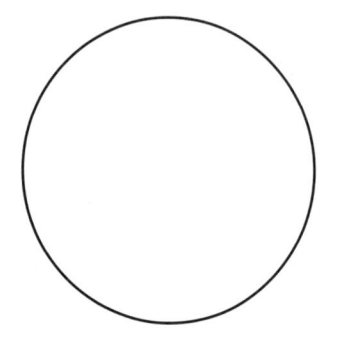

PRACTISE YOUR NEW SKILLS

1. Manjeet earns $550.00 per week.

   a) If he saves 14% of his salary, how much will he save in one year?

   b) If Manjeet's salary increases by 5% and he continues to save 14%, how much more will he save in one year?

   You may end up working in many places over your career.

2. Lena puts $3150.00 a year into savings. This represents 7% of her income.

   a) She would like to increase her savings to 10% of her income. How much will she save in one year if she makes this change?

   b) What is her annual income?

3. Sean is creating a monthly budget.

SEAN'S MONTHLY BUDGET

Income		Expenses	
Semi-monthly pay	$1300.00	Housing	$1200.00
Semi-monthly pay	$1300.00	Utilities	$175.00
Monthly tips	$150.00	Phone, cable, internet	$150.00
		Food	$325.00
		Transportation	$150.00
		Entertainment	$125.00
		Clothing	$175.00
		Miscellaneous	$100.00
		Charitable donations	$50.00
		Medical/health and other emergencies	$100.00
		Savings	$200.00
Total income		Total expenses	

a) Calculate his total income and expenses. Is his budget balanced?

b) Create a circle graph of Sean's spending.

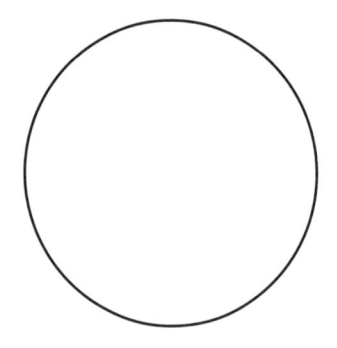

c) Spending guidelines suggest housing should account for 30–35% of total income. Is Sean's spending within these guidelines? What is the maximum amount he should spend on housing?

d) Sean has decided that he does not want to move, but he wants to increase his savings to 15% so that he has enough money for a holiday next summer. Suggest ways in which he could adjust his budget to do this.

Mountain biking can be a fun activity on a trip. What sort of vacation would you plan?

4. Gabriella's monthly budget is shown here.

GABRIELLA'S MONTHLY BUDGET

Income		Expenses	
Semi-monthly pay	$995.00	Housing	$840.00
Semi-monthly pay	$995.00	Food	$175.00
		Transportation	$125.00
		Entertainment	$175.00
		Clothing	$175.00
		Miscellaneous	$150.00
		Loan payments	$275.00
		Savings	$75.00
Total income	$1990.00	Total expenses	$1990.00

The suggested spending guidelines are as follows.

Spending Guidelines	
Housing	30–35%
Food	8–15%
Transportation	8–12%
Debt repayment	0–12%
Entertainment	8–12%
Personal	8–12%
Savings	at least 10%

a) Create a circle graph of Gabriella's spending.

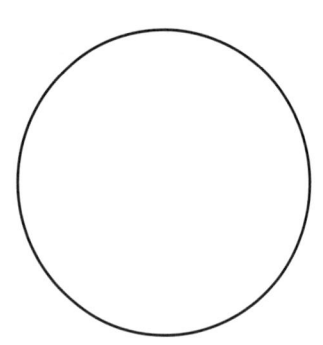

b) Calculate which of Gabriella's spending categories need adjusting according to the guidelines, and by about how much.

c) At her current rate of savings, how long will it take Gabriella to save $1000.00? If she wanted to save that amount in 6 months, by how much would she have to increase her savings per month? Would her savings fall within the guidelines?

CHAPTER TEST

1. Classify the following transactions as income or expenses. Identify the income as regular or variable, and the expenses as recurring, variable, or unexpected.

Item	Income	Expense
Biweekly paycheque: $735.00		
Monthly bus pass: $75.00		
Gas: $42.95		
Cell phone bill: $39.96		
New jacket: $69.95		
Tips: $52.00		
Debt repayment: $75.00		
Emergency vet bill for cat: $250.00		
Movie ticket and snack: $20.00		
Dinner at restaurant: $27.00		
Charitable donation: $25.00		
Commission: $100.00		

What type of expense is buying groceries?

2. Tamara has tracked her spending for four months. Her semi-monthly income is $975.00.

TAMARA'S MONTHLY BUDGET

Item	January	February	March	April
Rent	$575.00	$575.00	$575.00	$575.00
Utilities, phone, cable, internet	$155.00	$160.00	$145.00	$140.00
Groceries	$250.00	$275.00	$240.00	$300.00
Debt repayment	$100.00	$100.00	$100.00	$100.00
Gas	$109.00	$125.00	$95.00	$115.00
Parking pass	$100.00	$100.00	$100.00	$100.00
Entertainment	$50.00	$265.00	$300.00	$200.00
Car insurance	$110.00	$110.00	$110.00	$110.00
Clothing	$50.00	$100.00	$50.00	$75.00
Miscellaneous	$300.00	$100.00	$150.00	$130.00

a) Create a conservative budget for Tamara. Group the expenses into categories. If she has a surplus, allocate the extra money to savings.

b) If she follows this budget, how much money will she save in one year?

c) What percentage of her income do her savings represent?

3. Masaru works as a salesperson and earns an hourly wage plus commission. He works 35 hours per week, at a rate of $11.75 per hour. His commission is about $125.00 per week. His expenses account for about 85% of his income.

   a) How much money does Masaru put into savings in one year?

   b) Masaru spends about $7200.00 a year on rent. What percentage of his income does this represent?

4. Madeleine has begun creating a budget for herself.

   a) Complete her budget by calculating her total income and expenses and allocating any surplus to savings.

   MADELEINE'S MONTHLY INCOME AND EXPENSES

Income		Expenses	
Semi-monthly	$885.00	Rent	$595.00
Semi-monthly	$885.00	Utilities, phone, cable, and internet	$275.00
Tips	$250.00	Food	$295.00
		Transportation	$100.00
		Entertainment	$225.00
		Other	$350.00
		Savings	
Total income		Total expenses	

   b) What percentage of her income is Madeleine putting into each of the expense categories?

   c) If Madeleine's income increases by 5%, but she continues to put the same percentage of her income into savings, how much will she save per month?

5. Noah is a construction worker and he earns about $1200.00 semi-monthly. His average monthly expenses are as follows.

Expenses	
Rent	$795.00
Utilities	$150.00
Food	$500.00
Transportation	$375.00
Entertainment	$150.00
Clothing	$100.00
Savings	$30.00
Other	$300.00

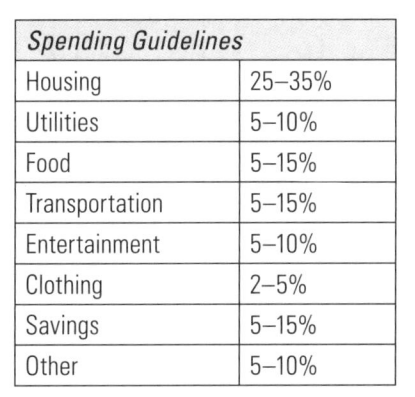

Like many jobs, construction workers need to use some form of math every day.

a) Compare Noah's expenses to the following spending guidelines. What changes would he need to make to fall within the guidelines?

Spending Guidelines	
Housing	25–35%
Utilities	5–10%
Food	5–15%
Transportation	5–15%
Entertainment	5–10%
Clothing	2–5%
Savings	5–15%
Other	5–10%

b) What is the minimum amount that Noah should put into savings per month?

c) Create a new budget for Noah that falls within the spending guidelines. Graph the expenses on a circle graph.

NOAH'S MONTHLY BUDGET			
Income		Expenses	
		Rent	
		Utilities	
		Food	
		Transportation	
		Entertainment	
		Clothing	
		Savings	
		Other	
Total income		Total expenses	

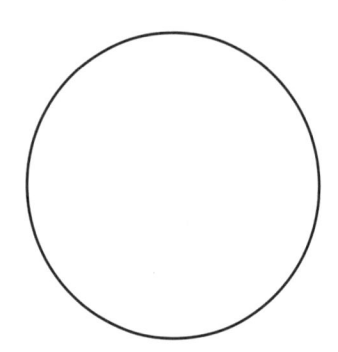

Glossary

amortization period: the time required to pay back a loan

base: one of the parallel faces of a prism

broken line graph: a graph that uses points joined by line segments to display data

budget: a balanced statement of projected income and expenses

capacity: the amount a three-dimensional object can hold

cash advance: a withdrawal of cash from an ATM or bank teller charged to a credit card; interest is usually calculated from the day of the withdrawal

component parts diagram: a two-dimensional scale drawing that shows each part of an object

compound interest: interest calculated on the principal plus interest earned in prior compounding periods

compounding period: the time between calculations of interest

default: failure to repay a loan

deficit: the amount by which expenses exceed income

dependent variable: a variable whose value relies on the value of another variable

discrete data: data made up of distinct values, where intermediate values are not possible

down payment: a partial payment sometimes required at the time of purchase

elevation: another term for view

exploded diagram: a 3-D representation of an object that shows how the components connect together; components are shown separated but in their relative positions, and dotted lines show where the pieces fit together

extrapolate: to estimate a value beyond a known range of values

finance charge: the total amount of interest paid to borrow a sum of money

grade: the slope of a physical feature such as a road or hill, often expressed as a percentage

horizon line: a horizontal line (not always visible) that is at the eye level of the viewer in a perspective drawing

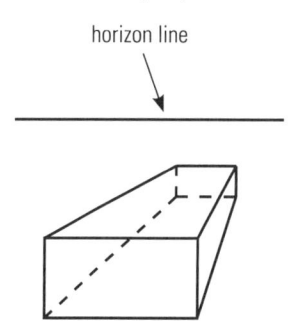

independent variable: a variable whose value can be freely chosen and which is not dependent on any other value

interpolate: to estimate a value between two known values

isometric drawing: a representation of a 3-D object where the same scale is used to draw the object height, width, and depth

lateral face: a face that connects the bases of a prism

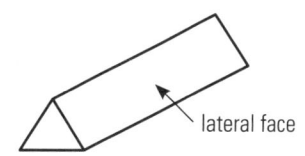

line of credit: an approved loan amount that you can draw on as needed, with interest charged on the money used

net: 2-D pattern that can be folded to make a 3-D shape

overdraft protection: an agreement with a bank that allows you to withdraw more money from an account than you have in it, up to a specified amount

payday loan: a small, short-term loan with a high interest rate

perspective drawing: a representation of a 3-D object in 2-D; objects appear smaller in the distance, and the vanishing point is used to create a sense of depth and space

principal: the original amount of money invested or borrowed

prism: a 3-D shape with ends that are congruent, parallel polygons and sides that are parallelograms

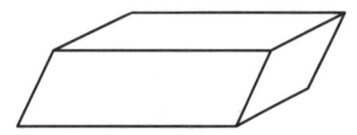

proportion: a statement of equality between two ratios

rate of change: the rate at which one variable changes compared to another variable

ratio: a comparison between two numbers with the same units

recurring expenses: expenses that occur on a regular basis

Rule of 72: a way to estimate the time it takes for an investment to double in value

scale factor: a number by which all the dimensions of an original figure are multiplied to produce an enlargement or a reduction

scale statement: a ratio that shows the relationship between the sizes of two objects

simple interest: interest calculated as a percentage of the principal

slope: a ratio of rise to run which indicates how steeply something is slanted

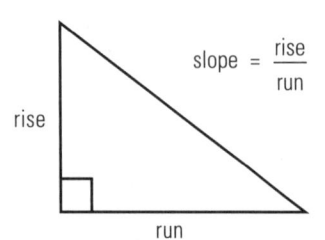

$$\text{slope} = \frac{\text{rise}}{\text{run}}$$

surface area: the area covered by the outside surfaces of a three-dimensional shape

surplus: the amount by which income exceeds expenses

term: the length of time over which money is invested or borrowed

vanishing point: the point on the horizon line at which parallel lines appear to converge in a perspective drawing

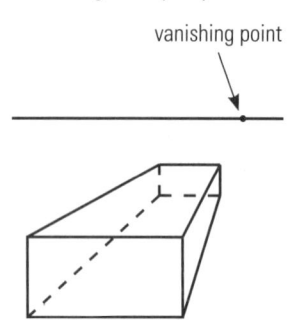

view: a scale drawing that shows one plane of an object

volume: the measure of the space a three-dimensional object occupies

Credits

Images in the text for which no page numbers are listed are copyright Pacific Educational Press.

Cover

Mason Morfix/Getty Images

Chapter 1

p.9 ©iStockphoto.com/Faulknor Photography; p.14 ©iStockphoto.com/Bailey Digital Images; p.17 ©iStockphoto.com/Cozart Photography; p.29 ©iStockphoto.com/Blazej Piotrowski; p.33 ©iStockphoto.com/tomallan; p.35 ©iStockphoto.com/kluk; p.52 Katrina Petrik.

Chapter 2

p.58 ©iStockphoto.com/DK Studio; p.59 Statistics Canada; p.65 ©iStockphoto.com/Jerry's Photo; p.69 Statistics Canada; p.74 ©iStockphoto.com/joxxxxjo; p.75 Statistics Canada; p.76 © David Smith | Dreamstime.com; p.77 Statistics Canada; p.79 ©iStockphoto.com/Mansi Ltd; p.80 Statistics Canada; p.84 Statistics Canada; p.85 Moose photo courtesy Katrina Petrik; Moose Jaw info courtesy Statistics Canada; p.87 © Can Stock Photo Inc./Avalon; p.90 Statistics Canada; p.91 Statistics Canada; p.92 Statistics Canada; p.93 © Fallsview | Dreamstime.com; p.96 ©iStockphoto.com/Anastasia Pelikh; p.99 Statistics Canada; p.101 ©iStockphoto.com/A. Korzekwa; p.107 © Can Stock Photo Inc./Feverpitched; p.110 ©iStockphoto.com/Felix Mizioznikov.

Chapter 3

p.124 ©iStockphoto.com/Francksudre Photographie; p.131 ©iStockphoto.com/Banks Photos; p.135 ©iStockphoto.com/Jack Davies; p.137 © Can Stock Photo Inc./Abv; p.143 © Can Stock Photo Inc./lastdays1; p.147 ©iStockphoto.com/lucato; p.148 © Can Stock Photo Inc./jewhyte; p.153 ©iStockphoto.com/Sara Gray; p.157 ©iStockphoto.com/Anton-Marlot; p.167 © Sophie Mcaulay | Dreamstime.com; p.168 © Can Stock Photo Inc./sprokop; p.173 © Can Stock Photo Inc./kadmy; p.177 © Can Stock Photo Inc./Elenathewise; p.183 © Can Stock Photo Inc./iofoto; p.188 ©iStockphoto.com/Yin Yang.

Chapter 4

p.197 © Can Stock Photo Inc./kadmy; p.199 © Andrew Emptage | Dreamstime.com; p.203 © Can Stock Photo Inc./endotune; p.205 © Claus Jepsen | Dreamstime.com; p.209 © Yobro | Dreamstime.com; p.212 © Valentyn75 | Dreamstime.com; p.213 © Can Stock Photo Inc./Pierdelune; p.220 © Can Stock Photo Inc./jabiru; p.225 ©iStockphoto.com/Sportstock; p.228 © Can Stock Photo Inc./ulga.

Chapter 5

p.231 © Can Stock Photo Inc./lisafx; p.237 Katrina Petrik; p.242 © Ene | Dreamstime.com; p.243 Taxiarchos228, Wikipedia Commons; p.244 © Can Stock Photo Inc./gvictoria; p.251 © Can

Stock Photo Inc./Pixart; p.255 ©iStockphoto.com/McCabe Design; p.255 © Yurchyk | Dreamstime.com; p.257 © Can Stock Photo Inc./pilgrimego; p.264 © Can Stock Photo Inc./javarman; p.273 © Can Stock Photo Inc./Maukun.

Chapter 6

p.279 © Olivier Le Queinec | Dreamstime.com; p.281 © Luchschen | Dreamstime.com; p.289 © Anatoly Tiplyashin | Dreamstime.com; p.297 © Can Stock Photo Inc./arekmalang; p.307 © Yuri Arcurs | Dreamstime.com; p.311 © Reflekcija | Dreamstime.com; p.314 © Yew Wah Kok | Dreamstime.com; p.317 © Mammoth | Dreamstime.com; p.319 © Nyul | Dreamstime.com; p.322 © Serdar Tibet | Dreamstime.com; p.324 © Roberto1977 | Dreamstime.com; p.328 © Tatyana Nyshko | Dreamstime.com.

Chapter 7

p.329 © Can Stock Photo Inc./Diego Cervo; p.330 © Lisa F. Young | Dreamstime.com; p.333 © Can Stock Photo Inc./photosoup; p.336 © Raynald Bélanger | Dreamstime.com; p.339 © Can Stock Photo Inc./Dusan; p.345 © Maksym Gorpenyuk | Dreamstime.com; p.348 © Can Stock Photo Inc./swimnews; p.351 © Diego Vito Cervo | Dreamstime.com; p.356 © Georgiy Pashin | Dreamstime.com; p.360 © Katseyephoto | Dreamstime.com; p.363 © Can Stock Photo Inc./Diego Cervo; p.365 © Candybox Photography | Dreamstime.com; p.367 © Can Stock Photo Inc./Leaf; p.371 ©iStockphoto.com/annmarie98121@gmail.com.